MW01129021

THE SOCIOLOGY
OF THE CHURCH

THE SOCIOLOGY OF THE CHURCH

Essays in Reconstruction

James B. Jordan, Th.M.

Wipf and Stock Publishers
150 West Broadway • Eugene OR 97401

1999

The Sociology of the Church
Essays in Reconstruction
By Jordan, James B.

ISBN: 1-57910-248-4

Reprinted by *Wipf and Stock Publishers* 1999
150 West Broadway • Eugene OR 97401

Previously Published by Geneva Ministries, 1986.

The cover shows the Jerusalem Cross. The cross is a symbol of the death of Christ for our sins, but more than that, the cross is the design of the world as created by God, with four rivers going to the four corners of the earth. The spreading Jerusalem Cross pictures for us the Good News of Christ's death and resurrection moving out to encompass the whole world. The smaller crosses picture the principles of the Kingdom coming to life in the hearts of believers, and in the life of the nations, as these are encompassed within the arms of Jesus Christ and His church.

TABLE OF CONTENTS

(An annotated table of contents is provided in the back of the book)

PREFACE

My grandfather, William Henry Jordan, was a Methodist minister. His father before him, and his before him, were also Methodist clergymen, and before that, the Jordans were Episcopal ministers. My father, Howard S. Jordan, did not go into the ministry, but instead became a Professor of French Literature, specializing in the Jansenist period (Pascal, Molière, Racine).

My mother, born Sarah Kathleen Burrell, came up in the Southern Baptist Church. She met my father at Salem College, a Moravian school in Winston-Salem, North Carolina. He was Head of the Foreign Languages Department there at the time. When they were married, they joined the Moravian Church.

In 1949, the year I was born, my father moved to Athens, Georgia, to assume headship of the Department of Modern Foreign Languages. There being no Moravian Church there, my parents became part of the First Methodist Church, where my father taught a men's Sunday School class. The Sunday School for young children amounted to very little, so my parents sent my brother and me to Sunday School at First Baptist Church.

My parents were distressed at the increasing liberalism in the Methodist church, and when a Lutheran mission started up a couple of blocks from our home, they began going there. They soon joined, and I was baptized at Holy Cross Lutheran Church (then part of the United Lutheran Church of America, now the Lutheran Church of America). My father served for years as an elder, or councilmember as it was termed. My brother and I were also confirmed in the Lutheran Church.

vii

My parents were not particularly impressed with public school education, and sent us to the parochial Roman Catholic school. I attended grades 2 through 6. This was in the 1950s, and I can recall discussions in class over whether we "non-catholics" could possibly be saved. The Sisters of the Sacred Heart were quite faithful to then-current dogma, and firm on the point that no one could be saved apart from the specific ordinances of the Roman Catholic Church. Pre-Vatican II Romanism was my earliest experience with the sectarian mindset; unfortunately, it was not my last.

My father would not have a television in our home when we were younger, and it was not until I was in high school that we got one. Entertainment in our home centered around the phonograph, and my father had a large collection of church music: Gregorian Chants, Eastern Orthodox services, passions and oratorios by Bach, sacred music by Couperin, Charpentier, Lully, and Lalande, and so forth. While we kept a critical distance from all these, we sought also to appreciate their contribution.

After we acquired a television, we used to watch Billy Graham's Crusades when they were aired, and I was influenced by his ministry. Just after graduating from high school, I read Graham's *World Aflame*, and for the first time came to grasp clearly justification by grace apart from works. After that, my interest in our Lutheran church waned, because the current pastor was rather liberal, though I continued to direct the choir and in other ways assist with the liturgy.

In college, I was active in a number of conservative political organizations (Young Americans for Freedom, Intercollegiate Studies Institute), and also in Campus Crusade for Christ. During my sophomore year, Francis Schaeffer's first books appeared, and I devoured them. I soon was listening to Schaeffer's tapes, and was also moving on to the works of E. L. Hebden Taylor, Herman Dooyeweerd, Cornelius Van Til, and Rousas John Rushdoony. Since all these men were Reformed or Presbyterian, I soon became oriented in that direction, though as a good Campus Crusader, I did my studies from a New Scofield Reference Bible.

After I went into the Air Force, in 1971, I spent a year attending Navigator Bible studies, but soon found my way into a Presbyterian church. I have remained a Presbyterian since, studying for a while at Reformed Theological Seminary in Jackson, Mississippi, and finishing at Westminster Theological Seminary in Philadelphia.

I thought it useful to explain my background, since it feeds into this book. In most ways, my experience was typically American. Christian views of man's sinfulness and the consequent need for limited government played a part in my involvement in antileftist political action during my college years (1967-1971), but I always felt a tension between conservatism on the one hand and Christianity on the other. That tension was resolved somewhat with my discovery of Francis Schaeffer, but the separation of "nature and grace" was still too great in Schaeffer to give me long lasting satisfaction.[1]

I thus soon found my way to the works of Rousas J. Rushdoony, whose rigorous Biblicism and presuppositionalism gave a much more sure foundation for Christian thought and action. Unfortunately, Rushdoony's low view of the sacramental body of the church served to reinforce my natural American bent in the same direction.[2] Thus, when I entered seminary it was with a rather low view of the church and a desire to learn "the faith," while bypassing the institutional church, which, after all, was but one social sphere among many. I tended to be deaf to the call of some of my teachers, most notably John Richard de Witt, to rec-

---

1. I have reference to Schaeffer's "pre-evangelism" set forth in his earlier books. Schaeffer's lack of clarity on this point becomes more obvious in his *Christian Manifesto*, where on the one hand he wants a Christian society, and on the other he shies away from any real Christian and Biblical law. For a critique, see the following three essays: Gary North, "The Intellectual Schizophrenia of the New Christian Right," and Kevin Craig, "Social Apologetics," in James B. Jordan, ed., *The Failure of the American Baptist Culture*. Christianity & Civilization No. 1 (Tyler, TX: Geneva Ministries, 1982); and Gary North & David Chilton, "Apologetics and Strategy," in *Tactics of Christian Resistance*. Christianity & Civilization No. 3 (Tyler: Geneva, 1983).

2. For a critique, see my remarks in the "Introduction" to Jordan, ed., *The Reconstruction of the Church*. Christianity & Civilization No. 4 (Tyler, TX: Geneva Ministries, 1986).

ognize the sacramental/institutional church as having a certain kind of preeminence in the kingdom.

The essays in this volume all in one way or another reflect my background and struggles in this area. To paraphrase C. S. Lewis, I have been dragged "kicking and screaming" into a higher view of the institutional church over the past decade. I feared that to take a high view of the church would result in my taking a lower view of the other aspects of Christ's Kingdom. I also feared that adopting a high view of the institutional church would move me in a sectarian direction, and cut me off from any real sympathy and understanding for the present condition of American Christendom. I hope that I have managed not to let either of these things happen.

Americans in general do have a low view of the sacramental church, and certainly tend to separate social action from liturgy. As I have written elsewhere, "To say that the root of our problems is religious is to say a great deal, but also to say rather little. . . . If this confession only amounts to the notion that religious *ideas* underlie any given culture, then the affirmation is [not particularly] radical. For to discuss religion only in terms of ideas or doctrine is to reduce religion to an ideology." A true presuppositionalist will not fall into the trap of the "primacy of the intellect and doctrine," but will recognize that social renewal must flow from the whole life of the Christian. "The practice of the Christian faith is most concentrated in the activity of the church. This is for the obvious reason that it is in the church that men devote themselves most rigorously to the practice of the faith."[3]

A true Christian social theory, I have come to see, means recognizing that the whole life of the church constitutes the nursery of the Kingdom of God. American Christians tend to isolate piety and prayer to the individual realm, leaving the social realm to political action. For there to be real reformation in our time, piety and social action must be integrated, and the Biblical way to do that is by a recovery of *corporate worship and life*, a recovery of the institutional church as a government and as a place of *public* worship.

---

3. *Ibid.*, pp. vii-viii.

In some ways these essays are a monument to my father, who, if he were still alive on this earth, would appreciate them. I feel, however, that what I have written here is so exploratory that I prefer that this book not be that monument — and this is a word to the reader as well. These essays will hopefully be challenging. They are hardly definitive.

I should like to thank a number of people, whose influence upon my life and thought has helped make these essays what they are. I imagine none of these men will agree with everything in this volume, but it would be ungracious of me not to mention them.

My intellectual formation as a presuppositionalist has been due to the writings of Cornelius Van Til and Rousas John Rushdoony, and also to various classes I was privileged to take under Greg Bahnsen at Reformed Theological Seminary and John M. Frame at Westminster Theological Seminary. I was challenged to apply the presuppositionalist "hermeneutic" to the question of ecclesiology by John Richard de Witt and Morton Smith, also then of Reformed Seminary. Norman Shepherd of Westminster Seminary tremendously reoriented my thinking about the covenant and the sacraments. Some of his insights play a large role in what I have presented in chapter 3, though I should not like the reader to saddle Mr. Shepherd with my own speculations! To Vern S. Poythress I owe many thanks, particularly for the wave-particle-field grid employed in chapter 2. My colleagues Ray Sutton and Lewis Bulkeley both challenged me to take a higher view of the governmental side of the church, and many of their insights are incorporated into these essays.

I need also to mention three writers whose books have been of great help to me. None of these men is an orthodox protestant presuppositionalist, but certain of their writings have been greatly stimulating to me and to others. They are a neoorthodox Presbyterian, Geddes MacGregor; a Roman Catholic, Louis Bouyer; and a Russian Orthodox, Alexander Schmemann. This book would not be what it is without their insights, as an examination of the footnotes will reveal.

And to all the men around Geneva Ministries I owe a debt of thanks for stimulating interaction and conversation, primarily

Gary North, Michael Gilstrap, Craig Bulkeley, Robert Dwelle, and David Chilton.

*   *   *   *   *   *

As a creature, man in intrinsically incapable of knowing anything exhaustively, but as a creature of time he inescapably knows things progressively. According to sin and grace, knowledge either progresses or regresses, but never remains the same. This elementary observation implies as a significant corollary that man's understanding of the church of God must increase, and to some extent alter, over time.

As a sinner, man has an inbuilt tendency to misunderstand and pervert the revelation of God. Even as regenerate, men still have this tendency. The Christian man, thus, may easily be and often is misled with respect to his understanding of the church. For this reason, the progressive corporate sanctification of the church in history dictates reevaluation and alteration in the church's self-concept.

Thus, because of man's creatureliness and sinfulness his understanding of the precise nature and definition of the church of God requires an ever-sharpening focus. We cannot, therefore expect to set forth a description of the church that will be valid in all of its particulars for all time, and we cannot expect the men of previous generations to have done so either. Just as the individual Christian, as he grows in grace over the years, acquires an increasing understanding of his uniqueness and definition under God, his name if you will, so also does the church. Just as the individual may and inevitably will have to correct some erroneous self-evaluations over the years, so also the church.

This volume seeks only to set out some lines of thought along which, it seems to me, the church could profitably reflect in seeking to resolve some of the problems currently facing her. The particular problems addressed here are those that concern the church's structure and relation to the other aspects of creation and society. It is in this broad sense that we are concerned with the "sociology" of the church, though inevitably such a concern draws us into matters theological and liturgical.

To attempt to resolve current problems in any field of theology simply by an appeal to historical theology is an exercise fraught with hazards. If theology historically has resolved the issue, we must ask why it continues to plague the church. (Of course, if we are willing to excommunicate from Christ everyone who disagrees with us, we can say that the issue has been resolved, and that only unregenerate people fail to see it.)

Moreover, it is usually the case that historical pronouncements were designed to meet problems current with their times, and are in the nature of the case inadequate for later difficulties. As history matures, new aspects of matters are disclosed, and new definitions of old problems come to the fore. This means that the church must sharpen her own definitions to meet the exigencies of the times. Old theological definitions are often not so much erroneous as imprecise. In the nature of the case, however, when an imprecise definition acquires the sanctity of tradition, its inadequacies are magnified and become errors.

* * * * * *

The essays in this book were published or distributed at various times and places. *Each has been revised for this publication.*

Chapter 1, "Reconstructing the Church," is based on a series of lectures delivered at Westminster Presbyterian Church in 1982. This essay was originally planned for inclusion in Geneva Ministries' volume *The Reconstruction of the Church* (Christianity & Civilization No. 4), but was transferred to this book to make room for other essays in the *Reconstruction* book.

Chapter 2, "The Sociology of the Church: A Systematic Approach," is a complete reworking of an essay I originally wrote for a class in Ecclesiology taught by Dr. Morton Smith at Reformed Theological Seminary. A later form of this essay was included in the Study Guide for Geneva Ministries' course on "Creeds and Confessions."

Chapter 3, "The Sociology of the Church: A Biblico-Historical Approach," was written for this volume. This essay, with some modifications, also appears as chapter 2 of my book, *Sabbath Breaking and the Death Penalty: A Theological Investigation* (Tyler, TX: Geneva Ministries, 1986).

The Introduction to Part II appeared in *Presbyterian Heritage* No. 8 (October, 1985) under the title "Ziklag Bivouac."

Chapter 4, "The Three Faces of Protestantism," originally appeared in *The Geneva Papers* I:31 (September, 1984).

Chapter 5, "Conversion," originally appeared in *The Geneva Papers* I:33 (November, 1984).

Chapter 6, "The Effective Church Splitter's Guide," was privately circulated by the author under the title and pseudonym, "How to be an Effective Roger Williams," by Robin Williams.

Chapter 7, "Propositions on Pentecostalism," appears here for the first time.

Chapter 8, "Christian Zionism and Messianic Judaism," incorporates an earlier essay entitled, "Jerry Falwell and the Heresy of Christian Zionism," *The Geneva Review* No. 11 (June, 1984).

Chapter 9, "Should Churches Incorporate?", originally appeared in *The Geneva Papers* I:30 (July/August, 1984).

Chapter 10, "How Biblical is Protestant Worship?", originally appeared in *The Geneva Papers* I:25 & 26 (February & March, 1984).

Chapter 11, "God's Hospitality and Holistic Evangelism," was first published in Gary North, ed., *The Journal of Christian Reconstruction* VII:2 (Winter, 1981), "Symposium on Evangelism." I have added considerably to it, and have changed my opinion on a couple of points.

Chapter 12, "Triumphalistic Investiture," originally appeared in *Presbyterian Heritage* No. 4 (September, 1984).

Chapter 13, "A Liturgy of Malediction," appeared originally in *The Geneva Papers* I:21 (October, 1983).

Chapter 14, "A Liturgy of Healing," appeared originally in *The Geneva Papers* I:22 (November, 1983).

I wish to reiterate that each of these essays has been revised for publication here, and some have been extensively added to or changed.

Preface (1999)

The Sociology of the Church was originally published in 1986, and subtitled *Essays in Reconstruction.* At that time, I was working in "Christian Reconstruction" circles, though somewhat on the fringe. The book was written to those interested in "Christian Reconstruction," as well as to a wider Reformed and evangelical audience, as an appeal to take the Church more seriously as God's ordained vehicle for changing the world. The United States of America is a nation of "parachurch" movements that tend to take a low view of the Church, and my goal was to address that situation.

At the time of this reprint, I am no longer involved in what is left of "Christian Reconstruction," and that is largely because my call for a higher view of the Church and worship was generally rejected by most (though not all) of those travelling under that aegis. At the same time, the need for a Biblical approach to Church renewal remains as pressing today as it was a decade ago. My hope is that the republication of this book, warts and all, will be of help and challenge to Christian people wrestling with such matters at the turn of the second millennium.

Those interested in more recent writings on this topic by the present author are invited to write to me at Biblical Horizons, P.O. Box 1096, Niceville, Florida 32588, for a catalogue of essays and more recent studies in worship and ecclesiology. Those with internet access can consult our website at:

www.hornes.org/biblicalhorizons

My thanks to Wipf and Stock Publishers for making this reprint available.

Part I

BUILDING BLOCKS FOR RECONSTRUCTION

The three essays in this section are an attempt to bring the insights of two schools of thought to bear on certain fundamental questions of ecclesiology. The two schools, which overlap one another to a large extent, are Vantillian presuppositionalism and Christian reconstructionism. Presuppositionalists such as Van Til himself, Norman Shepherd, and John Frame have concentrated on philosophical and dogmatic issues, while Vern S. Poythress has extended the school of thought to the areas of hermeneutics and exegesis. Reconstructionists such as R. J. Rushdoony and Gary North have concentrated on socio-political issues. To my knowledge, these efforts constitute the first time anyone has attempted in print to bring these insights to bear on ecclesiological questions. Of necessity, therefore, these essays are somewhat tentative, and are offered to the church at large as springboards for reflection, and certainly not as the last word on the subject.

Chapter 1 concerns two general areas that must be addressed if the church is to regain her role in society. These are the areas of government and worship. The church must once again become a genuine government, with her own courts, but for this to have any social impact the various churches must recover a genuine committment to catholicity in practice. Accordingly, a large part of this essay concerns catholicity. Since the sacraments, embedded in worship, constitute the primary juridical power of the church, a renewal of understanding in the areas of sacraments and worship is also absolutely essential, and so most of the rest of the essay deals with this matter.

1

Chapter 2 deals at more length with the place of the church in society. I have here brought to bear on the subject a valuable schema that arose in physics, was introduced to linguistics by Kenneth Pike, and was brought into presuppositionalism by Vern Poythress: the distinction between wave, particle, and field. This triple approach to the nature of the church, in my opinion, is of great help in sorting out certain fundamental questions that have plagued ecclesiological discussion for centuries. With this schema in mind, the essay takes up the question of the relationship between local and larger churches, and the problems of schism, denominationalism, and parachurch organizations.

Chapter 3 is the most "speculative" of the essays offered here. I have attempted to deal with certain legitimate questions raised by dispensationalism, to wit the relationship between Old Covenant Israel and the New Covenant Church. My resolution of this problem differs from traditional covenant theology and dispensationalism, in that I argue that the place of Israel in the Old Covenant was as a priest to the nations. The nations could be converted, and many were. There was no need for gentile converts to be circumcised, because circumcision was not a sign of salvation, but of the priesthood of Israel. This bipolarity of Israel-priests and Gentile-converts was overcome in the New Covenant, when all are priests in one body. This is a large matter to discuss in a short essay, and my purpose is not to deal with every aspect of the question, but to indicate the *prima facie* plausibility of my thesis. I can do no more in a book of this size, especially since it is addressed to an audience wider than only professional theologians. I must, therefore, ask that my more professionally educated readers bear this in mind as they consider my arguments.

1

RECONSTRUCTING THE CHURCH:
A CONSERVATIVE ECUMENICAL AGENDA

1984, the year in which this essay is being written, is a year made infamous in literature by a novel by George Orwell. Surely as far as the church of Jesus Christ is concerned, America in 1984 seems to be approaching Orwell's *Nineteen Eighty-Four* rather rapidly. The church in the United States of America cannot be said to have much credibility, power, or authority left. Men do not fear to rape the holy bride of Christ. What Emperors once did not dare to do is now done with impunity by gun-slinging "lawmen" in small American towns.

If I were to write an essay on what happened in Louisville, Nebraska, I should title it "Torture and Brainwashing in Nebraska." When fathers are arrested, thrown into county jail, and not permitted to speak with one another or with outsiders, I call it torture. When they are told that they will not be granted a trial until they identify their children (so that the court can steal them from their parents), I call it torture. When they are called out of isolation day after day, and shown photographs of children, and told to identify them, I call it torture.

Isolation, deprivation, and mental torture: These are standard torture and brainwashing techniques, used commonly behind the Iron and Bamboo Curtains (and made notorious when used against Americans during the Korean War). There is nothing strange about this, though, because these are the same techniques used to brainwash the children in Nebraska's public schools: isolation from their parents and the faith, and indoctrination with false and unGodly information.

3

Why were these men being tortured? Because they had their children in an "unlicensed" Christian school, run by an "unlicensed" Christian church. Nebraska had tried to shut down the school in 1983, and people all over America saw on their television sets a videotaped record of the sheriff of Cass County padlocking the doors of the Faith Baptist Church of Louisville, Nebraska. They saw armed officers of the state forcing their way into the church during a religious meeting, forcibly dragging a hundred or so clergymen from their knees, and hauling them outside the building.

In January, 532 A.D., there was a riot in the Hippodrome in Constantinople. (The Hippodrome was Constantinople's Colisseum.) The riot was a minor one, but those involved were protesting the tax policies of the Emperor Justinian, ruler of the entire Roman world. A few men were tried, and sentenced to be hanged. At the execution, the ropes hanging two of the men broke as they dropped from the scaffold. Undaunted, the hangman obtained a second rope and tried again. Again the rope broke, and the men fell to the ground. The sympathetic crowd surged forward, and bore the two men to the Church of Saint Lawrence, where they were granted asylum (or sanctuary).

The Emperor Justinian did not dare to order the arrest of the two tax rebels as long as they remained in the safety of the house of God, under the protection of the church. Though his soldiers stood guard to catch them if they came out, no soldier dared enter the church.[1]

But what Emperors and Roman soldiers once dared not do, local sheriffs and American policemen are now ready to do, without qualm.

The present essay consists of explorations and suggestions along the lines of reconstituting the Christian church. It would certainly be presumptuous of me to think that I have answers to

---

1. This was the beginning of the famous Nika Revolt. Standard histories of the reign of Justinian and Theodora describe these events. I have used the well written book by Antony Bridge, *Theodora: Portrait in a Byzantine Landscape* (London: Cassell Ltd. [MacMillan Pub. Co.], 1978), pp. 64ff.

every matter along these lines, all or most of which have been debated throughout much if not most of church history. As a result, this essay is somewhat rambling and is designed as suggestive rather than in any sense definitive. Much of what is contained here comes out of interactions with other men wrestling with these problems, but I am in no position to remember who said what when. The reader should be aware, however, that what I present here comes out of intense discussion and interaction with the other men who can loosely be described as a community of pastors and writers associated with Geneva Ministries of Tyler, Texas—men such as Ray Sutton, David Chilton, Gary North, Lewis Bulkeley, Robert Dwelle, and others. Ultimately, however, responsibility for what I have selected to write about is mine.

Since it is our responsibility always to clean our own house first, the reader should be alerted at the outset that I am addressing issues and problems that are found in American conservative, protestant churches—particularly those of baptist or presbyterian persuasions. All the same, I think that the "baptistification" of American culture,[2] and the fact that American ways are exported worldwide, mean that these issues are also relevant to Christians from other traditions as well. At any rate, I invite the reader to think with me about the matters discussed here.

True and False Churches

Which are the true churches? In today's mixed up ecclesiastical situation, can we say that some are and some are not? Not easily (though sectarians always think they can). It is important, however, to think about the question, so that we have some idea where we are in history, and can better figure out what God would have us to do.

When a person is brought to God, or when a baptized child is aroused or quickened to a more living commitment to God, one of the things that happens is a regenerating movement of the Holy

---

2. See James B. Jordan, ed., *The Failure of the American Baptist Culture*. Christianity & Civilization No. 1 (Tyler, Texas: Geneva Ministries, 1982).

Spirit.[3] Since the Spirit is the Author of the Bible, the newly aroused Christian immediately senses the need to cleave to the Bible as his source of information, inspiration, and law. If he is not sidetracked from this, he will come more and more to love and live out of the Scriptures.

Too often, however, he is sidetracked. Satan is the great enemy of the Word of God. It is his purpose to steal it from the hearts of God's people, and in the 20th century he has been particularly successful at this.

Conservative Christians, such as I am, are quite ready to point the finger at liberalism and neo-orthodoxy in this regard. And there can be no doubt but that at the theoretical and practical levels, liberalism and Barthianism gut the Scripture of its Divine authority and life-giving power. Various foolish theories about the origin of the Bible tell us that it evolved out of the developing religious consciousness of a primitive people. Thus, it is hardly the written Word of God. Practically, it is a matter of indifference to liberals and Barthians whether or not the Bible condemns abortion, homosexuality, or the ordination of women.

All very true, but is it really the case that every preacher and every church in liberal and/or neo-orthodox denominations is completely "sold out to the flesh" on these things? Hardly. Many people are simply mistaught and ignorant. This includes the pastors as well. Seeing how ignorant and mistaught the average fundamentalist and pentecostal pastors of today are, why should we think that pastors in liberal circles are any more self-conscious about their beliefs? Many of them were sidetracked early, and have never been encouraged seriously to consider historic, orthodox Christianity. Since we are in a time of reformation, we should

---

3. The Biblical doctrine of regeneration is not the same as that used in systematic theology. Theology uses the term "regeneration" to refer to the invisible one-time renewal of the elect, which brings about their faith and salvation. In the Bible, regeneration is a continual work, with peaks and valleys, and applies not only to individuals but also to society and the cosmos as well. Thus, the elect can experience turning points (conversions) or regenerations at a number of crisis points in their lives, in addition to the fact that every day brings with it the need for continual conversion and renewal.

not be too surprised if people from such circles begin to revive and take the Bible more seriously.

It is important to understand this. Just because a preacher or theologian voices a Barthian or semi-Barthian view of scripture does not mean that he is not a Christian, or that nothing else he has to say has any value. It may be that he is teaching and applying the Word of God, in spite of his bad theory, far better than some conservative theologians and preachers do. There are a lot of teachers and pastors in "mainline" churches who are only moderately liberal, and whose liberalism is more a matter of their being mistaught than of any self-conscious commitment on their part. The law of God distinguishes between sins of ignorance and high-handed sins, and so must we.

Among churches that give lip-service to the inerrancy and infallible authority of the Bible, the Scriptures are commonly negated in three ways. We may call these anti-Biblical tendencies by the names dispensationalism, pentecostalism, and bapto-presbyterianism.

How does dispensationalism destroy the Word of God? By two means. First, at the theoretical level, dispensationalism teaches that the entire Old Testament and much of the New Testament is not relevant to the life of the church or of Christian people today. Depending on which of various dispensational theories are used, theologians may *effectively* renounce from 7/10ths to 49/50ths of the Bible.[4]

Practically speaking, second, the ethos of dispensationalism directs its followers to focus primarily on end-time events rather than on present duties. Thus, there is always a plethora of books on prophecy emanating from dispensational outlets. Hal Lindsey is the most famous, but hardly the only, writer of this kind of escapist fantasy literature.

---

4. Scofieldian dispensationalism accepts only Acts through Revelation 3, thus putting aside 87%. Bullingerites accept only Paul's prison epistles, putting aside 98.2%. Modified Bullingerites (Grace Movement) accept all of Paul, putting aside the remaining 94% of Scripture. The popular notion that the Old Testament is gone and only the New Testament is canonical sets aside 69% of Scripture.

By these two means, dispensationalism undermines the practical authority of much of Scripture as thoroughly as any liberal theology does. Giving lip service to inerrancy is certainly inconsistent under these circumstances. Are all dispensational preachers and churches, then, anti-Christian? Of course not. Just as we saw with liberalism and neo-orthodoxy, many churches are far better than their official theories. And, happily, in recent years, dispensational theologians have become more sophisticated, and are willing to admit that Christians should pray the Lord's Prayer, and take other pre-Pentecostal portions of Scripture more seriously as authoritative for the present day.

Pentecostalism also all too often has little use for Scripture. The emphasis in the movement as a whole is upon direct, mystical experiences with God (roughly defined). The stimulation of glands has priority over the reformation of life. This is most pronounced in the various healing cults and "name it and claim it" sects, which are all over the airwaves today. This is nothing more than medicine man religion, and scarcely Christian at all. It has little more relation to Christianity than do the "cargo cults" of Polynesia.[5] Not all charismatics are this bad, of course, but the tendency is there in all too many of them. The effect is that the Word of God is rendered null and void.

The third conservative group that negates the Bible is the bapto-presbyterian group. These do so by means of their preaching and liturgy. That may seem a strange charge, but the fact is

---

5. The cargo cults make airplanes out of wood and sacrifice to them, in the hopes that the planes in the sky will be drawn back down to them, and give them more cargo (as they did during World War II)—cargo like liquor, good food, clothing, etc. This is all mixed up with "Jesus," as a result of confusion with white missionary endeavors. The pentecostalists endulge in self-stimulation in order to try to attract the blessings of their version of the Holy Spirit, and consequent cargo (such as a new Eldorado, lots of money, a new woman, etc.). To watch American cargoism in action, simply tune in your "Christian" radio or television station. To read about Polynesian cargoism, two studies are: Edward Rice, *John Frum He Come: Cargo Cults and Cargo Messiahs in the South Pacific* (Garden City, NY: Doubleday, 1974); and the chapter on "Commodity Millennialism" in Bryan R. Wilson's outstanding *Magic and the Millennium: A Sociological Study of Religious Movements of Protest Among Tribal and Third-World Peoples* (New York: Harper & Row, 1973).

that the text of Scripture is seldom preached in either Baptist or Presbyterian churches (and I mean conservative, "Bible-preaching" churches). Biblical exposition has often been replaced by screaming and yelling in the pulpit. Preachers preach against things that are not sinful (such as drinking wine), and when they do deal with genuine sin, they generally don't do so out of any text. In most (though not all) Baptist circles, the goal of preaching is to produce a conversion experience, and get people to engage in the ritual of walking the aisle, week after week. Biblical and theological content is kept to an absolute minimum.

Presbyterians may think they are better, but the dead homilies in some churches have been beating all interest in the Bible out of their people for years. The reason is simple: Presbyterian seminary students are taught, sometimes directly and sometimes indirectly, that laymen are stupid and can only be fed pabulum. (Laymen must take a lot of the blame here too, of course.) Thus, the student is told to take a text of Scripture, *process* it through some "analytic/synthetic" method (or some other method), *reduce* it either to one big point or three points, *spruce it up* with artificial illustrations (from some illustration book), and thereby mush out some *general thoughts* on the passage. Somehow, it just isn't "preaching" (or rather, *"PREACHING"*) if we simply go through the passage verse by verse and explain it, drawing together conclusions at the end. Not only does such a method give out far too much content for the cretins in the congregation to take in, but it also has the obvious disadvantage of sticking right with God's own words. Who wants that? How much better to use the process, reduce, and spruce method? (By the way, I've never found laymen to be all that dumb, particularly when they have an open text in front of them. Even if they are, it would be better to teach God's word and trust the Spirit to bring people up to that level, than simultaneously to insult God and feed processed leftovers to His sheep.)

Of course, some seminarians eventually manage to overcome what they were taught about how to preach. Far too many, though, do not. It is no wonder that people in these kinds of churches, if they want to be fed, wind up getting cassette tapes from some genuine Bible expositor.

Not only do all too many bapto-presbyterians gut the Scriptures through their non-preaching of it, they also remove it from effectiveness through their worship practices. Theologians in both groups give lip service to the regulative principle of worship, which says that our worship is supposed to be directed by and limited by Scriptural injunctions, but practically this has been interpreted and applied in an absolutely minimalist fashion. The psalter is not sung, let alone chanted. The patterns of worship seen in Scripture are ignored, and thus replaced either with nothing (the stoic deadness of much presbyterianism) or with the froth of modern entertainment (the showy circuses so frequently manifest in baptist and pentecostal circles). In this way, again, the Word is rendered null and void, absent from the church.

To summarize this section: We live in a confusing period of history ecclesiastically. The Bible is indeed God's inerrant and infallible Word — liberals are wrong to deny this. All the same, modern conservatives are all too seldom any better when they deny the applicability and relevance of most of Scripture. God is not going to judge men based primarily on what they gave lip service to on earth. He is going to judge them based on their faith, and on what they did, as all the judgment passages of Scripture make clear. And teachers will be judged by a stricter standard (James 3). This being so, we have to ask how many theoretical inerrantists will stand on that Day?

It must be admitted, of course, that churches committed to the inerrancy and infallibility of the Bible are, in general, in much better shape than are churches where this truth has been severely blurred. The point of my discussion, however, still stands, which is that it is practical, not mere theoretical, commitments that count before God.[6]

---

6. An interesting perspective on all this is the question of public opposition to abortion. How many "fundamental, Bible-believing" Christians simply refuse to get involved in picketing or any other public work against this hideous crime! At the same time, however, one occasionally finds laymen and leaders from "mainline" churches taking an open stand. Thus, this clear-cut moral issue is serving, at present, to cut across all kinds of ecclesiastical lines, separating the sheep from the goats as it were.

How do we respond in the face of this God-ordained historical situation? I suggest that the answer is by means of a carefully worked out policy of catholicity and integrity.

Catholicity and Integrity

How should one badly bruised and inadequate church relate to another? (I am not addressing the blessed possessors of absolutely perfect churches, naturally.) I believe there are three things to bear in mind.

First, we must be open to the values in other Christian traditions — even Roman Catholic and Eastern Orthodox traditions. Have we done such a great job in conservative protestantism that we are *certain* we have nothing to learn from these other churches? Simple openness and willingness to listen and learn from other churches is an important part of catholicity. I shall return to this concern in the next section of this essay.

Second, churches must become committed to a principle of mutual recognition of one another's orders and discipline. This requires self-discipline, or it will never work. How easy it is to receive disgruntled people from the church down the street! How easy to believe the bad report they bring! From my experience, however, people who are troublemakers in one church will be troublemakers in another. Why not call up the pastors of the other church, and ask them for their side? And if they say that this family is a problem, why not grant initial credibility to the findings of these shepherds?

Let me illustrate this with a couple of stories. We had a problem in our church caused by a man from another church. Eventually we found that we had to bring a written protest against this man before his church. We found, however, that they could not receive a "protest," since according to the definition found in their manual of discipline, "protests" can only come from within their own church. We were tempted to write another letter, calling it a "beef!" Moreover, some were not sure what they could do about it, since they did not "recognize" us as a church. Though in this situation the men were sympathetic, and did hear us out, this is the kind of problem that comes when open recognition of other churches is not the rule.

Similarly, we have on occasion been forced to declare certain of our members excommunicate from the church. These people, almost without exception, simply go down the street and join another church. Do the pastors of these churches phone us up and ask us about it? No. Never. Not once. Indeed, we have taken it upon ourselves, on occasion, to write letters or phone other churches when we hear that they have taken in excommunicated people, but we have seldom received any recognition.

Now, what is interesting is this. Recently, a presbyterian church in our town split. Who was right in the center of causing the trouble and the split? A couple of people excommunicated from another church. Also, recently, a presbyterian church in a nearby town also split. Who was right in the center of that split? Again, it was a couple of people excommunicated from another church. There is a price to be paid, it seems, for despising the government of other churches.

In our early days, a man came to us from another denomination. He had been excommunicated. He said it was because he had come around to Calvinistic doctrine that he had been persecuted. Instead of checking out his story, we believed him. Within six months we had had to excommunicate him also. *Then* we checked up on him, and found out that the real reason his former church had excommunicated him had nothing to do with doctrine! We had to learn the hard way. The next man who came to us with that story was sent back to his former church, not a presbyterian church, to set things right. Initially he was very angry with us, but after a couple of months he did go back and make his peace with his former congregation, and was enabled to transfer in peace to a presbyterian church.

Third, internally we need to work out a balance between catholicity and integrity. There are generally four ways to resolve the tension between the two.

(1) A church may strive exclusively for catholicity. In my opinion, this is what happens when the Lord's Supper is held, and the officiant invites everybody who thinks he is a Christian to par-

take. Visitors are not interviewed, and the elders make no attempt to fence the Table. Such churches sometimes have no written roll of members and accept virtually anybody who professes some kind of commitment to Christ. The problem comes when there is a need to make basic decisions, and everyone has a vote regardless of maturity and/or commitment to the (generally unspecified but very real) theology of the church. Somebody has to make a decision about this kind of thing, but the church is little more than a large Bible study. So the pastor or the elders must assume power in the middle of the situation, in order to do what they know to be right. This causes hostility, and can wreck the church. A similar problem arises from the unspecified theology of the church, so that people do not know exactly what they have to agree with and what they do not. Persons angry with the leadership can make hay with other members by charging, "You have to agree with the elders on every little point." False as this accusation may be, the fact that the boundaries of integrity are not defined leaves the elders open to this kind of charge.

(2) A church may opt for integrity, and ignore catholicity except in theory. Such churches rapidly become quite sectarian in character. Only people who believe exactly as they do are permitted to come to the Lord's Table. In theory they maintain that they are part of the church catholic, but there is no way in which such catholicity can come to expression sacramentally. This position is also quintessentially *congregationalistic*, because every member has to accept the whole theological package, and the congregation as a whole is seen as the guardian of orthodoxy.

(3) "Muddling through" is the third option: trying to come up with a blend of catholicity and integrity. This is a common way of handling the problem nowadays, especially in the presbyterian circles with which I am most familiar. The church maintains standards, and all the communicant members are supposed to come up to a certain par. Children must master certain details of dogma before they can be admitted to the Table. At the same time, the communion is open to all professing Christians. We recognize other churches if they are kind of like us, and if it is convenient.

Moreover, anybody who professes Christ can be not only a communicant but also a voting member of the church. The latter tends to dissolve integrity by opening the possibility of many people making decisions in the church who are not aware of sound doctrine. The check on this comes in the special officers (elders), who are supposed to know the faith more perfectly, but this again is compromised when "ruling elders" are elected only on the basis of being notable persons, and not on the basis of Spiritual and doctrinal maturity. We might pursue this, but it should be clear that catholicity and integrity are working against one another in this system. The more catholic we are, the more diluted we become, and the more integrity we try to have, the more exclusive we become.

(4) The fourth option is to combine a strong commitment to integrity with a strong commitment to catholicity. Here, integrity is committed to the province of the special officers, and anyone is permitted to come to the Table of the Lord who (a) has been baptized, (b) professes Christ as Savior and Lord, and (c) is under some ecclesiastical government. Such church members may be very ignorant of the doctrine of the church, and may be in considerable error, but as long as they are willing to listen to the preached voice of the Master, they are permitted to share at His Table.[7]

This position makes a distinction between voting and non-voting members. Children, people who are new to the faith, people who have not come to a knowledge of various fundamentals of the faith, and persons under chastisement for some sin clearly will not be permitted to vote in the selection of elders to govern the church.[8]

The guardians of orthodoxy in the church are not the people at large, but the special officers. Their integrity is in turn guarded by

7. I don't intend this to be taken in some simplistic sense. A person is initially admitted to the Table based on these three qualifications. Should he show himself in moral sin, or an avid advocate of some perverse doctrinal viewpoint, discipline would be in order.

8. Biblically speaking, the age of voting, of coming into the assembly, is 20; see Numbers 1:3. As regards new converts, Biblical data indicates that background should be taken into account; see Deuteronomy 23:3-8. The power of the New Covenant is such that, I believe, it is not necessary to wait several generations; but perhaps the wait of a sabbath period of six years would be advisable.

making sure that voting membership is properly restricted. The advantage of this fourth position is that it preserves the integrity of the church, her morals, government, and doctrine, while allowing for a very broad catholicity. Virtually any kind of Christian can be welcomed to the fellowship of the Lord's Table, without jeopardizing the standards of the church.

Who is our Examplar in this? Was there ever anyone with more integrity, and who made greater demands, than Jesus Christ? Yet look at the catholicity of His practice: He ate with publicans, harlots, and sinners, and He took nursing infants into His arms and thus to Himself. Who complained about all this? The Pharisees. How could Jesus, the spotless Son of God, associate with such evil people? Simple: They were (a) members of the visible church, even though that church was borderline apostate (run by Sadducees and Pharisees). They were (b) not excommunicate from that visible church. They were (c) willing to listen to what He had to say. Now, of course, after they listened for a while, most of them departed, not willing to persevere. They excommunicated themselves. But initially, they were welcomed according to the catholic principle we have outlined. Notice that Jesus *ate and drank* with them. It requires a clever bit of nominalism to miss the sacramental implications of this. Pharisees, beware![9]

By following the fourth option, then, our Savior's example can be imitated, and we can avoid falling into the kind of sectarian practice that so often characterizes the most thoroughly conservative churches.

What Might We Learn from Episcopalianism?

Let me now return to my first point about catholicity: openness to other traditions. To do this, I should like to present a brief

---

9. Beware indeed! Jesus reserved His most ferocious threats of hellfire for those who refuse to recognize other Christians. See Mark 9:38-50, and also Numbers 11:27-29. Jesus articulates an important principle of catholicity in Mark 9:49-50. The man who has salt in himself—the fire of self-purification and humility—will be a peaceful man, esteeming others better than himself, and with that attitude he can correct the wayward.

essay on Episcopalianism. I offer it as an example of the kind of openness we need to have if we are going to make significant progress toward the reconstruction of the church and of our culture.

Some of us like to believe that our American Christian culture is based on Presbyterian and Baptist values. Obviously this is to a great extent true. The fact is, however, that both in Britain and in America, the dominant religious group has been Episcopalian. Like it or not, the Episcopalians have exercised more effective social dominion than have the rest. The strengths of Presbyterians and Baptists have been harnessed, monitored, directed, and overseen by Episcopalian rulers in both nations.

Why is this? Why are the Episcopalians, as a group, the strongest, and that in spite of the fact that after the War of Independence they were associated with despised loyalists? I should like to isolate what I regard as certain key factors, at which points Episcopalians differ from Presbyterian and Baptist groups. All three have a heritage of Calvinistic or Augustinian orthodoxy (in soteriology and the doctrine of God), and thus all three far surpass all other churches in dominion (counting the Methodists, for now, as a variant of Episcopalianism in this regard). The Episcopalians (as distinguished from Methodists here) have been on the top, always. There is something different about Episcopalians that brings this about. What is it?

I believe that the salient factors are three: the promotion of excellence, the respect for tradition, and a certain primacy of the institutional church.

First of all, it is my impression that the Episcopal churches, more so than any others, are careful to advance and promote their best men. If this is true in their church, it will also be true in their society at large. If one looks to see who the big name theologians of Episcopalianism are, they are frequently bishops. The Episcopalians identify, promote, protect, and prosper their best men. They provide large salaries, good homes, secure retirements. For their scholar-bishops, they provide domestic servants and secretaries, so that the man of the cloth is free from ordinary worries and duties and can devote his time to pastoral and literary work.

Is anything like this *ever* done in Baptist and Presbyterian circles? I dare say not. To my knowledge, there has never been, in the entire history of Presbyterianism, a man who was set aside to be a scholar and writer. Without exception, Presbyterians load their best men down with detail and trivial tasks, so that they accomplish little. Their best thinkers are made teachers in theological institutions, where they are made to spend their days going over basics with young, immature men just out of generally worthless college educations. The rest of their time is taken up with committee meetings and administrative tasks. It is a wonder that any of them ever get any writing and research done. It is no surprise that the most brilliant of them, Cornelius Van Til, seldom was able to get his writings into polished English style — he had no time for it.

We can contrast this with the armies of scholars maintained by Rome, and the small cadre maintained in Episcopalian circles. The difference is marked, and points to the fundamental difference between these two groups. The catholic party (Roman and Anglican) is frankly elitist. It strives to convert and control the elite in society, and it arms its best men for that task, giving them time for reflection and writing. The evangelical party (Presbyterian and Baptist, especially the latter) is infected largely with the heresy of democracy, and believes (wrongly) that the conversion of society comes with the conversion of the masses.

Americans (evangelicals) like to believe the myth that society is transformed from the "bottom up" and not from the "top down." This flies squarely in the face both of history and of Scripture. The history of Israel, as recorded in Scripture, is not a history of revivals from the bottom up, but of kings and their actions. Good kings produced a good nation; bad kings a bad nation. The order is always seen from the top down, though of course with real feedback from the bottom up.

This is no surprise. From Genesis 3 onwards, society is likened to a large man, with a head and hands and feet. The head obviously governs the rest of the members. To destroy the body, you crush the head. This is seen over and over in the book of Judges. Sometimes the head is literally crushed, as with Sisera and Abimelech. Sometimes it is the social head that is crushed, as with Eglon, Oreb and Zeeb, Zebah and Zalmunna, and the five lords of the Philistines.[10]

Christ is the head of the church, the New Testament repeatedly tells us. The church, however, is also a body politic, with eyes, hands, and feet (1 Cor. 12). Each part is necessary, but each part does not have the same function. There are rulers and governors — a hierarchy — in the church. There is no virtue in trying to evade this obvious fact, by objecting to the term "hierarchy," or by ignoring the issue. Clearly, the greatest danger to the church comes not from wayward sheep, but from false leaders, savage wolves (Acts 20:30, etc.).

Of course, we must say by way of a comprehensive philosophy of history that the Triune God always moves all at once, reforming from the top down at the same time as He reforms from the bottom up. The point, however, is that there is a small group of elite leaders and controllers — a hierarchy — in every society. There always will be. Whoever ministers to that elite group will control society. Paul knew that. That is why he wanted so badly to get to Rome.[11] The Episcopalians also know know it. The Presbyterians and Baptists have tried to pretend that this is not so, and have thus left the elite to others, as much by default as by anything else.

Life and death flow from the head. This is true of Adam and his posterity, and of Christ and His. In smaller ways, the same principle is true in all of life. Good kings bring up a good nation; bad kings a bad one. That is why kings are likened to fathers and mothers in Scripture (Is. 49:23). Influence, for good or bad, flows from the head. People imitate those who are high and mighty.

This is the invariable posture of Scripture. It was the belief of the early church, which arranged its elders, each of which had the

---

10. For an extended discussion of this, see my book, *Judges: God's War Against Humanism* (Tyler, TX: Geneva Ministries, 1985).

11. Compare the way God moved Joseph and Daniel into positions of influence with the ruling emperors of the world, as well as the more subtle discussion of the same theme in the book of Esther (e.g., Mordecai's initial schemes for advancement are thwarted, but upon his repentance, eventually rewarded).

same power, in ranks according to the pattern of Exodus 18. Modern presbyterians, infected with the heresy of democracy, try to make all elders equal in function as well as in office. This does not work, of course, as lay elders do not have the same time nor the same degree of concern for the day to day workings of the church as do fulltime elders. Their speciality lies elsewhere. Modern presbyterians, arguing against the Episcopalian notion of the bishop as a separate office, have gotten rid of higher ranks of elders (bishops) altogether, so that age is not really respected, and a truly spiritual hierarchy is never groomed. One bad result, because hierarchy is inescapable, is that power often, though not always, falls to those least qualified to wield it. Another bad result is that the Biblical pastoral hierarchy is replaced, in democratically-infected denominations, with impersonal bureaucracies.

Along with this goes a polemic against envy. A society that is openly hierarchical, as is the Episcopalian church, does not have near the problem with envy as does a society that pretends to democracy. A society that recognizes that there is a diversity of gifts, and that actively promotes its best men, has gone a long way toward stripping the envious of their power. Baptist and Presbyterian bureaucracies not infrequently have their least capable men in high position, in part due to the greater prominence of envy in their midst.

We may question whether Baptist and Presbyterian bodies really even want to minister to the elite. It is easy to say "there are not many mighty called." So what? What about those who are? And what about influencing those who are not? Men who are big frogs in small ponds have a vested interest in keeping the pond small. They don't want an invasion of elite people, who have more money, more education, and more power than they do. Thus, they really don't want to minister to the elite. They don't want to take over the elite. They don't prize excellence, and they don't reward it. They move to cripple the capabilities of their best men, as I have described above. They cling to the myth that literature oriented toward the masses will do more than scholarly material oriented toward the elite. That this is baloney does not bother them, because they really *do not want dominion.*

We might make a case study of the mass literature of evangelicalism and dispensationalism. Are there any people in the ruling
elite in America who are even aware that such literature exists?
No. Dispensational literature has not actually affected American
life at all, simply because nobody in any position of power and
prominence ever reads any of it.[12] The power elite in America is
humanist and liberal, not dispensational. The conservative elite is
Roman Catholic or Episcopalian (and therefore largely influenced
by Catholic writers). The production of literature aimed at the
masses has its place, of course; but it does not affect the transformation of society. It is a legitimate ministry, but it will not change
the world. In fact, in the history of the church, to my knowledge it
has never been possible to reduce hard, intellectual, elitist theology to the level of the common man. The effort to do so seems
wasted. (This is not to reject the need for genuinely content-full
Biblical preaching.)

This is not to despise the poor and the simple. One of the ministries of Episcopalian churches in town after town is the Episcopal Thrift House, where the used clothing of the wealthy is made
available to the poor at extremely low cost. I got through college
wearing coats from the Episcopal Thrift House. These stores are
staffed by volunteer ladies from the Episcopal church, ladies
whose husbands make so much money that they can afford to
donate lots of time free to this ministry. This kind of ministry is
simply impossible among churches that do not have wealthy
members.

The second factor that has made Episcopalianism strong is its
respect for tradition. Unlike most other Reformed churches, the
English church was blessed with reforming bishops. The bishops
were not the enemies but the friends of reform. As a result, the
English church never *reacted* against the Medieval tradition, and
sought to conserve the best that was there. All the Reformers were

---

12. This situation has changed somewhat with the rise of the New Christian
Right, which translates dispensational theology into "pop-dispy" support of
present-day apostate Israel. The influence of such men as Jerry Falwell and Pat
Robertson is felt in the formulation of American-Israeli policies. See the chapter
on "Christian Zionism and Messianic Judaism," pp. 175-186 in this volume.

experts in the early church, and also in the Medieval theologians. After a century, however, the other Reformed groups had begun to ignore the Fathers and the Medievals. The myth arose that the Medieval church was wholly evil from A.D. 606 on. The great advances of the Christian centuries were overlooked. The real accomplishments of the Papal See were rejected. Only among the Anglicans did Patristic and Medieval scholarship retain a strong footing.[13]

Thus, the Episcopalian churches have never lacked a strong sense of tradition. They subordinated tradition to Scripture, but never threw it out altogether. They have built enduring institutions, both physical and literary. They are here to stay.

In their respect for tradition, they are like the Jews, who are the other group that makes up the elite in British and especially American culture.

Third, the Episcopalian churches have put the visible church in first place, before theology and before personalities. The history of the Baptist churches is a history of personalities (preachers). The history of the Reformed churches is a history of combating theologies and theologians. Both groups have a history of one schism after another. This is not true of the Episcopalian churches. This is because they permit various theologies to exist under the common umbrella of the institutional church.

Is this bad or good? Before answering that, let us look at how it works, and how strong it is. The Episcopal churches bind their people to the church and to the tradition by the careful and plenary use of profound symbol and beautiful ritual. These things, contrary to the rationalistic and intellectualistic criticisms of it heard in the Presbyterian and Baptist world, sink deep into the consciousness of the people.[14] The result is that the church be-

---

13. Take up Cunningham's *Historical Theology*, and read his scathing contempt for the Apostles' Creed, to see an example of Reformed historiography at its worst.

14. If this seems "unspiritual," remember that Peter was rightly impressed by the sight of the transfigured Christ, though he had to be reminded of the need for ministry. Similarly, John was rightly enthralled by the sight of the glorified Christ in Revelation 1.

comes something more than merely a collection of people, and it transcends their differences. Not until the Episcopal church began ordaining women and homosexuals, and openly denying the faith, did any schism come.

This makes for a strong church, if a rather closed one. There are a lot of analogies to the Jews here, not least in the failure of either group to evangelize for itself. (Elites seldom feel any need to evangelize.) Provided the various theologies tolerated in the church are each basically orthodox, and in line with the historic creeds, there is no problem with having a strong church. The problem comes when liberalism creeps in, and of course the Episcopal churches today have rotted out as much as any others have.

Doubtless Episcopalian readers have been amazed at how I have described their church. Doubtless if I were an Episcopalian rather than a Presbyterian, the grass would look greener on the other side. Doubtless what I have written here is more an occasion to set out some of my own thoughts than it is an accurate description of Episcopalianism. We ought, therefore, in closing to look at the glaring problem in Episcopalianism.

That problem is the lack of discipline in that body. Do Episcopalians ever declare anyone excommunicate? (Nobody else does either, but for different reasons.) Episcopalianism has been tied to the cultural elite, with the result that Episcopal churches often can become little more than religious country clubs. The cart (the elite) begins to pull the horse (the church). This is the danger and corruption of Episcopalianism.

The answer to this problem is seen only in the Roman Catholic church. That body alone has retained a ministry to all levels of society. The result is that no particular cultural group controls it. A second result is that there is no reticence about disciplining apostates.

Clearly, the reconstruction of the Christian church must take a catholic (though reformed) approach. The point of this essay is that there are things in evangelical protestantism today, which is basically Presbyterian, that prevent this wholistic type of ministry. In particular, if we want to capture the leadership of society, we have to take seriously those things that enabled the Episcopalians, in the early days of America, to emerge as the dominant social force.[15]

Let us now turn from the general question of true and false churches, and look at some specific matters that belong on our reformation agenda. First of all, then: the Bible.

The Bible

Obviously, the Bible lies at the heart of the church. It is not true to say, as many do, that the church produced the Bible, except in a very limited sense. Rather, the Bible, as the Word of God, produced the church. It is the Word that calls the church into being. To be sure, churchmen (the prophets) wrote the Bible, but only under Divine inspiration. It is sometimes argued that the church has authority over the Scriptures insofar as it was the church that, under Divine guidance, determined the limits of the canon. Even this, however, must be challenged. We must maintain that God's Word is instinctively recognized by His image, man, and thus that His Word is "self-attesting." The fact that some men react against and actively suppress this witness only shows that the witness is real. Thus, as portions of the Bible were written, Godly men immediately recognized them as truth, and incorporated them into the existing canon. The only thing the early church did along these lines was *defend* the self-attesting canon against heretics.

Formerly, the Bible was translated and published by the church. A rather grotesque situation developed in England, due to the statist character of the Reformation there, in which the civil government commissioned a translation (the "authorized" version, aptly called by the name "King James") and then only authorized certain favored printers to publish it. With the breakdown of this form of statism in America, the publishing of Bibles became the province of free enterprise printers. There was nothing wrong with that until men began to make new translations *and*

---

15. An informative, if somewhat scandal-mongering study of the social power of Episcopalianism is Kit and Frederica Konolige, *The Power of Their Glory: America's Ruling Class: The Episcopalians* (New York: Wyden Books, 1978).

copyright them! We now have the spectre of the Word of God copyrighted by groups of men, either groups of scholars or publishing houses.

This is a preposterous situation, and ought to be remedied. Let me make a proposal, and use the fine new version put out by Thomas Nelson as an example. They put up the money to create the "New King James Version." I have no problem with their putting a *temporary* copyright on this translation, so that they can obtain royalties and get back the money they put into it. On the day, however, when they have recovered their cost, they ought to remove the copyright. They could still make money printing and selling the NKJV, but so could anyone else. Scholars would no longer have to write to *obtain permission to quote the Bible* (!). Not only would this be a fine gesture of goodwill, it would also guarantee the NKJV a strong running for adoption as the Bible of our culture, a running that it deserves in my opinion.

Still, it would be good for the church to become sufficiently reconstructed to undertake the translation and publication of a church Bible.

Another question along these lines is the order of the books of the Bible. From earliest times, there was a definite order and grouping of the books of the Old Testament, and of the New. That order is no longer used today. High on our agenda should be a discussion of going back to publishing the Bible in its original order.[16]

Practically speaking, the Bible needs to be restored to centrality in our worship. I shall have more to say about Biblical liturgics later in this essay. For now, let me propose that a Composite Psalter for worship is desperately needed. Each psalm (and also other Biblical canticles) would be given in at least three forms. First would be the text of the psalm, set out for responsive reading along the lines of Hebrew parallelism. Next would come a chanting version, with the words placed within the staves of music in-

---

16. On this question, see Ernest L. Martin, *The Original Bible Restored* (Pasadena, CA: Foundation for Biblical Research, 1984; available from Geneva Ministries, Box 131300, Tyler, TX 75713). Much of this book is speculative, and highly debatable, but it raises many important points that need discussion.

stead of below them. Third would be at least one, preferably two or three, paraphrases of the psalm in the form of rhythmic hymns. The "Genevan jig" tune, with complete harmony and the words printed between the staves for several stanzas, might be included, as well also as a Gelineau version, and other hymnic renderings as well, such as those of Isaac Watts and those found in *The Trinity Hymnal* and *The Book of Psalms for Singing*. Such hymnic renderings ought to make use of the greatest of church music, such as the Lutheran chorales and the great Anglican tunes of the 19th century. Such a project should command the support of all churches interested in genuine reconstruction, but where is the money for it now? A genuinely usable and catholic psalter is nowhere to be found.[17]

Worship

Evangelicalism needs a return to formal and Biblical worship. Worship is a public act, performed on the surface of God's true altar, the world, before His throne. Man's chief end is to glorify and enjoy God, and worship is done for God's pleasure. It is man's highest privilege to dance before the throne of the King of kings, to make a public ritual affirmation of the primacy of God.

Public worship is also done for the edification of men. To "edify" is to build up, as we see in the word "edifice," which means building. God's appointed pastors oversee and organize worship, because they are in charge of overseeing the building of the edifice (1 Cor. 3:10-15; and 14:26). At the same time, edification does not mean "good feelings." We are not to worship as we "feel led," but as God requires.

The basic regulation of worship is found in John 4:24, "in Spirit and in truth." "Truth" refers not just to ideology but primarily to *covenant faithfulness*. The Hebrew words that lie in back of the New Testament word for "truth" have to do with faithfulness, reliability, trustworthiness, sureness. (One of them is the word

---

17. For further remarks on this, see my essay "Church Music in Chaos," in James B. Jordan, ed., *The Reconstruction of the Church*. Christianity & Civilization No. 4 (Tyler, TX: Geneva Ministries, 1985).

"amen.") Jesus said, "I am the Truth," and He is more than a mere intellectual ideology. Truth involves discipleship (John 8:31f.), so that we are commanded to "do" the truth (John 3:21; 1 John 1:6).

Truth is presented as a dialogue between man and God. God speaks first, and man returns speech to God. God speaks His Word to man in more than one way: The Word is read to us, taught to us, preached to us, made visible to us in the Supper, sprinkled upon us in baptism, embodied to us in the lifestyle of Godly men and women. Then, we return God's Word to Him, by listening, submitting to baptism, eating the Supper, singing and praying Scripture, and so forth. This is the dialogue of Truth at the heart of life, before the Throne, and it flows out into all of life.

The second element in true worship is Spirit. If we read John 4:24 in its context (verses 20-26), we realize that it is talking about *environment*. Worship in Spirit means worship in the environment established by the Spirit.[18] In the Old Covenant that was Mount Zion. In the New Covenant, it is wherever Jesus Christ is present. Worshipping in Spirit does *not* mean (a) worshipping internally, or (b) worshipping enthusiastically, or (c) worshipping with *my* spirit. Rather, it means worshipping in the glorious environment of heaven itself.

This is made clear in Hebrews 12:22ff. The Spirit brings heaven to earth during the time of worship (compare Acts 2), and we are taken up into this heavenly environment (compare Revelation 4 and 5). We are present not only with other Christians ("the assembly of the Firstborn who are enrolled in heaven"), but also with "myriads of angels in festal array," as well as the departed saints ("spirits of just men made perfect"). This is the environment of worship, and it is described throughout the book of Revelation. The slain Lamb and the Book in the center of the scene mean that Scripture and sacrament should be prominently displayed at

18. The Spirit proceeds from the Father and the Son outward to manifest a glory-environment around the Godhead. This glory is called heaven, and also is seen as a cloud. It is architecturally modeled in the Tabernacle, in the Temple, and in the world itself considered as an altar under a canopy of sun, moon, and stars. For an introduction to this, see Meredith G. Kline, *Images of the Spirit* (Grand Rapids: Baker, 1980).

the center of visual attention in the church, for the glory-environment of the Spirit is established around Christ, Who is specially present in Word and sacrament.

The essence of worship, according to Romans 12:1, is for us to offer ourselves as living sacrifices. Leviticus 9:15-22 shows us the proper liturgical order of sacrifice: confession, consecration, and communion. First comes the sin offering, which means worship must open with an act of confession of sin. After the sin offering comes the whole burnt offering and the cereal offering, which are acts of consecration: of self and works, respectively. Last comes the peace offering, which is the sacrifice of communion, a meal shared with God.

In terms of the dialogue of Truth, God speaks to us each time, encouraging us to the triple act of sacrifice. First, we are exhorted by the minister to confess sin, and then we do so (hopefully praying together a prayer provided for the occasion). The sanctuary — God's corporate people — must be cleansed by the sprinkling of blood before worship can be offered, and we affirm that by the blood of Christ it has been so cleansed, once and for all.

Second comes the *synaxis* or service of the Word. Passages of Scripture are read (Old Testament lesson, Epistle, Gospel, Psalm), and then comes the sermon. This is all designed to lead us to the second act of sacrifice: the Offertory. The Offertory is not a "collection," but the act of self-immolation (in and through Christ) of the congregation. In union with Christ, and not apart from Him, we offer ourselves ("whole burnt sacrifice") and our tithes and gifts ("cereal sacrifice") to God. In the early church, the bread and wine for communion were also brought forward at this time, along with tithes and other gifts. Thus, the offering plates are brought down front to the minister, who holds them up before God ("heave offering") and gives them to Him. God then gives the offering back to the elders to use in His name. Then comes the long prayer, the prayer "for the whole state of Christ's church," ("incense offering"), which also is part of the Offertory. With this prayer, the synaxis is over.

Now begins the third act of sacrifice, the *eucharist* ("thanksgiving") or Lord's Supper. Prayers are offered, and the people are exhorted to eat of the meal God has provided, His holy Peace Offering. After the eucharist, the people are sent out. Perhaps the Song of Simeon is sung: "Lord, now let Your servant depart in peace, according to Your Word. For mine eyes have seen Your salvation. . . ." The people are ordered to leave: "Go, the service is over." It is good for us to remain within the glory cloud on Mount Tabor, but there are demon-possessed children outside that need our attention (Matt. 17:1-20).

The Bible taught the early church how to worship, but in the later Middle Ages, great corruptions set in. The Protestant Reformers were primarily interested in the restoration of worship, rightly perceiving it as the center of the Kingdom. After all, when God called Israel out of Egypt it was not first and foremost to establish a theocratic nation, but to engage in a third-day worship festival.[19] Unfortunately, within a hundred years, the liturgical dreams of the Reformers were mostly in shambles.

The Reformers wanted three things. First, they wanted a return to Biblical regulation of worship. Almost immediately, however, this concern was sidetracked by a minimalist approach. The rule, "we should do in worship only what is actually commanded in Scripture," was taken in an increasingly restricted sense. The Reformers had realized that God's "commands" are found in Scripture in "precept, principle, and example." Their heirs tended to exchange this wholistic openness to the Word of God for a quest for "explicit commands." Instead of reading the Bible to see the patterns presented there for our imitation, there was an attempt to find the bare minimum of what is actually "commanded" in the New Testament. The book of Revelation, which shows how worship is conducted in heaven ("Thy will be done on earth as it is in heaven"), was ignored. Anabaptist minimalism soon overwhelmed the Reformed churches.[20]

---

19. See my book *The Law of the Covenant* (Tyler, Texas: Institute for Christian Economics, 1984), p. 41f.

20. J. I. Packer has written: "The idea that direct biblical warrant, in the form of precept or precedent, is required to sanction every item included in the public worship of God was in fact a Puritan innovation, which crystallised out in the course of the prolonged debates that followed the Elizabethan settlement." Packer

Second, the Reformers wanted a return to Old Catholic forms, as they understood them. A reading of the liturgies they wrote shows this.[21] Though all of the Reformers tended to over-react against anything that reminded them of Italo-Papal imperial oppression, they were not so "anti-catholic" as to reject the early church. Soon, however, sectarian reaction against anything that "smacks of Rome" overwhelmed their concern.

Third, the Reformers wanted participation in worship from the whole priesthood of all believers. They wrote dialogue liturgies in which the people had many things to say and sing. They had their congregations singing, for instance, the creeds, the Ten Commandments, and the Lord's Prayer. Soon, however, the strength of the Medieval devotional tradition reasserted itself— the "low mass" tradition in which the people only sat and watched and listened, while the minister did everything. *This Medieval tradition was the essence of the Puritan view of worship.* In worship, the Puritans departed from the desires of the Protestant Reformers.

It is important to understand that although the Puritans did uphold the theology of the Reformers, they rejected the Reformers' views on worship at some crucial points. After the Puritan Revolution failed and Charles II came to the English throne, there was a conference at Savoy between Puritan Presbyterian churchmen and the newly restored Anglican bishops. It is very interesting to note what the Presbyterians proposed. They wanted "to omit 'the repetitions and responsals of the clerk and people, and the alternate reading of Psalms and Hymns, which cause a confused murmur in the congregation' : 'the minister being appointed for the people in all Public Services appertaining to God; and the Holy Scriptures . . . intimating the people's part in public prayer to be only with silence and reverence to attend there-

---

goes on to note that, in rejecting such things as prayerbooks, kneeling, the Christian year, and weekly communion, "they were not in fact reverting to Calvin, but departing from him, though . . . it is doubtful whether they realised this." Packer, "The Puritan Approach to Worship," in *Diversity and Unity*. The Puritan and Reformed Studies Conference Papers (Kent: PRSC, 1963), pp. 4, 5.

21. See the collection in Bard Thompson, *Liturgies of the Western Church* (New York: Collins World, 1961).

unto and to declare their consent in the close, by saying *Amen.*' "[22]
In other words, no dialogue, no responsive readings, no congregational praying of the Lord's Prayer or any other prayer. The Anglican bishops replied that "alternate reading and repetitions and responsals are far better than a long tedious prayer." They also noted that "if the people may take part in Hopkins' why not David's psalms, or in a litany?"[23] In other words, if it is all right to sing metrical paraphrases of the psalms, why is it wrong to read responsively the very words of Scripture?

Originally the Puritan movement had not been opposed to prayerbook worship, but in time the combination of state persecution with the continuing strength of the Medieval quietist tradition led the Puritans into wholehearted opposition to congregational participation in worship.

Worship and Ceremony

So, "ceremony" came to be a bad word. The Puritan approach greatly influenced the whole Calvinistic world, and so came into virtually all of what today is called evangelicalism. Gradually, however, the Puritan extremes were watered down. Congregations began to pray the Lord's Prayer together. Choral recitation of the Apostles' Creed was reintroduced. Responsive readings crept back in. Christmas and Easter became acceptable, as did the use of the cross as a symbol. At the same time, however, little has been done to recover the actual perspective and principles of the early church and of the Reformers. To a great extent, these catholic practices have crept back into evangelical churches not because they are clearly seen to be part of Biblical precept, principle, and example, but because of a *de facto* abandonment of any commitment to Biblical regulation at all.

Ceremony is still thought of with suspicion; it is just that certain compromises have been made. On our agenda today, however, must be a rethinking of the whole matter of ceremony. In

---

22. See Francis Procter and Walter H. Frere, *A New History of the Book of Common Prayer* (London: MacMillan, 1908), p. 172.
23. *Ibid.*, p. 173.

this section, I lay out three considerations that bear on the subject of ceremony: the priesthood of all believers, the heavenly pattern, the nature of performative language. A fourth principle, the action of the eucharist, is given special attention in the next section of this essay.

The priesthood of all believers means we need whole-personed participation in worship. Worship is a dance. It is a command performance. It is not a spectator sport. The Greek notions of the primacy of internal feeling, or the primacy of the intellect, have nothing to do with Scripture. In fact, if anything, the Scriptures give us the *primacy of eating*. Alexander Schmemann has written that "in the biblical story of creation man is presented, first of all, as a hungry being, and the whole world as his food. Second only to the direction to propagate and have dominion over the earth, according to the author of the first chapter of Genesis, is God's instruction to men to eat of the earth: 'Behold I have given you every herb bearing seed . . . and every tree, which is the fruit of a tree yielding seed; to you it shall be for meat. . . .' Man must eat in order to live; he must take the world into his body and transform it into himself, into flesh and blood. He is indeed that which he eats, and the world is presented as one all-embracing banquet table for man."[24]

Schmemann goes on to note that "it is not accidental, therefore, that the biblical story of the Fall is centered again on food. Man ate the forbidden fruit. The fruit of that one tree, whatever else it may signify, was unlike every other fruit in the Garden: It was not offered as a gift to man. Not given, not blessed by God, it was food whose eating was condemned to be communion with itself alone, and not with God. It is the image of the world loved for itself, and eating it is the image of life understood as an end in itself."[25]

At the climax of worship is the Lord's Supper. Jesus did not say, "*Understand* this in memory of Me." What He actually said

24. Alexander Schmemann, *For the Life of the World* (New York: St. Vladimir's Seminary Press, 1963), p. 11.
25. *Ibid.*, p. 16.

was "*Do* this *as a memorial* of Me." The doing takes precedence over any theory of what is being done. If this simple fact were understood, it would be possible for churches to recognize one another and cooperate in true Biblical catholicity. At any rate, I do not want to be read as pitting knowledge against action, or as saying action is more important. I am saying, however, that knowing and doing are equally important, and in terms of the sacrament, doing is more important.[26]

The whole-personed priesthood of all believers means not only congregational participation (which requires prayerbooks), but also wholistic "doing." It means singing, falling down, kneeling, dancing, clapping, processions, and so forth. The recovery of all these things for worship is not the labor of a week or even of a year, but that recovery must be our eventual goal.

The second perspective on ceremony is the heavenly pattern. John was "in the Spirit" on the "Lord's Day" (Rev. 1:10). This is the day of worship, and John was ready to "worship in Spirit and truth." Thus, he entered the heavenly environment. He saw a liturgy conducted in heaven, which is our model. Just as Moses saw the model on the Mount, and then came down to build the Tabernacle on the plain, so we pray "Thy will be done on earth as it is in heaven."

When we read Revelation 5:9-14, 11:15-18, 15:2-4, and 19:1-7, we see that worship is organized, planned, prepared, and done in unison. We see the "rote" use of standard phrases, such as "amen" and "alleluia." We see dialogue, *responsorial* worship between the leader and the people. We see *antiphonal* worship between the choir and the congregation. We see physical actions.

In short, we see ceremony.

A third perspective comes from the nature of language. We use language for various purposes. Some language is primarily *informative* ("My name is Jim.") Some language is primarily *ceremonial* ("How're you doing?" "Fine; and you?" "Just fine, thank you.")

---

26. That is, so long as the Word is also present, as read and preached. The essence of the sacrament, qua sacrament, is doing, not saying. See Dom Gregory Dix, *The Shape of the Liturgy* (Westminster: Dacre Press, 1945; reprinted by Seabury in the U.S. in recent years), especially chapter 2.

Some language, and this is the point, is primarily *performative*. Such speech actually performs an action. Here is an example: "I now pronounce you man and wife." Here is another example: "I baptize you in the Name of the Father, and of the Son, and of the Holy Spirit."

Ritual is not "mere ceremony," though it can become that. Ritual worship is supposed to be performative. We as a congregation perform the following acts in worship: We confess sin. We accept forgiveness. We offer ourselves as living sacrifices. We take vows. We give gifts. We eat. We say "amen," which is a covenant oath implying "May I be ripped in half and devoured by the birds and beasts if I do not confirm these words to do them." The officiant also performs certain acts in worship: He baptizes. He declares us forgiven. He gives us Christ in bread and wine.

The Lord's Supper

The fourth perspective on ceremony is that of the action of the Lord's Supper. As we noted above, the inauguration of the Lord's Supper preceded its interpretation. Jesus did not at that point give an explanation of it. He just said to do it. A truly Christian philosophy must take this into account. Knowing and doing are equally important. Each is the context for the other, and each is under submission to the Word.

A faith-commitment to the Word comes before both understanding and obedience. It is sometimes naively thought that the Word is addressed first of all to the understanding, but a moment's reflection will show that this is not so. Frequently in Scripture God tells people to do something without explaining in context what it means. For instance, in Leviticus 12 there are a number of rules for the separation of women after childbirth. In context, however, no explanation is given for these rules. Examples could be multiplied, and of course, right before us is the example of the Lord's Supper.

Apart from faith, obedience is nothing but "works of the Law," and stands condemned. Apart from faith, knowledge is nothing but vain imaginings. We must have faithful works, and faithful understandings. Each leads to and reinforces the other. Obedience yields understanding, and vice versa.

Knowing and doing form the foci of the ellipse of worship. The most concentrated form of the "knowing" side is the actual reading of the Scripture, done by an officiant whose voice stands for Christ's. The most concentrated form of the "doing" side is the action of the eucharist, performed by the hands and voice of the officiant as Christ's representative.

The secondary stage of these things is performed by the church, who has been called and privileged to assist Christ. The preacher takes the Word from Christ and in the sermon makes applications from it, "distributing" it to today's situation. The servants of the church take the bread and wine from the hands of Christ and pass them out to the people.

When the church falls into doing without saying, as in the Middle Ages in both East and West, then false teaching arises, and false understandings of the "doing" part. Then, there is feedback of error into the "doing" itself. As we know, the "doing" came to be seen as magical, and then people were afraid to do the sacrament, rejecting the cup and forbidding their children to come.[27]

Similarly, when the church falls into teaching without doing, as in protestantism, then false activities arise, with feedback into the teaching itself. Some of the false activities that have arisen because of the protestant failure to practice weekly communion are:

(a) extreme negative sabbatarianism, which fails to see the Lord's Day as a celebration at God's house and table;

(b) the altar call ritual, in which unfed hungry saints seek relief in other actions;

(c) pentecostalism, because the weekly miracle of Christ's special presence is not maintained;

(d) extreme negative views of worship that reject all kinds of worship actions commanded in the Bible (such as kneeling, dancing, processions, etc.).

---

27. One of the finest discussions of this process of corruption can be found in Alexander Schmemann, *Introduction to Liturgical Theology*, trans. by Asheleigh E. Moorhouse (New York: St. Vladimir's Seminary Press, 1966).

But then comes the feedback into the area of doctrine, and in protestantism the failure to keep the sacrament equal to the reading of the Word in worship has led to the doctrine that faith and works are separate and opposed one to another. The failure to "do" has led straight to antinominianism.

Well, then, what is this action? It is what Jesus did, and commands us to do. Originally it was a nine-fold action. Jesus —

1. took bread	6. took wine
2. gave thanks	7. gave thanks
3. broke it	
4. gave it	8. gave it
5. they ate it	9. they drank it.

This reduces to a five-fold action of taking, blessing, breaking down and restructuring, sharing, and consuming.[28] Notice that there is in this no "setting apart of the elements from common use," as if man had such a power. Nor (surprisingly) is there any invocation of the Holy Spirit. These things are not necessarily wrong, but they are not the essence of the rite.

A comparison of the steps in this rite with Genesis chapter 1 is most revealing. As we read that chapter, we see God repeatedly take hold of His creation, break it down and restructure it, and then distribute it to various kingdoms of creatures. We also see God evaluate His work ("And God saw that it was good") and enjoy it (resting on the seventh day). There are five steps here, to which man as a creature would add a sixth: the giving of thanks to God.

In this action there is a world-view. Man the priest is called upon to *take* hold of the creation. He is not, however, to do like Adam, and take hold of it autonomously; he is to *give thanks*. Having done so, he is to work with the creation, *breaking* it, restructuring it, and then *sharing* it with others through giving or trading. At

---

28. See Dix, *op. cit.*, chapter 4. Dix is noted for his discussion of the "four-fold" action. He does not see breaking as a separate act, but simply as necessary for the act of sharing.

various stages, he will *evaluate* what he and others have done. Finally, he is to *consume* or enjoy it.[29]

This is the Christian worldview, and it also proclaims the death of Christ. Because of human sin, it was necessary for God to lay hold on man, break and restructure him, and send him back into the world. Only thus could God give man a positive evaluation and enjoy him in common sabbath rest. This Christ accomplished for us. Even though not a bone in His body was broken, yet He experienced the curse of the covenant, which is to be ripped in half and devoured by the lower creation. As in all the Old Testament sacrifices, His blood was separated from His flesh.[30] Thus, the bread is broken. Similarly, before Jesus gave the cup to us, He drank it Himself, and this is explained as His death: "Father, if it be possible, let this cup pass from Me." Accordingly, while the eucharist does not recrucify Christ, nor extend the action of His death, it does *"proclaim* the Lord's death until He comes" (1 Cor. 11:26).

This proclamation is not only to men, but also to God. The covenant memorials were given by God for man to use to remind Him to keep the covenant. It is not as if God forgets and must be reminded, but that for man's own good God requires us to remind Him. The proclamation is made to men, but unless men add their "amen," thus returning the proclamation to God, the proclamation is not salvific. This amen-proclamation to God is almost certainly what is in view in 1 Cor. 11:26.[31] Thus, the rainbow was es-

---

29. I have developed the "six-fold action" as a worldview in an essay, "Christian Piety: Deformed and Reformed," *The Geneva Papers (New Series)* No. 1 (September, 1985); available for $4.00 from Geneva Ministries, Box 131300, Tyler, TX 75713.

30. This is why the bread is eaten, and then the wine drunk, as two separate actions.

31. Leon Morris asserts that *katangello* in 1 Cor. 11:26 can only refer to the proclamation of the gospel to men. See *The First Epistle of Paul to the Corinthians.* Tyndale New Testament Commentaries (Grand Rapids: Eerdmans, 1958), p. 162. While I am reluctant to differ with so eminent a scholar, Morris's assertions at this point betray the weakness of leaning too heavily on word studies to do theology. By itself, *katangello* means "show, proclaim." We have to look at context or theology to determine to whom the proclamation is being made. In the light of the Biblical theology of covenant and covenant memorials, it surely stands to rea-

tablished not first and foremost to remind us of the covenant, but to remind God (Gen. 9:12-16). Similarly, when God gave His covenant Name to Israel, it was a memorial Name, and we see Moses citing God's Name to Him as he argues that God should keep the covenant and not destroy the people (cp. Ex. 32:9-14; Num. 14:11-19; Ex. 34:5-7; and Ex. 3:13-15). The incense offered under the Old Covenant is called a memorial, to remind God (Lev. 2:1-3; 24:5-9; Gen. 8:21). The names of the tribes of Israel were engraved on Aaron's vestments, so that when he entered the sanctuary God would be reminded of the covenant (Ex. 28:29). Compare also Acts 10:4-5, 31-32. Thus, we pray "in Jesus' Name," reminding God of the death of our Savior, and asking Him to keep His promises because Christ has died in our stead. Similarly, the eucharistic memorial is done before the throne and eyes of God, for Him to see, to remind Him of the death of Christ, and to argue blessings from Him.[32] God has established the eucharistic memorial as the preeminent means of arguing covenant blessings from Him. The importance of weekly communion should be obvious from this.

---

son that the proclamation is both to God and to men, but primarily to God. Since the world is not present in the sanctuary when the Supper is held, it is hard to see how an evangelistic proclamation can be in view in any event.

32. This was the position of the French Reformers, and of the early church. Max Thurian has summarized it well in writing that "the Eucharist is the liturgical presentation by the Church of the sacrifice to the Father. This liturgical presentation is the action that recalls to God the Father the unique sacrifice of His Son, which is eternally actual, and implores Him by this sacrifice to grant mercies and blessings to His people." See Thurian, *The Mystery of the Eucharist: An Ecumenical Approach,* trans. by Emily Chisholm (Grand Rapids: Eerdmans, 1983), p. 23. See also Louis Bouyer, *Eucharist* (Notre Dame: University of Notre Dame Press, 1968), which in its entirety is a discussion of this theme. Bouyer shows that the structure of Jewish prayer was always to remind God of what He had already done in creation and redemption, and then to ask Him to complete His work by rebuilding Jerusalem. This also became the structure of Eucharistic prayer in the early church. It is implied in 1 Cor. 11:26, in that we proclaim the Lord's death *until He comes;*" that is, we remind God of the finished work of Christ, and petition Him to complete His work by bringing creation to consummation. Also see Joachim Jeremias, *The Eucharistic Words of Jesus* (Philadelphia: Fortress Press, 1966), pp. 237ff. My use of the work of Thurian, Bouyer, and Jeremias should not be taken as an endorsement of every aspect of their overall theological positions.

Worship is a response to truth, not a technique to manipulate God. Thus, God gives us truth in the verbal proclamation, and we respond with the verbal amen of prayer. The same thing happens in the eucharist. As we noted above, citing Schmemann, God gives man certain food to eat, denying him other food. Setting this special food before us is God's proclamation to us of the covenant. Eating the food given by God is our reproclamation to Him, our memorialization of the covenant. It is important to see this. We remind God of the covenant not in the act of holding up the "consecrated elements," or even in the prayer of thanksgiving. Though these things are not wrong in themselves, it is the doing of the rite itself, culminating in the act of eating, that is the reminder to God. When God hears us take His word and amen it back to Him in prayer, He is reminded to keep the covenant. When God sees us take the body and blood of His Son and amen it by eating it, He is reminded to keep the covenant. The heart of the eucharistic action, thus, is not some act of "consecrating the elements," but the act of eating itself.

The eucharistic action is not a silent ritual. Jesus spoke while He performed it. There is a prayer of thanksgiving to be offered. Indeed, the act itself "proclaims" something. The action does, however, precede understanding. Just as Adam needed to eat of the Tree of Life *before* he ate of the Tree of Knowledge, so the Christian needs to come humbly before Christ and do what He says and eat of His gift *before* he begins to try to understand this great mystery. The failure of the Western churches is seen precisely at this point. By requiring knowledge before communion, the church cut its children off from the Table, and also initiated a series of schisms over eucharistic doctrine. If we are to have reformation, we must reject this residuum of gnosticism and return to an understanding that the act of the eucharist precedes the interpretation of it. An understanding of "eucharistic prevenience" will result not only in the restoration of paedocommunion to the church, but also can form the foundation for a true catholicity of practice and an end to "closed communion."

The Keys of the Kingdom: Word and Sacrament

Man was created the guardian of Eden, but when he fell, he lost this post (Gen. 2:15; 3:1-5). God gave the keys of Eden's doorway to new cherubic guardians (Gen. 3:24). In Christ, however, the keys have been restored to man, and Christ has given them to His representatives to use for Him (Matt. 16:18f.). We are only supposed to bind on earth what we know has already been bound in heaven, and the way we know that is from Scripture.

What are the keys? Protestants have answered this question by saying that there is a general and a specific aspect to the administration of the keys. The general aspect is the proclamation of the Word to all men, drawing them in or sealing them out (2 Cor. 2:16). The special or particular aspect is the judicial power of church discipline, admitting to the church by the sacrament of baptism, and expelling from the church by excommunication. This is seen in Scripture imagery again in that the *key* locks or unlocks the *gate* of the city, and the gate of the city was not only the place of (general) traffic in and out, but is also the (special) place where the elders sat as a court of law.

What is the relationship between Word and Sacrament? Are they two different ministries of God? Is the sacrament merely attached to the Word as a seal? Are they equally ultimate?

According to Hebrews 6:13-18, God always gives two or three witnesses of His truth. Here the two primary witnesses are called "word and oath." In the Old Testament, God's Word was always accompanied by a sign. The sign was either a momentary miracle, or a lasting memorial (such as a memorial pillar, a memorial rite like Passover, or a memorial action like circumcision). This testimony of two witnesses is not God's condescension to our weakness, but is a manifestation of the fact that He is Three and One. The Triune God always reveals Himself by two or three witnesses: Word and Sign; or else Word-Sign-Image (men).

The sacrament is the standing memorial of the death of Christ. When Jesus said, "Do this in memory of Me," He was not advocating that they break bread simply as an aid to devotion, a reminder of Jesus' death. The context for this statement is the theology of memorial in the Old Testament. A memorial is a reminder, yes, but it is a reminder that exists whether people make use of it or not. The memorial stones Joshua set up by the Jordan were standing memorials, even on days when nobody came by to look at them. Thus, there is an objective "thereness and thatness" to a memorial that precedes our subjective appreciation of it.

The "thereness and thatness" of the memorial means that the memorial is always present before the eyes of God. If men pray to God for blessing on the basis of the memorial (e.g., "in Jesus' Name"), then the memorial reminds God to bless them. If men ignore the memorial, forgetting God's mighty acts, then the memorial still stands before God, but it calls down His curse. The blood of Jesus Christ reminds God of those wicked men who crucified His only Son just as much as it reminds Him of the payment for the sins of the elect. Thus, the eucharistic memorial is never neutral, but always works either blessing or curse (1 Cor. 11:30).

The sacrament, as a memorial, is also a continuing miracle. The fascination with the miraculous that has crippled the American churches since the days of the Great Awakening can only be overcome when the Lord's Supper is once again part of the center of our worship, for that is where Christ is specially present in our midst. As a miraculous memorial, the sacrament has a real influence or effect. It is never neutral. For the faithful, it magnifies the grace of the gospel, and for the unfaithful it magnifies the curse. The sacrament works positively in response to faith, but it also works negatively in response to faithlessness. In this sense, we must say that the sacrament does indeed work *ex opere operato*.

Because the pluriform revelation in Word and Sacrament is a reflex of the triunity of God, it will always ultimately evade our attempts to explain it rationally. At the same time, some things can be said. I should like to propose that the Word is more the work of the Son, for obvious reasons (John 1:1), while the Sacrament is more the work of the Spirit. It is the Spirit Who makes Christ present at the sacrament, and baptism — water descending upon us from above — also is a sign of the Spirit. I say "more" the work of one or the other, because in the *opera ad extra* of God, no one Person works exclusively.

What, then, is the relation between the Second and Third Persons of God? If we say that the Spirit proceeds from the Father only, then Word and Sacrament are independent, separate revelations. Each stands alone. This has been the position of some Eastern Orthodox theologians.

If we say that the Spirit proceeds from the Father through the Son, then the Sacrament is only a confirmation of the Word, and secondary to it. It is a supplement, which we can take or leave. This is the unconscious view of most protestants.[33]

If we say, rightly, that the Spirit proceeds from the Father, and also from the Son, then the Sacrament is tied to the Word inseparably (proceeding from the Son), yet is also a separate line of testimony (proceeding from the Father). Because the Spirit proceeds from the Son, the Sacrament should be done liturgically *after* the proclamation of the Word. Because the Spirit proceeds from the Father, the Sacrament should be regarded as a distinct revelation of God, different in mode, but not in content, from the Word.

Another slant on this is to see the Word as primarily sign, and the Sacrament as primarily seal. When the Word is heard (from reading or preaching), and received in faith, then certainly the Spirit also seals it to our hearts. And, when the Sacrament is rightly viewed, it is a sign that proclaims Christ as well as the seal of the covenant. As the work of the Spirit, however, the Sacrament is primarily the seal of the gospel, the oath that comes in to confirm the Word; and as the work of the Son, the Word is primarily the sign and content of the gospel.

Church Rulers

The third witness is the image of God, man himself. The Ethiopian eunuch was reading the Bible, but could not under-

---

33. This unspoken belief finds expression in various ways in protestantism. Believing the Word and being baptized is wonderful, but to really enter into the fullness of the kingdom one must be confirmed, or receive the second blessing of the Holy Spirit. Any notion of the Spirit's giving a second-stage work of grace implies this kind of subordination, and it is no surprise that it is in circles where the sacrament is regarded as only an adjunct to the primary work of salvation that such doctrines arise.

stand it until a man explained it, for "how will they hear without a preacher?" (Acts 8:31; Romans 10:14). It is an amazing truth that God involves men in His work. He normally gives not just two witnesses, but three. The fact that the saints, in their persons, are a revelation of God and of the gospel is an important theme in 2 Corinthians (especially 2:14 - 4:6).

In a general way, all members of the royal priesthood are church rulers. All sit on the Divine council. That council is seen initially in Genesis 1:26, and had then only three members. Had Adam persevered, he and Eve would have been the next two. We see in Genesis 18:17-33 that Abraham was a member. The Biblical word for council-member is "prophet." A prophet is a member of the council who brings the decisions of the council to men, or who prosecutes the covenant lawsuit against men before the council. Abraham is called a prophet for just this reason in Genesis 20:7. In meetings of the council on earth, all have a voice, but in different ways and at different times. Thus, in certain weighty matters of doctrine, or embarrassing matters of ethics, only elders meet in the council (Acts 15). At church council meetings where judgment must be passed, only men may speak (1 Cor. 14:34 in the context of v. 29). At other meetings, women may speak, but need to have a sign of authority on their heads (1 Cor 11:5).

This is the general work of the council, and because it is a heavenly council, its members are called "stars" (Phil. 2:15). There are, however, also special members. These are the guardians of the church, the elders. They are called stars in Revelation 1:20, and also called angels. Why angels? Because they have taken the place of the cherubim at the door of Eden, and they have the special use of the keys committed to them. (Indeed, in the Eastern Church liturgy, there is a hymn that begins, "Let us who mystically represent the Cherubim. . . .")

According to Exodus 18:21, the elders of the church are supposed to be arranged in hierarchical ranks.[34] The angels of Reve-

---

34. For some odd reason presbyterians, who make the most fuss about elder rule, generally ignore the Biblical prescriptions for the hierarchical organization of the eldership. The Reformers, however, were not opposed to bishops. See

lation are the bishops, or elders over myriads, of the churches in the seven cities. Why do modern exegetes assume that the angels later on in Revelation are not these same bishops? Because after chapter 4, we are in heaven. We have seen, however, that in worship, on the Lord's Day, heaven and earth are joined. Thus, the simplest understanding of the Book of Revelation is that the angels continue to be bishops. If, however, someone wants to insist that the angels in Revelation 4 and following are spirit-angels, I shall simply call attention to the obvious linguistic linkage of the angels in heaven and those on earth (bishops), and remind us that we pray "Thy will be done on earth as it is in heaven." The angels in Revelation, at the very least, show us what the earthly bishop-angels can and should be doing.

What happens in Revelation? It is a worship service. First of all, the Lamb ascends the Mount to the Throne, takes the book, and begins to open it. Historically, this has been acted out in that the altar-table and pulpit in the church have been placed on a raised platform (mountain). The minister ascends this mountain between the Epistle and Gospel lessons, while the Gradual is sung. This ascent corresponds to the breaking of the seals and the opening of the Word.

The angels then sound trumpets. This is the preaching of the Word, a word of judgment to the wicked and salvation to the righteous. Let us consider the awesome power committed to the elders of the church when they join in unity. When the wicked united at Babel, God said that nothing would be withheld from them (Gen. 11:6). God did not want them united, but Jesus prays in John 17 that we will be. Since we are, nothing will be withheld from us, either; and the more visible that unity becomes, the more visible will be the blessings. Read Revelation 8:6-13. This is how we should deal with those who dare to rape God's holy bride. In a *performative act*, we should ritually bind them to destruction by proclaiming the trumpet of judgment against them. Then, since

Geddes MacGregor, *Corpus Christi: The Nature of the Church According to the Reformed Tradition* (Philadelphia: Westminster, 1958), chapter XI, "The Episcopate in the Reformed Tradition."

eucharist follows synaxis, the angels pour out chalices of wrath. Here the saints administer judgment on the world. This interpretation is rendered the more obvious when we read the description of the seven angels in Revelation 15:6.

Revelation shows us the actions of the three witnesses: Word (trumpet), Sacrament (chalices), and the Image of God (angels). Since worship is the heart of culture and history, the liturgy seen by John is also a revelation concerning immediate events (the fall of Jerusalem, and of Rome), and a revelation concerning the nature of all of history as judgment, restoration, and transfiguration.

The Woman Question

Having moved to a discussion of church officers, we naturally come to the question of the place of women in the church. This question has come to occupy a very large place in modern ecclesiological discussion. Liberal churches have simply ignored what the Bible says on the subject, and have ordained women to every office that formerly only men might hold. Some orthodox protestant churches have debated whether or not women might be "ordained" to the "office" of deacon, while others have reopened the question of whether or not women may be permitted to vote in congregational plebiscites. Certain charismatic churches (in the radical Wesleyan tradition) present a confused face, with their female preachers.

The question before us is this: What may women do, and what may they not do in the church? I fear that conservatives have become so taken up with answering liberal critics of the historic position, or else so taken up with detailed spadework in the texts of various important passages (both of these labors being necessary), that there has been a dearth of good theological, and therefore practical, reflection on the subject. I hope here to make some contribution to this last area.

The question comes: May women prophesy? May they rule in the state? In the church? May they act as priests? Before trying to answer these questions, it would be well to step back and examine the questions themselves. What hidden assumptions are involved in the way these questions are asked?

I believe that the hidden assumption is this: It is assumed that the human calling to serve God as prophet, priest, and king is more universal than sexual differentiation. Protestants especially start from the assumption of the "universal priesthood of all believers," and from this it follows that "both men and women are priests" in this sense.

This in my opinion obscures the issue. Suppose we were to say, "No, it is not true that both men and women are prophets, priests, and kings. Rather, only men are prophets, priests, and kings; women are prophetesses, priestesses, and queens." If we phrase our canon in that fashion, we are asserting that the differentiation of humanity into male and female must totally qualify the notion of office or function.

On the basis of what is said in Genesis 2 and 3, we have to think in this latter fashion. Man was given his calling to dress and to guard the garden before the woman was created. The woman was then brought to be his helper. She also dresses and guards the garden, but as a woman, not as a man. She guards and dresses in a way different from the way a man guards and dresses.

Let us return to our questions. May women prophesy? It seems so. There are prophetesses in both the Old and New Testaments, and while they are few in number, nothing in the text indicates anything unusual about them. In the Bible (as opposed to systematic theology), a prophet is simply one who speaks for another, in terms of God's council. Thus, the first reference to a prophet in the Bible is to Abraham, who is said to speak to God on behalf of Abimelech (an activity generally seen as priestly by systematicians). May a woman speak for her husband? Certainly. This being the case, it is certainly proper for a woman to speak to the whole church on behalf of God, the heavenly Husband.

But, a prophet prophesies not only as a representative of the Father/Husband/Son, but also as a symbol thereof; while the prophetess prophesies simply as a representative, as the Mother/Bride/Daughter.

May women be judges? It seems so. Deborah is the premier example here. Does that mean that a woman may exercise authority over a man, in this sense? Clearly, yes. The whole theology of Judges 4 and 5 revolves around Deborah as the Mother of Israel, whose sons hearken to her voice and thus win the battle (the Mother, then, of the Seed). May a woman exercise authority on behalf of her husband? Certainly. This being the case, it is certainly proper for a woman to be involved in making judgments in the church.

But, a king rules not only as a representative of the Father/ Husband/Son, but also as a symbol thereof; while the queen is only a representative.

May women be priests? Clearly not, at least in the special sense. There are no priestesses in Scripture. Protestants (and also Catholics) are not clear on why, however. The question is this: What is the kernal of the priestly office that men have, and that women do not? The following answers are inadequate:

1. The priest offers prayers and sacrifices on behalf of the people. But if the people are the Bride of God, then surely females would make better representatives. It cannot, then, be the case that the priest is simply a representative of the people. Besides, to say this and no more makes the priest the same as the prophet.

2. The priest represents God in passing judgments on the people. Again, this is not enough. After all, a woman may represent her husband, as we have seen in the case of Deborah. And if the church is our Mother, rearing us as her children, why not have women as rulers in the church? Besides, to say this and no more makes the priest the same as the king.

The correct answer is this: The priest is a guard, and as a guard, he must guard something. What he guards is the Bride, and as the guardian of the Bride, he must be a figure (symbol) of the Father/Husband/Son. That is, he must be a male.

We can go back to Genesis 2 and 3 for more insight into this. In brief we find the following:

God gives man two tasks: the kingly task of dressing the garden, and the priestly task of guarding it.

First of all, God teaches man about the kingly, shepherding, wisdom task. He brings animals to man, for man to name, acquire wisdom, and so forth. Man learns from the animals that he lacks something, something needed for his kingly task. God provides what man lacks: a helper fitted for him, a queen.

Second of all, God teaches man about the priestly, guarding, sacramental eating task. He brings an animal to man, for man to guard against. The animal assaults the wife, offering a demonic substitute for the sacrament. The man guards the wife, rejects the animal, and has a sacramental meal with God, feeding his wife. From this, the man learns that he lacks something, something needed for his priestly task. God provides what man lacks: a robe of judicial authority.[35]

Of course, this is not what happened. Man failed the priestly task. He stood by and permitted his wife to interact with the serpent. He failed to guard her, or the garden.[36] He permitted her to partake of the table of demons. He received instruction from her mouth, and food from her hand, the reverse of the proper order.

Now, the important thing to note at this point is that the woman was not present when the man entered into the kingly task. She was brought in to help him with it, making her a queen. But, when the test regarding the priestly task came about, it was precisely in terms of whether or not the man would guard his wife.

We have to note that the Bible repeatedly says that Eve was deceived (1 Tim 2:14; 2 Cor. 11:3). She was not constitutionally created to be able to guard the garden, and she is not blamed for the fall. But, when Adam is called on the carpet, he advances from failing to guard his wife, to attacking her openly. In this, Adam totally reverses the relation he should have, and becomes the precise antithesis of what he was to symbolize: God's relation to His Bride.

Are women priests then? No, at least not in this ultimate, special sense. But what about the "priesthood of all believers?' What the Reformers meant by this phrase is that any person can and

---

35. For an extended defense of this interpretation, see James B. Jordan, "Rebellion, Tyranny, and Dominion in the Book of Genesis," in Gary North, ed., *Tactics of Christian Resistance.* Christianity and Civilization No. 3 (Tyler, TX: Geneva Ministries, 1983).

36. The connection between the woman and the garden, as environments for man, runs all through the Song of Songs.

should approach God without having to go through any mediator except Christ alone. In terms of what they meant, they were right. But, what they should have called it was not "universal priesthood," but "universal Bridehood." The privilege of approaching God is not a priestly privilege, but is the privilege of the Mother/ Bride/Daughter.

All the same, women do perform priestly tasks. They do guard the home. They do instruct their children (and informally they can instruct men). They do prepare meals and serve them. Are these not "priestly" tasks? Certainly, but we have to make two distinctions.

The first is the same one we have already made concerning prophecy and rule. Women are never priests, but priestesses. A priestess can only guard under the authority of a priest.

Second, we have to distinguish between the general and the special. There is a special meal, and special office, in the church. In connection with these, the priestly task must be performed in an exclusively masculine fashion, in order that the relationship between God and His Bride may be set out clearly.

Having noted this, we may now go back and assert the following propositions:

Both men and women may perform the task of prophecy in both the general and special areas. Women may be teachers.

Both men and women may perform the task of ruling in both the general and special areas. Women may be magistrates.

Both men and women may perform the task of guarding in the general area, but only men may perform the task of guarding in the special area. Women may not be elders.

How about women as deacons? Impossible, because to be a deacon you have to be a man. How about deaconesses, then? No problem. Both in the Old and in the New Testament, certain women are set aside to assist the elders with certain tasks (Ex. 38:8; 1 Sam. 2:22; Jud. 11:40;[37] Matt.27:55-56; Luke 8:2-3; Rom. 16:1; Phil. 4:2-3; 1 Tim. 3:11;[38] 1 Tim. 5:3-10). This, of course, is

37. On Jephthah's daughter, see my book *Judges: God's War Against Humanism* (Tyler, Texas: Geneva Ministries, 1985).

38. If this verse referred to wives, it would not be imbedded in the section on deacons. It clearly, in my opinion, refers to deaconesses.

not a special ruling function.

A deacon is an assistant and an apprentice elder. Joshua was Moses' deacon. Elisha was Elijah's deacon. The twelve were Jesus' deacons, until they ascended to eldership, and then they selected other trainees under them. A deaconness is an assistant to the elders, but never an apprentice.

Conclusion

This is only the beginning of an agenda. Other matters need to be thought through as well.[39] For instance:

Church Architecture. The Bible shows us that the Spirit makes a glory environment visible around the throne of the Lamb. Historically, the architectural model seen in the Tabernacle, the Temple, and in the Book of Revelation has been viewed as the norm for church architecture. Curiously, evangelicals, who make the most out of doing things the Bible's way, pay the least attention to these architectural examples.

Children and Catechisms. Protestants historically have kept their children from Christ's Table. This entire matter is being re-thought today. Moreover, we need to ask if the best way to teach the faith to children is by their memorizing a catechism consisting of little more than a series of definitions of terms (for instance, "What is justification?"). Biblical pedagogy for children seems to consist of two things: stories and proverbs. In my opinion, catechizing, while important, has historically assumed far too large a place in the Christian education of children, though it should not be done away with altogether.

Church and State. The Biblical model is the interrelationship of avenger and sanctuary. One of the social functions of the church in society is to act as a restraint on the state. Today, however, church buildings are no longer regarded as sanctuaries. The church needs to recover the concept that her courts are real, her property inviolable.

---

39. Some of these matters are taken up in this book's companion volume, James B. Jordan, ed., *The Reconstruction of the Church*. Christianity and Civilization No. 4 (Tyler, TX: Geneva Ministries, 1985).

Preaching. Because protestantism was originally a prophetic movement, protestant preaching has tended to be along the lines of a prophetic rather than a priestly model. This needs to be reassessed. I do not believe that the sermon during worship should be denunciatory, but rather encouraging and comforting. In the Bible, prophetic denunciation is directed against sinners, not against those in the church. Obviously this is not a hard and fast rule, but I believe that great weight of emphasis in preaching should be on *encouraging* the saints to lay hold of the power of the gospel and grow from grace to grace and from glory to glory.

2

THE SOCIOLOGY OF THE CHURCH:
A SYSTEMATIC APPROACH

In this essay we are concerned with a variety of problems that can generally be put under the umbrella of the "sociology" of the church. That is, we are not concerned directly with a (sacramental) theology of the church, but with how the church relates to other spheres and institutions of life in this present world. We shall be concerned first of all with an investigation of the nature of the church in her threefold manifestation: the people of God, the special government of Christ, and the institution of organized public worship. We shall be concerned with how we are to *recognize* the church in these various aspects or manifestations. Then we shall turn our attention to the institutional church in its relationship to itself, to other "denominations," and to the parachurch phenomena. To assert that the church should not be divided into denominations, and that parachurch organizations should not exist, is of little help in trying to discover why God has brought it to pass, and how the matter should be understood and resolved.

The Three-fold Nature of the Church

Without too much difficulty we can see that the church has three aspects. First and foremost, the church is a specific governmental body with a specific governmental power. I say first and foremost, because this specific power is nothing other than the power to admit to or expel from the sacramental Body of Jesus Christ. It is at the sacraments that Christ is specially present, and manifests His special and central rule on the earth. The special

51

presence of Christ in her midst constitutes the center and foundation of His church, and thus the sacramental/governmental aspect
of the church has a certain primacy over the other aspects. This
governmental aspect can be contrasted with the two other governments God has instituted on the earth: the state (with the power of
the sword) and the family (with the power of the rod).

The second aspect of the church, an aspect that flows from the
sacramental Presence, is the church as the institution of special
public worship. When we speak of "going to church" we mean attending worship.[1] This is the church as a gathered body, not as a
governmental body. We can contrast this gathering for worship
with other kinds of activities that Christians engage in, such as
business, recreation, family, civil affairs, and so forth.

Finally, the church can be viewed, not only as a governmental
body and as a worship assembly, but as *the people of God.* Here we
use the word "church" to designate God's holy people, separated
from the "world." Flowing from Christ's special governmental
manifestation is the manifestation of His general government of
all human affairs, exercised through His people in all walks of life
as they strive to reform and transfigure all of life according to His
commands. God's people leave His assembly on the first day of
the week, and go out into all of life to work and harvest His world.
In everything they do, they are *the church* at work, in contrast with
the unconverted or worldly.

So we have three aspects of the church.[2] Ultimately, these
three are one, according to the analogy that exists between the
Triune God and His human image. All the same, just as we must
not confuse the Father, the Son, and the Spirit, so we must be
careful not to confuse the three aspects of the church.[3] Also, we

---

1. If we want to say we are going to a church supper, we say "going to *the*
church," using "church" to refer to the building. "Going to church," without "the,"
means attending worship.

2. For a more detailed discussion of these three aspects, going into the
Hebrew terms that are involved, see Appendix A.

3. This is not to say that each of these three aspects corresponds to one of the
Persons of the Trinity. I am simply arguing that the unity and diversity seen in
the creation arises from the unity and diversity present in the Creator. A case
might be made, however, for seeing government as related primarily to the Father

should be careful not to reduce the church to one aspect or another. Liberalism and Roman Catholicism have manifested a tendency to reduce the church only to the institutional (governmental) aspect.[4] American Fundamentalism, on the other hand, has had a tendency to reduce the church to the people of God aspect, downplaying public worship and governmental authority.

Recognizing the Church

We have said that the people of God can be recognized over against the world by their holy lifestyle, the government of the church by her officers and sacraments, and the worship of the church by the distinction between appointed times of worship and other times. We have the problem, however, that what is clearly visible to God is not necessarily clearly visible to man. The Belgic Confession states (chapter 29) that the true and false churches "are easily known and distinguished from each other." At the same time, the Westminster Confession of Faith states that the church "has been sometimes more, sometimes less visible. And particular churches . . . more or less pure" (chapter 25:4). There is no necessary contradiction between these two statements as they stand isolated here, because God kindly leads his children to sense, if not to understand fully, whether a church is true or false, regardless of how weak or astray it may be. It is not so difficult to judge particular churches in the concrete situation, when you get to know the people. In the abstract, however, formulating a theory that will enable you to tell true from false churches at a glance is quite difficult.[5]

The Belgic Confession, for instance, tell us that a true church "maintains the pure administration of the sacraments as instituted

---

(Christ being His agent), sacramental worship as related primarily to the Son, and procession (mission) into all the world as related primarily to the Spirit.

4. In the recent "theology of liberation" we see an unhealthy reaction against this institution-centeredness. Now the Church is said to exist "where the action is," which today means Marxism, but yesterday (in Europe) meant Nazism.

5. Of course, Christendom is littered with sects who think they have found the precise formula, the exact "marks" of the true Church.

by Christ." But what does this mean, practically? Most followers of the Belgic Confession would argue that Baptists do not practice baptism as it is taught in the Bible. The Bible, however, nowhere speaks *directly* to the issue of infant baptism. "Well," it may be replied, "the whole Bible makes it clear that infant baptism is to be practiced. Since Baptists reject this, they are not 'pure' in their administration." But what about Reformed churches that use grape juice for Communion? How "pure" are they, since the Bible "makes it clear" that wine is to be used? And what about Reformed churches that do not have Communion each week, when the Bible "makes it clear" that weekly Communion is the rule? How "pure" are they?

The hard fact is that there is no abstract formula that can be used as a procrustean measure of whether a given church is true or false. In practice, such Reformed churches demand of other churches that they be as pure as they need to be to be regarded as pure enough by such Reformed churches. How pure do you have to be? As pure as we say you have to be.

This is not helpful. The Bible nowhere gives us any "marks" of the true church, at least not in the sense of abstract formulae. We need something that is a little more practically relevant to the question, especially in a time of ecclesiastical chaos such as we are in today.

Wave, Particle, and Field

Modern physics has contributed to linguistics and to philosophy the notion of three basic perspectives available to man as he views existence.[6] The "Particle" view focuses on a discrete thing, in terms of its identifiable features. The "Particle" view answers the question: What are the characteristics of this thing?

The "Field" view focuses on the interrelationship of the thing with other things. It answers the question: How does this thing relate to other things?

---

6. The best overall theological treatment of this is Vern S. Poythress, *Philosophy, Science, and the Sovereignty of God* (Phillipsburg, NJ: Presbyterian and Reformed Pub. Co., 1976).

The "Wave" view focuses on how the thing moves and changes in time. It answers the question: How much can this thing change and still remain itself?

There are hierarchies of particles, waves, and fields. That is, large particles may be seen as composed of smaller particles, large waves of smaller waves, and large fields of smaller fields.

An important phrase in the preceding paragraph is "seen as." We are talking about different *perspectives* on a given matter. Each perspective is valid, but needs to be balanced by others. The idea that there is only one valid perspective is an effective denial of the doctrine of the Trinity (denying diversity).

The People of God

Let us apply this first of all to the church as the people of God. What are the identifying marks of the people of God, considered as "Particles"? They may be summarized by the moral law and the fruit of the Spirit. The people of God live a holy life in their callings. They show forth visibly that they are God's people, and not His enemies. In terms of the "Field" perspective, the people of God exist in a "Field" with one other group, the enemies of God. That is, in the "Field" of the world there are two groups: God's people and God's enemies. In terms of the "Wave" view, we notice that the people of God are more or less faithful at different times. Sometimes they are making progress in subduing all things to Christ. Sometimes they are being driven back because of their own sin or because of persecution. They make mistakes and correct them; they sin and repent; they triumph and go forward. Sometimes the people of God are so weak morally that it is hard to tell them apart from the world, but then a revival comes and they "Wave" into greater visibility.

We said that there are hierarchies among these things. Considering the church as the people of God, there are various particles that come into view, such as Christian individuals, families, businesses, clubs, schools, states, churches, etc. There are also various "Fields" that come into view. As noted, the basic "Field" is people of God versus enemies of God, but the people of God also function in such "Fields" as neighborhoods, businesses, political parties, etc. Finally, there are a variety and hierarchy of "Waves." To take an example, a Christian may wish to give up some sin. He may wave in and out of victory over this sin on a daily basis, but he will also (if he perseveres) eventually wave into a condition of largely continual victory, so that his small, daily "Waves" are part of a larger "Wave."

The Gathered Church

How about the church as a gathering for public worship? What are the identifying marks of such a "Particle"? Here we have to be careful. Shall we say that unless a particular liturgy is used, the group in question is not a real church? Obviously not. There are certain things, however, that we can expect to see as characteristics of the gathered church. We can expect some reading and/or preaching of the Bible. We can expect to see the sacraments administered (however rarely). We can expect to hear prayers and praise. There are hierarchies and varieties of such gatherings, such as home Bible studies, Wednesday night prayer meetings, local church meetings, meetings of wider church organizations (presbyteries, councils, etc.), and so forth.

The gathered church is set in a "Field" consisting of itself and the other, cultural activities Christians engage in.[7] We don't expect to see a man sawing wood (in the literal sense!) as a part of worship. This is labor, and is to be set aside for sabbatical worship. There might be some overlap, however, between sabbatical and cultural activities. A group of Christians might perform a Bach Cantata in German on Friday night for money, and perform it again in English on Sunday afternoon free of charge as a form of worship. Looking at hierarchies and varieties, we have for instance the Christian family at play over against the family having its devotions, and we have the Christian community doing the same, and the Christian individual.

---

7. The "people of God" concept contemplates these spheres of life as zones of moral action. The "gathered" concept contemplates them as areas of intensional activity. The "organization" concept contemplates them as zones of exercised dominion.

The church as a gathered assembly "Waves" through its liturgy, proceeding from confession to consecration to communion. It "Waves" through the Church Year. It "Waves" into special festivals. There are a hierarchy and variety of such "Waves", as when the individual "Waves" in and out of his daily private devotions, when the family does the same, when the institutional church does it publicly, and so forth.

The Church as a Government

Finally, the church as a government: What are its characteristics? We may speak of two: the sacraments (which are her power) and the officers (who administer the sacraments). These are visible to the eye of man, although the primary visibility is in the sacraments.

Considered from the "Field" perspective, the church as a government is set off against other governments. God has set up two other governments: the state and the family. Man has analogously set up others, such as the business firm, or the school. Since there are various levels in the organization of the institutional church, there are various "Fields" in which she operates. For instance, the National Council of Churches has some interaction with the policies of the Federal Government, while local churches interact with local governments, and so forth. One "Field-view" question is the question of the interrelationship between the diaconal work of the church as an institution and the diaconal work of the church as people of God, the question of so-called parachurch organizations.

Considered from the "Wave" perspective, the church as an official institution is more or less faithful, and thus more or less visible. This is what the various sectarian groups do not wish to admit. Each sect believes it has encoded and encapsulated the final formulation of the truth, and is therefore in a position to demand that all other Christians get into line, or else be regarded as counterfeits. The fact is, however, that the worship of the church "Waves" in and out of closeness to God's standard. When the church is faithful in worship, the Bible is the standard; the Psalms are chanted (as well as good hymns); the congregation is active in prayer and praise; a Biblical philosophy undergirds architecture, decor, color, lighting, vestments, etc.; infants are claimed for Christ in baptism and admitted immediately to His Table; the proclamation of the Word is never separated from the sacramental seal, so that Communion is held every week; and we might go on. When the church "Waves" out of faithfulness, however, these things diminish.

The "Wave" of Church History

The "Wave" perspective is so valuable and important that I wish to expand on it a bit more. These "Wave" motions in the church also have a variety and hierarchy to them. If we look only at particular churches, they seem to be rising and falling at different times and in different ways. In the overall history of Christ's Body, however, the "Waves" are not small, nor are they local. It took a long time for the church in America to get into the bad fix she is in today, and she will not be reconstructed overnight. Moreover, while there are superficial differences among the various kinds of churches, they all have the same fundamental problems. We are all together in this boat, deep in the present trough (low point) in the "Wave." It is not just the Baptist, or the Fundamentalist, or the Presbyterian, or the Reformed, or the Episcopal, or the Lutheran churches that have waved into liturgical slovenliness. They are all about equally guilty, though in different ways.[8] And, just as the churches all fell together, they will not rise unless they rise together.

The problem with sectarianism is precisely that it militates against a catholic and wholistic reconstruction of the church. We shall consider schism and separation later on, but for now consider these two different options: On the one hand, a conservative catholic Christian church may separate from a liberalizing denomination without saying that the liberal denomination is a

---

8. Episcopalians sitting in church and passively listening to the choir sing the liturgy are in the same position as Baptists sitting in church and passively listening to the choir and preacher do everything. The music differs; the problem of passivity is the same.

"synagogue of Satan." It is possible simply to say that the local church cannot function properly as a part of the larger body, because that larger body is so weak and relatively unfaithful. There is no need to pronounce a final judgment. The sectarian, on the other hand, believes that he may not separate until he can confidently pronounce the larger body apostate.

An historical example of this is seen in the Pilgrims and the Puritans. The Pilgrims regarded the Church of England as part and parcel of Antichrist, and they left England with a curse upon the English Church. The Puritans, however, took the catholic approach. They were insistent that they did not regard the Church of England as apostate, but as a wayward mother. They prayed for her reformation, even while they had to flee her borders. "Shortly before leaving Yarmouth, Governor Winthrop addressed an historic letter to the Church of England, calling her 'our deare Mother,' and adding these significant words: 'Wee leave it not therefore, as loathing that milk wherewith we were nourished.' This document shows that the Bay colonists were non-Separatists. A further confirmation of this fact is that when Separatist Roger Williams came to the Bay in 1631, he refused a position in the Boston church because it would not renounce fellowship with the Church of England."[9]

The sectarian compares the weakness of other churches to his own supposed strength, and pronounces them apostate on that basis. The catholic notes the weakness of other churches, and because of that tries to work with them, and prays for them. The sectarian thinks history has ended; the catholic realizes that it has not. (If anything, by the way, "postmillennialists" should be even more flexibly catholic than others, because they believe that history has a long way to go, and that theology and ecclesiology will be developing for centuries to come.) The "Wave" view notices the impact the church in general has upon the cosmos, as the redeeming work of Christ steadily transforms society. As regards the

---

9. Smith, Handy, and Loetscher, *American Christianity: An Historical Interpretation with Representative Documents* (New York: Scribner's, 1960) I:98. And see John Cotton on the same issue, pp. 103ff.

church as institution, the "Wave" view notices the establishment, growth, decline, increasing and decreasing visibility, and differentiation of the church. This matter of differentiation is extremely important. When the gospel of Christ penetrates a pagan society and the church has been instituted in a new place, initially all the functions of the church as the people of God tend to be placed under the church as an institution. As the church permeates and influences society, however, it differentiates. Christian families, civil magistrates and business enterprises begin to spring up. Where formerly the church's courts tried all Christian offenses, now the Christian magistrate also takes up his proper place. Moreover, a variety of necessary diaconal duties performed by the church in its early years tend to be farmed out to parachurch agencies especially erected for certain specific purposes. Finally, the church as an organization develops into an advanced institutional organization, well equipped to handle its duties in the world.

Now, what can and has happened is this: The church begins to "Wave" out of fellowship with God. The recreating, sustaining power of the Holy Spirit is gradually quenched. As this happens, society is left with a large number of highly-developed *shells* in which there are sometimes no organisms. A number of peculiar problems arise from this, problems that can be seen abounding in the 20th century. The "Wave" view can help us address these problems. We shall return to this when we discuss the problem of schism later in this essay.

* * * * * *

We have seen that there are three general aspects of the church. We can consider the church as God's people, as a worship assembly, and as a sacramental organization or government. We have also seen that the church becomes visible before men in three ways. It becomes visible as Christians live holy lives, when they gather in a place for worship, and in the sacraments and government of the organization we call "the church." Finally, we have seen that these visibilities vary in degree and in purity according to whether the church is in a time of deformation or a time of reformation. What we have here discussed should make us wary of trying to reduce the visible "marks" of the church down to some pat formula.

Let us now turn our attention particularly to the sociology of the institutional church. By this we mean the church as an organization for worship and for Spiritual (sacramental) government. At this point we are concerned with certain problems that may be placed under the umbrella of the sociological: the question of local versus larger churches, the problem of schism, the question of denominationalism, and the parachurch question.

Local and Larger

In the organization of the Israelite church there was a bipolarity between local and larger church. On the one hand there was the sacramental worship, organized on an annual basis, administered by God-appointed priests, and centralized in one location. On the other hand there were the local synagogues, engaging in non-sacramental, prayer- and teaching-oriented worship, organized on a weekly basis, administered by elected officials working with local Levites.[10] There was, thus, a local and a larger church in Israel, with carefully separated duties. We should also note that the larger church was not a national one, but was international in character. Thus, when northern Israel separated from Judah (with Divine sanction), it was still the case that Israelites were to pilgrimage to Jerusalem for annual sacramental worship. It was the goal of Jeroboam I to prevent this, because he placed national sovereignty before Spiritual order (1 Ki. 12:25ff.). One of the essential failures of the Protestant Reformation was the forfeiture of a truly international ecclesiastical organization, and too close a tie of the church to national interests.[11]

---

10. The synagogue was created by Leviticus 23:3. Levites were found in all the towns (Dt. 12:12, 18, 19; 26:11; Judges 17:7ff.; 19:1ff.). They were salaried by part of the tithe (Dt. 14:28f.; 26:12ff.). Those administering the tithe, and thus running the local churches, were the elders of the gates.

11. See chapter 4 below, pp. 137-150.

The administration of the local synagogue is a matter of curiosity for us. Any Bible encyclopedia will describe the synagogue of the rabbinic period, and we learn that its officials were elected representatives of the members of the congregation. For earlier times, however, we have little information. Since the tithe was administered by the elders of the gate, it may be that the local "civil" rulers were also the directors of the local synagogue. If that were the case, the autonomy of the church from the state was safeguarded, we may suppose, in the person of the Levitical teacher who was also present in each synagogue.

Because this whole organizational system was intimately tied to the sociological structure of the Old Covenant, it is transfigured in the New Covenant. We find in the New Testament only that the church is run by "elders." No particular statements can be found to indicate how these elders are to be organized, but the use of the term throws us back to the Old Testament to see how elders were organized then.

The elders of the Old Covenant seem to have been primarily civil officers. Their organization is set out in Exodus 18:21-22, "Furthermore, you shall determine out of all the people (1) able men who (2) fear God, (3) men of truth, (4) those who hate dishonest gain; and you shall place these over them, as leaders of thousands, of hundreds, of fifties, and of tens. And let them judge the people at all times; and let it be that every major matter they will bring to you [Moses], but every minor matter they themselves will judge." This gives us a series of hierarchical courts of appeal. The problem addressed was that all matters were being brought to the supreme court (Moses), instead of originating at the local level. The solution clearly points to the doctrine that judicial matters must originate at the local level with higher courts only serving as courts of appeal.

There is reason to believe that there were two such hierarchical court systems in Israel, one for the state and one for the church. This is indicated by 2 Chronicles 19:11, "And behold, Amariah the chief priest will be over you in every matter that pertains to the LORD; and Zebadiah the son of Ishmael, the ruler of the house of Judah, in every matter that pertains to the king. Also the Levites shall be officers before you." There is a clear distinction made here between civil and religious jurisdictions. The same double court system is implied by Deuteronomy 17:8-13, but how this was organized is yet undetermined.

The New Testament, by referring to church officers as "elders" and "overseers," ties them to the organizational structure of Exodus 18. Thus, there is every reason to believe that there should be courts of appeal in the church. Also, as we have seen, there is every reason to believe that this church organization should be international in character. We can see this in Acts 15. The Jerusalem council was truly international, and the decisions were made by the elders, and not simply by apostolic decree (vv. 2, 4, 6, 22, 23).

For the present we have only a couple of observations to make. The first is that the question of local and larger institutional church concerns the hierarchy of particles. In the world, the hierarchy of particles, whether in matter or in language or in social structure, is simply the created reflection of the One- and Many-ness of God Himself. The institutional church also reflects this equal ultimacy of the One and the Many. We cannot say that the larger church is really more the church than the local, or vice versa. The former is a deviation in the direction of hierarchical*ism* (either monarchical or bureaucratic), the latter into individualism. It is wrong to say that the local church is only a creation of the larger body, and thus can be closed down simply by action of the larger body. On the other hand, it is wrong to say that the larger body is nothing but a creation of a group of local churches. While the precise delineation of duties and responsibilities has been problematic in this area, and can vary according to times and seasons, we ought to be committed at the outset and in general to a Trinitarian presupposition in dealing with the problem.

Second, the Bible always speaks of the church *at* or *in* a given place, such as the church at Corinth, or the church in Jerusalem. This means that in many ways it is far more important that ties be developed with other local churches than with denominational fellows located far away. Without denying the value of the latter, we wish to emphasize the former. Only at the local level can practical and Biblical ecumenism take place. Biblically speaking, God is more interested in the "Church at Tyler, Texas" than He is in the "Association of Reformation Churches." The local church of which I am a member has ties in both directions, but our primary concern should be with the former. Once we get rid of the Greek notion of the primary of the intellect (and thus of dogma), we can see clearly that the Bible teaches the importance of local connections over ideological (denominational) ones.

Schism and the "Visible" Church

The distinction between the Church Visible and the Church Invisible has a long, confusing, and often unhelpful history. The Bible does not speak in these terms, and this has rendered the discussion highly problematic. The distinction is used to safeguard some important truths, but the question may justly be put as to whether these same truths might be better safeguarded in some other way.

Our concern is not directly with the Church Invisible, however conceived. Rather, we are concerned with the nature of the visibility of the church. How does what is visible to God become visible to man? Earlier in this essay we discussed three forms of visibility corresponding to the three aspects of the church: moral and dominical visibility (people of God), gathered visibility, and institutional visibility (sacraments, officers, buildings, political influence, etc.).

We must now ask the question: What is the mainspring of visibility? It is common for people to think that the church's source of visibility is historical institutionalization. In this view, the church is a visible institutional empire or bureaucracy that flows down through history from the time of Christ, or Abel, to the present. Christ is unalterably committed to this institution. He died for it. He must always revive it. Outside of it there is no ordinary possibility of salvation. To disrupt it is the awful sin of schism. The extreme view associates salvation simply with incorporation into the institution. The mild view holds that it is sinful for a local church to leave the institution. If a separation occurs, it is "they" who left the true institution, and it is "we" who preserve it. We may call this a successional view of the church, whether the succession be apostolic or merely institutional.

This is, however, not the Biblical view of the mainspring and origin of the church in history. The church proceeds out of eternity into time at every moment of time, as a creation of the Holy Spirit. The essence of the church is the covenant: God with us. In John 17:20f., this is straightforwardly asserted by Christ Himself: "My prayer is not for them alone. I pray also for those who will believe in Me through their message, that all of them may be one, Father, just as You are in Me and I am in You. May they also be in Us so that the world may believe that You have sent Me." The unity, oneness, and communion of the church is communion with the Trinity. The heart and essence of the church thus is the communion of the Triune God with Himself. The people of God are covenantally (not ontically) incorporated into that Divine fellowship. That is, Christians are not merged with the being of God, but are woven into the Divine fellowship of the blessed Trinity. The result of that incorporation is visibility: "so that the world may believe that You have sent Me." This is clear: Contact with God is the mainspring and only source of the church. Jesus said the same thing in Matt. 18:20, "Where two or three are gathered in my name, there am I in their midst."

What this means is that the church will be visible only so long as and to the extent that it participates in communion with the Persons of the Blessed Trinity. Where that communion begins, the church begins, even if there be no "official" connection with any institution whatever. Where that communion grows, the church becomes visible, organically and institutionally. Where that communion declines, the church loses visibility in both respects. This is a "Wave" view of the visibility of the church.

As regards the "Particle" view, as the church becomes more visible, it becomes more visible to itself. As a result, divisions are healed. Often mutual recognition of visibility occurs more readily among parts of the church as a people than among various sects of the institutional church.

What we have just outlined may be called a "processional" view of the church, as opposed to a "successional" view. The church proceeds out of eternity into time, by the work of the Holy Spirit, Who proceeds from the Father and the Son. The church is not like a steam locomotive, which takes on coal and water at the beginning and then moves under its own power down the track of history. The church is rather like an electric train, which runs only when it is in contact with the wires above it. Grace (power) is not deposited into the church; rather, grace is imparted to the church continually.

The church is God's new creation. Every generation born into the world is born dead in trespasses and sins. There is no inheritance of grace. Each new generation must be born again. We do not baptize people, and children in particular, because they are already Christians, but because they are dead and need to be renewed by water and the Spirit. Water baptism is the outward confession of the church that only the regenerating work of the Spirit can save a man. While the succession and inheritance of the church is very real, it is only valid when based upon the recreating work of the Spirit. In other words, underlying all apparent historical continuity is the continual discontinuity of the recreating activity of the Spirit. Procession is the ground of succession. Every new generation should seek to preserve the inheritance of the past, but its right to that inheritance is gained only through faithfulness to its calling to live as a new creation.

With these general observations in mind, let us look a bit more carefully at the problem of visibility. First of all, we need to keep in mind that the First Church is the fellowship of the Holy Trinity. That Church is eternal and divine. As we saw above, the essence of the church as far as human beings is concerned is the fellowship of the Holy Trinity. Thus, when we ask how the church becomes visible in history, we are really asking first of all how God becomes visible in history. And the answer to that question is: in Christ.[12]

---

12. Or more carefully: God becomes visible in His glory. Since man is the very image of God, man was designed to show forth the nature and glory of God. Jesus Christ, the Second Adam, who is also very God of very God, is the fullest revelation of the glory of God. Cf. John 1:18, "No man hath seen God at any time; the Only-begotten Son, who is in the bosom of the Father, He has explained Him."

The Divine and eternal Church becomes visible in Christ, and by extension in His body.

Now we can ask this question: What aspects of the church centrally and most pointedly make Christ visible? These will be the irreducable symbols or signs of Christ, without which the church cannot be said to exist at all. They are three: the proclamation of the Word of God, the administration of the sacraments, and the ordination of special officers. These three correspond to the traditional "marks" of the church: Word, sacrament, discipline. They also correspond to the three basic perspectives and concerns of ethics: the normative (law, Word), the situational (sacramental incorporation into the body of Christ), and the personal (human administration, under the Spirit). Finally, they correspond to the three aspects of the church, as follows: The Word gives direction to the people of God in all that they do; the ritual of the sacraments structures special worship in the assembly; and the officers provide the government for the church as an institution or organization.

The Bible is the Word of Christ, specifically instituted by Him through the power of the Holy Spirit. The sacraments of Holy Baptism and the Lord's Supper were specially instituted by Christ. The apostles and their successors were specifically set apart by Christ to govern the church. Two of these three elements (sacraments and officers) are directly "institutional" in character. This means, contrary to the opinions of most of American popular Christianity, that *there is an irreducible institutional character to the true church of Christ.* The church is not first and foremost a group of people who have come together to worship, and who set up officers from among themselves, and who do the sacraments. Rather, the church is first and foremost the visibility of God on the earth, set up by Him. The people are called by the officers and the sacraments, first and foremost. Thus, if a missionary and his wife go into a pagan land and make the sacraments visible, and call men by preaching the Word, the church is fully visible in that place in its essence, because Christ is visible. This is the wellspring of all other, wider forms of visibility.

We now have a paradigm for visibility. There is special

visibility (God manifest in Word, sacraments, officers), and there is general visibility (all other aspects). The general visibility flows from the special.

Earlier we criticized the "institutional" view of visibility. We need now to purify our critique, for the irreducible heart of visibility is institutional in character. All the same, there are wider aspects of institutional visibility that grow around the three central elements, such as architecture, liturgy, vestments, an elaborate court system, bureaucracies, and so forth. Let us liken these to the shell secreted by some ocean animal. The living organism secrets a shell around itself, for various reasons. First, it is its nature to do so. Second, it provides additional protection and reinforcement for the organism. Third, it is a thing of beauty. Just so, the institutional organic heart of the church creates around itself an institutional shell. There is nothing wrong with this, and the tendency of Quakers, Puritans, Anabaptists, and Brethren churches to fight this shell-secreting activity is misguided, for shell-secreting is part of the natural life of any vital organism,[13] and part of the natural dominion of the living, thriving church. The shell helps greatly with the work of the church, providing protection and reinforcement. The shell can also be a thing of beauty (in vestments, architecture, and liturgy).

The point to keep in mind is this: The shell is not of the essence of the church. The shell is not essential to the *being* (*esse*) of the church, though it is valuable for her *well-being* (*bene esse*). Moreover, as we can see from the Old Covenant, it is important for her eschatological *full being* (*plene esse*). While Abraham, in his exile from the possession of the promised land, worshipped at simple altars, when Israel grew to a multitude, God established a more splendid tent of meeting, the Tabernacle. With the full conquest of the land, under David, the time came for the erection of the glorious Temple of Solomon. Later, the Jews idolatrously regarded the Temple as important in itself, confusing the shell with

---

13. This is true in the broad sense in which I am discussing the secretion of "shells." Higher forms of animals secrete "shells" through territorialism, schooling, flocking, herding, and so forth.

the church, at which points in history the shell (Temple) was destroyed that the heart (the presence of the Lord) might be clearly seen (cf. Jer. 7:4; the whole book of Ezekiel; and Jesus' words in Matt. 12:6; etc.). Keeping this in mind will help us get at the problem of schism.

We have seen from John 17 that the church ultimately consists of the Three Persons of God and those in fellowship with Them. We have also argued that the visibility of the church is "processional" rather than "successional" in character, because it is the influx of the revitalizing power of the Holy Spirit that is the sole impetus for visibility. What happens historically is that the Spirit of God makes the church visible before men in the officers, sacraments, and proclamation of the church. As long as the church is growing in communion with God, visibility will *appear* to be successional. This very real historical succession is, however, due solely to the influx of Spiritual power and life. In time, however, it often has come to pass that the church in a given place will wave out of fellowship with God. The influx of Spiritual power is then cut off. This grieving or quenching of the Spirit is what the sin of schism really is. Schism is not first and foremost the sin of breaking with a shell, for the shell may be in sin. Schism is breaking fellowship with God. The fracturing of a shell follows schism as a consequence.

When the church drifts out of fellowship with God, several things happen. First, there are ethical patterns created by the church that persist for a time, but that are not well understood, if at all. Obedience becomes legalistic, not Spiritual. An example of this is the notion that adultery is wrong, and that men and women should be virgins when they marry. For a while after the direct influence of the church has actually died, this pattern of belief or prejudice persist in a society, but eventually it collapses.

Second, there are institutions created by the church as a people and by the institutional church, such as orphanages and colleges, that fall into enemy hands and are misused. More important is the fact that the institutional shells of the church fall into enemy hands. In the days of its power, the institutional church was a force to be reckoned with. Its institutional shell continues to wield power. As a result, it attracts men who want to play god by wielding power. The power of God being withdrawn, the shell is the helpless prey of these vultures. They entrench themselves, and the outer shell of the institution becomes corrupt.

Third, the time comes when people begin to seek God once again, and He lets Himself be found by them. As a result, Christ is in their midst. They enter into communion with the Blessed Trinity. They may grow up within an historical shell, or they may grow up alongside of one. The history of the "remnant" in Old Testament illustrates this sociological factor. How this "remnant" should relate to the older shells will be taken up below.

The process we have just delineated has repeated itself countless times in history, even in the period before Christ. Yet theologians generally have not been able to formulate a theological rationale for this movement, due to a preoccupation with the "Particle" view and ignoring the "Wave" view.

All the same, there are certain legitimate questions that have to be asked about the recognition of the church as a "Particle." If the shell is corrupt, does that mean that the organic heart is corrupt (officers, sacraments, Word)? We have to say, first, that men cannot corrupt the sacraments. They can fail to administrate them, and thus corrupt the sacramental order, but even if the officer doing the sacraments is a thorough renegade, the sacraments remain God's work, and are not corruptible by man. The heart of the Donatist controversy was over this issue, and the church determined from Scripture that the power and authority to administer the sacraments lies in the office itself, and in God's work, not in the person of the office-bearer. Thus, we submit to the office, not to the person, and it is the office and not the person who administers the sacraments.

All the same, churches do become corrupt, and men should separate from them. On what basis do we determine the corruption of the church? Which is more corrupt, the Baptist church that makes Christ visible each week in the sacrament, but that refuses the sacrament to children, or the Reformed church that administers baptism at least to children, but that makes Christ sacramentally visible in the Supper only four times a year? As we noted earlier in this paper, it is virtually impossible to come up with a list of abstract characteristics that help us determine that a given group is not a church. Still, there are some things that can be said. First, groups that do not practice the sacraments at all are not part of the church of Jesus Christ. These include Quakers and hyper-dispensational sects. (I am not saying that nobody can ever be saved in these groups; I am saying that *we* cannot recognize them as churches and as Christians. Man looks on the outward, visible, appearance; God alone judges the heart.)

Second, groups that have completely replaced the Scriptures in worship are not part of the church of Jesus Christ. This would include some extreme quarters of liberalism, but it might also include some pentecostalists and fundamentalists (oddly enough). Listening to the radio in some of the more backward parts of America, one suspects that there are those in the latter two groups who never sing any psalms at all, and in which the preaching consists only of ranting and raving, with no Biblical reference whatsoever.[14]

Third, groups that have no government at all, and no recognized officers (regardless of what they call them), can hardly be considered churches. No one is binding and loosing; no one is retaining and remitting sins; no one is guarding the Table.

But what about groups that have not gone so far? What about a liberal Episcopal church, let us say. They still have officers. The sacraments are still rightly administered (far more so than in Reformed churches, since Christ is made visible weekly). The Word is still sung in the liturgy and in the psalms, and read in appointed readings, even if the sermons are heretical. On the basis of what we have seen, such a church should be counted and treated as part of the church of Jesus Christ. Strange as this may seem, coming from an arch-conservative like myself, it is the clear teaching of the Bible. The people of Israel were not permitted to renounce the Temple and its worship during those times that the priests were apostate. The people did go to prophets for outside nourish-

---

14. Anyone who has ever heard a radio screamer lapse into the "hut-to-huhs" will know what I mean.

ment, but the proper procedure was to pray and prophesy, that the visible church might be restored.

It is precisely at this point, however, that the New Covenant differs from the Old. Recognizing a liberal Episcopal church as a true church does not carry with it a requirement that no one may ever transfer from it to a better church. The New Covenant situation, being multi-centralized, provides such options. Moreover, any local church is free at any time to sever its ties with the larger church, because the local church does not receive its existence from being part of the larger.

The practical question of when to give up on an historical shell and move to create a new one can be answered by taking a "Wave" view of the matter. What is important is not the position of the shell at any given moment, but its settled trend. A shell may be doing the sacraments in a basically correct manner, and have a fine constitution on paper, but be in a trend away from God. This trend can be observed. An observable trend away from God does not fully indicate that the shell is apostate. The conservative office-bearer must wait for God to bring to pass an issue that requires a careful, polite, but firm and intransigent confrontation over the drift, using matters clearly and unmistakably revealed in the Word[15]. This is required by Ezk. 3:17-21. The confrontation will surely reveal the situation (1 Cor. 11:19). Repeated confrontations will make it clear to all. If what is revealed is a settled determination to defy the clearly-revealed laws of God, departure is mandated. The Christian should not be enslaved to an evil institutional shell simply because of a false successional view of the church.[16]

---

15. For instance, a man commits adultery, forsakes his wife, and renounces the church. If the elders flatly refuse to excommunicate this man (because he is a relative of some of them, or a power in the community), then matters are clearly and unmistakably revealed.

16. It is not the place of non-officers to provoke such confrontations. The layman (or, general officer) should approach a special officer whom he trusts, and ask him to provoke the confrontation. If there are no special officers who care enough to fight for orthodoxy, then the general officer should quietly and peaceably transfer to another church. God never blesses insurrection, even if the cause is just.

In this way we may repeat our answer to the question of schism. The only real schism is between God and man. Where this break occurs, pernicious effects inevitably follow. The institutional shell of the church is not the first concern of Christ, for it is a byproduct of communion with Him. That communion has primacy, and must have primacy in our actions. The unity of institutional shells is a desideratum, for it facilitates discipline. It can only be accomplished, however, in Christ.

To make this clear, let me ask you (the reader) some questions. First, is the Word read and preached in your church? Second, are the sacraments of Baptism and the Lord's Supper performed in your church? Third, do you have officers who oversee your church? I assume you have said "yes" to all three. Now, my church has the same three things. On this basis, I wish to assert firmly that your church and mine do not need to become united, because *we are already institutionally one.* We do not need to become one, because we already are one in Christ. This is not just "mystically" true, it is really true because we both eat of exactly the same bread.

Now, let me make a pledge to you. If your church excommunicates someone, we will recognize it, and will not serve that person communion. Will you make the same pledge to me? If someone will not make that pledge *he is a schismatic*, because he is denying the oneness that already really exists. That oneness exists whether he recognizes it or not, and because of that *we will recognize his government even if he does not recognize ours.*

The church is called to a task. That task is not a bare minimum of keeping in contact with the three forms of the special visibility of God in the church. That task includes the expansion of the faith and of the church into all of life and the world. To put it another way, the task is to create beautiful and proper shells that adorn and protect the gospel in all its purity. When a local, orthodox church decides to break from a liberal denomination, this is not schism. Rather, the local church is simply saying that in order for her to perform her task, she believes she must break with the corruption that has infested the old shell. It is not necessary to determine that the old shell is totally corrupt. It is still possible to recognise the sacraments and orders (officers) of the older body (otherwise we would have to rebaptize and reordain anyone coming from that older body after the split).

We should be quite clear on this. Regardless of what they might sometimes have said, the Reformers continued to recognize that the Roman Catholic Church was in some sense part of the true church. We know that because they continued to recognize Holy Baptism as performed by that church. The shell was definitely corrupt. Yet, the corruption of the shell was not seen to defile the very heart of the church. At the same time, the corruption of the shell did require a separation.[17]

Thus, we may say that a church may separate from its former association for any number of practical reasons. The reasons do not even have to be very great.[18] It is not necessary to anathematize the former body in order to leave. Such separations are not in themselves the sin of schism. Rather, the sin of schism, which is separating from Christ through sin, is the cause of the fracturing of the institutional shells of churches.

The situation is different regarding the individual. If an individual leaves a local church, without transferring, then he has apostatized from the church. He is no longer part of the church of Christ. But for a local church to leave a denomination does not imply apostasy, for the local church remains a true church.

Denominationalism

The question in the problem of denominationalism is not the question of the visible unity of the church. The church is always

---

17. Until Vatican II, the Roman Church denied the validity of protestant baptism, while the churches of the Reformation generally have accepted Roman Catholic baptism. If anything, then, the churches of the Reformation have shown themselves more truly catholic than has the Roman Church.

18. For instance, in our town there are three conservative presbyterian churches, which are in three different conservative presbyterian denominations. Maybe someday these three will decide that since local connections are more important than national ones, they all should come into the same denomination. For that to happen, two of the churches would have to leave their present associations. Obviously, however, this would involve no condemnation of the associations being left behind.

visibly united. There is one Lord Jesus Christ, one audible Word making Him visible, one pair of sacraments making Him visible, and one conception of special officers making Him visible. Moreover, speaking of the church in general, we see her united against sin, abortion, homosexuality, pornography, united in favor of the family, family property, etc. There is organic visible unity to the church insofar as Christians share a common witness against evil and act for Christ. There is unity visible in the cooperation of the churches. There is unity visible in local interrelationships among churches, including common Eucharistic worship on occasion. There is unity visible in the cross-fertilization of the parachurch organizations. In view of all this, much of the grief expended over the lack of unity in the church has been misplaced. It is due again to a failure to distinguish the various aspects and dimensions of the church.

The Father has never failed to answer the Son's prayer in John 17. It is wrong to act as if He has. We must confess unity by faith (not by sight), and on that basis work for greater visible manifestations of it.

The question in the problem of denominationalism is the question of shell unity. It is a genuine problem, because it prevents the church from functioning in a proper way as a government (since various denominations do not recognize one another), and as a local ministry (since the churches in a location will be of varying denominations). The proliferation of shell diversity is due to at least three factors. First, with the Reformation there was a great burst of understanding with respect to the Scripture. God and His Word being infinite, and man being finite, it is understandable that different men would see and appreciate different aspects of Christianity. This diversity would not have sparked disunity except that, being sinners, men tend to fight over their differences in perception. If this were the only factor involved in shell diversity, we might call for a council and synthesize all the apprehended truths.

Second, communication is an important factor in shell disunity. Differing theological traditions often use words or key phrases in slightly different ways. Skill and effort is needed, as well as a gracious spirit, to understand, for instance, if the Scofield Reference Bible *really* teaches that people were saved by their own works under the Old Covenant.[19]

Third, sin is a major factor. Unfortunately, not only do the various groups focus on different aspects of revelation, they also do so with varying degrees of admixture of error and heresy.

All of this is to say that the reasons for denominational diversity are deep-seated, complex, and cannot be removed by a wave of a magic wand or anathema. The problem can only be effectively resolved by local communication, cooperation, and prayer. It must be recognized by all parties that there are legitimate strengths and weaknesses in all the branches of the church. The relative proportion of strenghts to weaknesses may and does vary, but the presence of them does not. The Puritan branch of the church, for instance, may be thought to have the greatest collection of strengths, but its weaknesses are visible to true Christians in other groups. The devout Lutheran or Anglican has in some ways a better understanding of what it means that the world is restored in Christ, so that he does not pit worship against the world, and is thus able to honor his King with the very best of his meager cultural attainments. Local discussion and interaction on these and other matters would redound to the benefit of all participating, and would tend toward the unification of the shells of the church.

It is, as we have seen, only as men draw near to God and participate in the fellowship of the Holy Trinity that the church becomes visible in any wide and outwardly powerful way. What this means for the current discussion should be obvious: The visible disunity of the institutional shells of the church cannot be healed directly by political measures. The very best, and indeed only way to overcome disunity is to take as much of the truth as possible, make it as visible as possible through life and proclamation, and suffuse one's life with as much communion with God as possi-

---

19. Another way to put this is that Christians not only differ over particulars, but operate with different *secondary paradigms*, or systems of truth-and-world organization. Theological disputes are often little more than ships passing in the dark precisely because of a failure to be sensitive to varying presuppositions and models.

ble. These radical steps may seem calculated to separate the church further from itself, and they are indeed the opposite of the worldly lowest common denominator approach to unity, but they are the only steps God will honor. Unity can only be built on Truth, and the more the Truth is set out in clarity (not belligerently, but clearly and precisely), the more a new and more profound consensus will appear, which will lead to increased unity among the churches.

The problem of denominationalism is the problem of shell unity. Shell unity is a byproduct of union with Christ, and often a byproduct of organic unity in the church as a people. Organic unity in Christ always exists, though not always as fully and forcefully visibly. Christ's prayer in John 17 has always been answered, though the fullest manifestation of the Father's answer awaits the eschaton, when there will be a fullness of unity unmixed with the smallest tare.

Shell disunity is not a sin, for if it were, we should not have any way of avoiding sin by participating in the church, and 1 Corinthians 10:13 tells us that we never have any excuse for sinning. This takes us back to the nature of the sin of schism. Shell disunity is not schism, but an historical byproduct of schism. The schism is the failure to maintain communion with God, and to recognize the sacramental presence of Christ in other churches. The only way to heal the effect is to correct the cause, and so the only way to achieve shell unity is to maintain communion with God. Disease and famine are not sin but the byproduct of sin; so it is with shell disunity.

Parachurch Organizations

We are not concerned here with the manifold problems created by the inadequate theologies of various parachurch organizations in our day (which correspond to inadequate theologies in the various churches in our day). Rather, we are concerned with the nature of their place in the church at large.

The "Wave" perspective helps us with this, I believe. In its early days, the church as people of God is virtually identical to the institutional church, being few in number, living in a hostile environment. As the church grows in strength and influence, it is not necessary for the church in its official and institutional aspects to maintain a stance over against the rest of society. The "world" is not the things outside the wider shell of the church, but the things outside of Christ.

The institutional church is the nursery of the Kingdom, and thus as the church grows and develops, many of its earlier diaconal responsibilities can be taken over by separate organizations, aspects of the church as people of God. Thus, there is no need for the institutional church to run Christian hospitals, orphanages, schools, etc. On the other hand, it is not wrong for the institutional church to institute or run such organizations, if the people of God cannot organize to do so. For instance, the enemy secular state in our day has made plain its hostility to Christian schools. These schools may be better protected by becoming part of a local church, even though ideally the Christian school is not part of the institutional church's but of the Christian family's responsibility.

"But such things are the charge of the institutional church's deacons," one might object. Not necessarily. In chapter 11 of this book I argue that the Biblical concept of the diaconate is apprenticeship, not permanent charitable service. The diaconate in the institutional church is not a separate office, but is composed of men set aside to assist the elders, some of whom at least will become apprentice elders. In my opinion, the deacons in a local church should not form a separate board, but should simply do what the elders assign them. During those "Waves" in history when the church is small and weak, virtually all charitable work will be done within the institutional church, and so will be the charge of the deacons. This need not always be the case, however. In its ages of ascendancy, the deacons will, I believe, be sent out to learn from charitable organizations run by the church in general, but their specific charitable responsibilities will simply be to the more general needs of the members of the local church. Specialized work, such as hospitals and orphanages, schools for the deaf, etc., will be carried on not by deacons but by service organizations independent of the institutional church.

"What kind of power, then, does the institutional church have over these independent parachurch organizations?" The same power it has always had: the power to deny them or admit them to the sacraments. This is the basic and most awesome power entrusted to humankind, and it is entrusted to the officers of the institutional church. It is noteworthy that no parachurch organization sees itself as a sacramental body. Campus Crusade for Christ considers itself "an evangelistic arm of the church," not a sacramental body parallel to the institutional church. This is the right way to look at it. (Remember, we are not here concerned with such doctrinal or practical errors as we may believe are present in Campus Crusade or any other parachurch organization, only with their "sociology.") If members of some parachurch organization get out of line seriously in their lives or beliefs, they can be disciplined or excommunicated by the institutional church to which they belong.

"What about groups that engage in evangelism and instruction?" This is a bit trickier, since these tasks are more associated with the eldership than with the diaconate, but the deacons in Acts 6 - 8 obviously spent much of their time in evangelism and teaching. Indeed, it is all the rage nowadays to insist that every Christian has a duty to engage in evangelism. (Depending on how we define "evangelism," this might be right or wrong. Some people are obviously not called to engage in "cold turkey" evangelism, though all Christians should live out a Christian witness before their friends and neighbors.)[20] If the church as the people of God has a general responsibility to evangelize, we can hardly object to parachurch organizations set up for that purpose. The following strictures need to be kept in mind, however:

(1) Parachurch may never administer the sacraments. I do not believe that the sacraments should be administered at parachurch meetings, even if "under the auspices" of some local church — as at the Triennial Urbana Conference. In my opinion, it is a sentimentalistic abuse bordering on the magical to use the sacraments that way. Keep the sacraments in the context of the Lord's Day liturgy of local church where they belong.

---

20. See chapter 11 below, pp. 221-258.

(2) Parachurch officers must never demand the same degree
of respect or submission as the elders of the institutional church.
This heinous offense is committed by some parachurch organizations, where an almost monastic degree of submission is required.
Not even the institutional church can require such submission,
though there is nothing wrong with a special temporary vow of
special submission for the purpose of special discipleship. Parachurch organizations should be thought of as businesses with em-
ployees, not as churches with officers.

(3) Teaching conducted in parachurch has no official weight.
It has only the weight of an informal Bible study. The teaching
conducted in the institutional church has official weight, which
does not mean that the people are required to accept it willy-nilly,
but does mean that they are required to take it with utmost ser-
iousness. The churchmember is to be a Berean (Acts 17:11), studying Scripture to make sure these things are true, but giving them
special weight. Also, the teacher in the institutional church has a
right to expect a special power from the Holy Spirit in his teaching
that the parachurch teacher cannot claim.

We conclude that parachurch evangelistic and teaching orders
are not in themselves wrong. Many such organizations have
sprung up because the institutional church has fallen down on the
job. The proper corrective to present abuses is not to preach the
parachurch organizations out of existence as an evil, but to so outshine them that they wither away as their members are drawn into
the institutional church. A couple of years ago the leader of a large
parachurch organization became a Reformed Christian. Suddenly
he dissolved his entire organization, "because parachurch is
wrong." Instead of turning the organization into a Reformed
group, working with the churches for good, he dropped the whole
thing, leaving his sheep to scatter. Such is the effect of hyper-
institutional thinking on the church and on the people of God.

"May the tithe be used to support parachurch organizations?"
I have dealt with this at length elsewhere.[21] All the tithe is owed to

21. James B. Jordan, "Tithing: Financing Christian Reconstruction," in Jordan, *The Law of the Covenant: An Exposition of Exodus 21 - 23* (Tyler, TX: Institute
for Christian Economics, 1984).

the sacramental sanctuary. The determination of what to do with tithe money is to be made by the special officers, not by the person paying the tithe. Gifts above the tithe may lawfully be given to parachurch organizations, and local churches may choose to give part of the tithe they receive over to parachurch groups.

It is best to play the parachurch tune by ear. In the area of Bible translation, Wycliffe has done a good job over the years. (Questions might be raised nowadays, unfortunately, because of the rise of "dynamic equivalence.")[22] There is really no crying need for each denomination to have its own Translation Society. Missionaries can be trained by Wycliffe and sent out by the churches, if desired. The same can be said of other groups.

The major advantage that accrues to the church from the multiplicity of diaconal organizations is this: They tend to break down artificial barriers and work for cross-pollenization and unity among the churches. If our long term goal is the unification of the whole institutional shell of the church, it is to our advantage to work with existing parachurch and diaconal organizations, and add them to the melting pot, rather than set up new ones.

In summary, my point is this: Given the Biblical understanding of the church as the people of God, there is nothing wrong in principle with parachurch organizations. The independence of these organizations is a problem no different from that of denominationalism. The only serious issue in the problem of parachurch organizations is whether the organization in view is doing an effective, Biblical job or not. If the matter were debated on this material ground, rather than on formal abstract grounds, more would be accomplished. If some parachurch group is inadequate, it is not because it happens to exist at all, but because its theology and practice are truncated. Independent mission boards should be examined in the same way.

Conclusion

The main point of this essay has been to examine the notion of the institutional church. The Reformation started out assuming

---

22. On "dynamic equivalence," see Jakob van Bruggen, *The Future of the Bible* (Nashville, Thomas Nelson, 1978).

that a Christian church and a Christian state were different but correlative powers, and that membership in the one was equivalent to membership with the other. Thus, they retained a largely institutionalistic or bureaucratic view of these structures. Soon, however, it became obvious that Christians would often have to separate from, quietly disobey, or even flee some supposedly Christian states, because these states were actually hostile to the faith. Later, the Puritans found the same thing to be true of the institutional shell of the church.

Theology has never quite caught up with these phenomena, probably because of inadequate presuppositional tools with which to work. Each Scottish church, for instance, that separated from the state church, has continued to insist that it deserves to be the state-supported church.

The sociological phenomena surrounding the church in America have been relatively unique in the history of the church. The problems surrounding the relationship between local and larger churches, the problem of denominationalism and the concomitant problem of schism, and the problem of parachurch—these did not exist until the 17th century.[23] Splits began to take place in European churches then, creating the problem of denominations. But it is especially in America, where immigrant groups simply brought over their own churches, that we find such ecclesiastical chaos. The purpose of this essay has been to explore these problems, and to seek afresh from the Scriptures insights into their resolution. Repeating old answers has not helped, because the old answers were not designed to deal with these new questions. As Christian reconstruction progresses in America, the twin virtues of catholicity and integrity will be sharpened, and true reformation will inevitably result.

---

23. At least not in the protestant form. Conflicts between local churches and monastic parachurches, between secular and regular clergy, run all through the history of the Catholic churches, West and East.

3

THE SOCIOLOGY OF THE CHURCH:
A BIBLICO-HISTORICAL APPROACH

In this essay we are concerned to investigate the relationship of Israel to the nations under the Old Covenant, and how this relationship compares with that of the church to the world under the New Covenant. My purpose is to challenge directly the assumption that Israel were the only saved people during the Old Covenant period. I assert that while Israel alone were priests, God generously redeemed many other people before the coming of Jesus Christ. It is the burden of this essay to demonstrate this thesis from the Scriptures, although perforce this investigation must be rather tentative and preliminary.[1]

Looking at the Old Covenant we find, as we usually do, that the situation was much more complex then than it is today. There were many different sacrifices/sacraments and rites of initiation (cleansing, circumcision, cutting the nails and hair of a war-bride, etc.). Now there is but one of each. Sociologically, there were Israelites, nations, Levites, priests, and the High Priest, not to speak of Nazirites and others. Now there are just special officers (elders), general officers (laymen), and unbelievers. A consideration of how things were then, and how they differ now, should help us to avoid mistakes in our practice and organization.

Before looking at the matter in detail, let us take a general

---

1. Throughout this chapter there are references to "sabbath enthronement." The reader is referred to my study, *Sabbath Breaking and the Death Penalty: A Theological Investigation* (Tyler, TX: Geneva Ministries, 1986) for more on this. Chapter 2 of that study repeats a great deal of what is contained here, but with a focus on the sabbath rather than on the sociology of the church.

overview. When God created Adam, He made him out of the dust
of the ground. When Adam sinned, a curse spread from him to
that dust. The curse also spread to all men. Thus, the entire
"world," whether considered as a cosmos (dust, etc.) or as a society
(humanity), became estranged from God. Cherubim were placed
to bar the way back into Eden.

The original arrangement of the world in this First Covenant
was this: There was a central sanctuary with symbolic, sacramental trees, and a priest-king (Adam) maintaining it. The sanctuary
garden was located in a particular land (Eden), and there were
also other lands outside the sanctuary, but which were fed by
rivers that originated in the sanctuary land. There were, thus,
two geographical dualities to the organization (sociology) of the
world. There was the distinction between Garden-sanctuary and
Land (in this case, Eden), and the distinction between the First
Land (Eden) and all other outlying lands.[2] The fall of the priest-
king in the sanctuary spread the influences of the curse downstream to the whole world.

Throughout the Old Covenant period, these geographical
dualities were maintained. God kept restoring certain chosen men
to the Edenic sanctuary, establishing them as priests, and tieing
the salvation of the rest of the world to them. When these sanctuary priests were faithful, they led the downstream nations into
faithfulness, though these nations did not themselves become special priests. When these sanctuary priests fell, they brought the
entire world down with them.

With the coming of the New Covenant, these dualities were
transformed. The New Covenant embodies the fulfillment of
what the First (or Old) Covenant with Adam was supposed and
designed to bring to pass, but never did. The New Covenant is,
thus, not simply a replacement for the Old one, fallen in Adam; it

---

2. This can also be seen as a three-sectioned world: Garden, Eden, and Lands
(corresponding to Heaven, Earth, and Waters under the earth). At the same
time, what we see most often in Scripture is a discussion in terms of a series of
dualities: Garden and Eden; Eden and Lands. Both perspectives are valid, and
the ambiguity exists in part because these distinctions are all pre-eschatological,
designed eventually to be overcome in the new heavens and earth.

is also the fulfillment of that original one. In the New Covenant, the sociology is different. There is no one Edenic earthly central sanctuary; rather, the sanctuary exists in heaven and wherever the sacramental Presence of Jesus Christ is manifest. The equivalent to being in the holy land is now to be in the Body of Christ.

Israel sustained a relationship to the nations analogous to the relationship between Eden and the world. Believers in the nations were ministered to by the priests in Israel. Gracious influences spread from Israel to the nations. To be saved, one did not have to become an Israelite and be circumcised, but one did have to put faith in the system God had set up, and permit the Israelites to function as one's priests. From this perspective, there were both faithful and unfaithful persons in both Israel and the nations. Abraham was the "father" of both groups, the faithful circumcised and the faithful uncircumcised. There were spiritual leaders (priests) among the nations (such as Jethro), but these always had to look to Israel (Eden) as the special priests God had established in the center of the earth.

As we shall see, these dualities were both multiplied and strictly enforced in the Old Covenant by a series of exclusionary laws. It is helpful, before looking at these, to meditate on the original creation situation in this regard, for such exclusions would not have existed had Adam not fallen.

The Original Design of the World

According to Genesis 1:1, God created two things initially: heaven and earth. On the second day of creation week, God placed *within the earth* an image of heaven (1:8). This by itself is sufficient to indicate that the world is supposed to be brought into conformity with the heavenly model. God created man as His very image to be the priest and king overseeing this project. Man was to "subdue" the earth (1:28). Was the earth in revolt? No. Then what does "subdue" mean? In context it means that man is to take the good world and work with it, bringing it gradually into a condition of glory. With his eyes on the glorious heaven as a model, man is to raise the world to glory. This glorification of the earth was man's original task. "Thy will be done on earth as it is in heaven."

Within the world itself, however, God established three different environments for man. There was the land of Eden. Within Eden, to the east, there was the Garden (2:8). Outside of Eden there were other lands, downstream (2:10). In a generally ignored but all-important paragraph of Genesis 2, we are told how the world was organized when it was created:

> 10. And a river went out of Eden to water the garden; and from thence it separated and became four heads.
> 11. The name of the first: Pishon. It encompasses the whole land of Havilah, where there is gold.
> 12. And the gold of that land is good. There is bdellium and the onyx stone.
> 13. And the name of the second river: Gihon. It encompasses the whole land of Cush.
> 14. And the name of the third river: Tigris. It runs east of Assyria. And the fourth river: Euphrates.

Here we have a world model. In the center of the world is the land of Eden. On the east side of the Land of Eden is the Garden of Eden (Gen. 2:8). In the center of the Garden of Eden are the two trees (Gen. 2:9).

In short, the world was organized in terms of a primordial duality between the central sanctuary of Eden, and the outlying world watered by four rivers extending to the four corners of the world. The design of history was for man to start in Eden, in fellowship with God. Then, obedient to the cultural mandate (Gen. 1:28ff.), man was to extend his dominion over the earth, following out the four rivers. He would bring his tithes and offerings to the throne of God in the Garden and eat of the sacramental Tree(s) from time to time. Ultimately, the entire world would be brought from its primordial to its perfected condition, and then the world would be transfigured into a New Creation, with a perpetual sabbath. Man's work would have been accomplished.

Let us try to formulate a theory as to how this world would have worked. God did not make the world an ugly place, or a barren wilderness. The world already had an initial, natural glory. The Garden was the most beautiful, glorious place in the world. It was the sanctuary, where God and man would meet on the sabbath day. By letting man meet with Him on the sabbath, God was promising that man would someday finish his labors, as God had His, and enter fully into God's own rest (Gen. 2:1-3).

Thus, like any good father, God gave Adam a head start. The Garden was, partially at least, a special model of heaven on earth. Outside the Garden was the land of Eden. Part of man's project would be to extend this Garden into Eden, glorifying all of Eden into Garden. Simultaneously, however, man would be glorifying the Garden itself, moving it from glory to glory, according to the degrees of glory (2 Cor. 3:18). How would he do this? By *taking* hold of the creation, *giving thanks* for it (thus orienting his labors toward God), *breaking down* the creation and reshaping it, and then *sharing* the fruits of his labors with others, who would then *evaluate* them and *enjoy* them.[3] For instance, man would take grain, break it down into flour, mix it with other things, and bake bread. He would engage in the same general process turning grapes into wine. He would also extract gold and jewels from rock, to adorn the Garden.

Now, in order to do this he would have to make a trip downstream to Havilah, where the gold was. Thus, the glorification of the Garden would not be possible without assistance from the downstream areas. Neither the Garden nor Eden was self-sufficient. It would not be possible to glorify one part of the world (Garden) without beginning to reprocess and glorify other parts. Glorification would be a holistic process.

Just as Havilah would contribute gold to the Garden, so the Garden would contribute things to Havilah as well. In particular, the heaven-model would be brought by Adam's descendants from the Garden into other lands. And, along with that, seeds from the Garden would be planted in other lands. In time, new Trees of

---

3. I have discussed this sequence of actions elsewhere in this volume; see pp. 35-36. See also my study, "Christian Piety: Deformed and Reformed," *The Geneva Papers* II:1 (available for $4.00 from Geneva Ministries, Box 131300, Tyler, TX 75713).

Life would grow, establishing other sanctuaries downstream from Eden. There would be a sanctuary-Garden in Havilah, in Cush, and in every other land.

Sometimes this is called the distinction between cult (worship, sanctuary) and culture (downstream labors). As history moved forward, the distinction between cult and culture would tend to disappear, but it would never fully disappear. This is because until man's work was finished, he would still have a sabbath day set aside for worship and rest. Thus, both sanctuary places (Gardens) and downstream places (lands) would go from glory to glory, but the distinction would remain until man had finished getting from this creation all its potential. At that point, there would be a new heavens and a new earth, a transfigured cosmos.

The geography here is all important. The Garden was on the east side of Eden. The river arose in the Land of Eden, flowed to the Garden, and from the Garden to the other lands. When man was cast from the Garden, he was tossed out the "back door," so to speak, to the east (Gen. 3:23f.). Thus, Adam was blocked not just from the Garden, but from the whole Land of Eden, and that Land could only be reached by going through the Sanctuary-Garden. (Eden was on a high plateau; we know this because water flows downhill, and the river arose in Eden and flowed elsewhere.) As men went farther in sin, they moved farther east (Gen. 4:16; 11:2). Throughout Scripture, men had to come in a westward movement to the east gate of the house of God (tabernacle/Temple). Only those who were admitted into the Sanctuary area (by circumcision and Passover) might press through to live in the land of Eden (Israel). We shall investigate this more fully

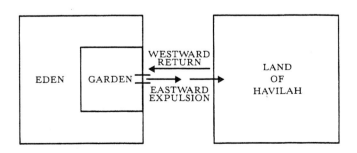

below.[4]

Thus, there was originally one sanctuary for the whole world, located on the east side of Eden. The program of downstream dominion did not exclude the multiplication of sanctuaries. The fact that there was only one central sanctuary during the Mosaic, Davidic, and Post-exilic periods does not mean that by the design of the first creation there was never intended to be but one. Indeed, even within Israel we find that there were several secondary sanctuary cities, and that these were established according to commonsense rules of geographical centrality. There were six of these sanctuaries, spread out on both sides of the Jordan (Num. 35).

We may draw from this, and from the analogy of the New Covenant (when the Edenic program is once again back in force, though transformed, as we shall see), that as men multiplied, and the distance to the central sanctuary became prohibitive, they would have established other places of worship, under Divine guidance. Indeed, even in Israel, there were synagogues in every place, though the annual feasts were only to be celebrated at the central sanctuary.

All of this implies a program of spreading gardens. It makes sense to assume that, just as there was a garden-sanctuary in the land of Eden, so there would eventually be one also in the lands of Havilah, Cush, and so forth. The two sacramental trees would also reproduce themselves, finding appropriate places in these new sanctuaries. After all, the Bible pictures trees growing where water goes (Psalm 1, for instance), and the pictures of eschatological development in Ezekiel 47 and Revelation 22 show Trees of Life spreading wherever the restored rivers flow. Indeed, a pri-

---

4. There is another interesting aspect to the world-design of Genesis 2. The water that formed the river in Eden actually arose from the "waters under the earth" (Gen. 2:6). This water went into the sanctuary, and then flowed out to the rest of the world, eventually returning to the "waters under the earth." Similarly, the wealth of the nations is seen in Scripture to be brought to the Edenic people (Israel), who then take it and adorn the sanctuary with it. The sanctuary, thus adorned, then becomes the fountain of life to the world. Agreeable to this model, in the New Covenant men bring the bread and wine made by their labors to the Church, and it becomes the sacramental food of the Kingdom, feeding in a special way the people who brought it in the first place.

mary symbol of the failure of the sanctuary to spread and multiply
is the laver of cleansing, which has no outflow until it is tipped
over in Ezekiel 47 (and compare Zechariah 14).[5] Thus, the reason
for the restriction of sacramental worship to one and only one
place during the Old Covenant lies in the sin of man and consequent curse and exclusion, not in the design of creation.

Of course, sin wrecked this original program, but God never
gave it up. Accordingly, throughout the Old Covenant period, we
continue to see a duality between central sanctuary and outlying
world. We have a seed-throne nation of priests, who maintain the
sanctuary; and we have outlying peoples who engage in cultural
tasks "downstream from Eden." The plan of redemption is always
set out in terms of this duality in the Old Covenant. The difference is that instead of an outflow there must be an influx: The
peoples must come to the sanctuary, specifically to the gate of the
sanctuary because they are not allowed in. Only in the New Covenant is the outflow reestablished.

When he fell, Adam had already taken up his general or kingly
task, beginning with naming the animals and receiving a helper.
This task continues down through history, though under curse.
Adam had failed to take up his special or priestly task of guarding
the garden and his wife. As a result, cherubim were appointed
guardians, and men were excluded from the priestly role and the
sabbath enthronement that goes along with it. Only a special people, symbolically raised to priesthood, would act the role of
priests, on a provisional basis, until the Second Adam had
become enthroned on behalf of all righteous men.

Thus, we find that the gentiles carried out kingly tasks and not
true priestly tasks, but that Israel carried out both, though its
peculiar calling was to show forth the priestly task to all men, as a
prophecy of the Messiah. The nations labored only in the general
area, while Israel labored in both the general and the special
areas, with emphasis on the latter.

---

5. Following on the observations in footnote 3 above, it is interesting to note
that the laver of the Tabernacle becomes a "sea" in the Temple. It is that "sea" that
is the source for the waters that flow out of the sanctuary.

The prototype is Abraham. The period before Abraham is obscure as regards its sociological organization. We know that Cain
and Abel "brought" their offerings to the Lord, and that Cain was
"driven away" from the Lord's presence (Gen. 4). From this we
can infer that they brought their offerings before the cherubim
who guarded the gates of Eden. Men were downstream, and cherubim were the sanctuary guardians. Man was originally supposed
to be the guardian (Gen. 2:15), but when he fell, the cherubim
were appointed to the task (Gen. 3:24). The cherubim continued
to be the guardians until the coming of the New Covenant, for
even the High Priest was not permitted to come into the ultimate
sanctuary, the cherub-guarded Holy of Holies, except once a year,
and then only very carefully.

Downstream Sabbath Worship

We may draw from this that all humanity lived downstream
from Eden in the period between Creation and the Flood, and after
the Flood until the time of Abraham, or maybe until the time the
Levitical priesthood was set up. After the Flood, they brought their
sacrifices at many places, but always with the understanding that
these altars were cherubim-guarded, and always with the understanding that they were still outside, looking in. From the silence of
Scripture, we can infer that none of these sacrifices was ever a sacrament; that is, the flesh was never shared as a meal between God
and man. Such sacramental fellowship is the essence of the peculiar
sanctuary privilege, and the first time it is seen is when the sanctuary people are reconstituted by Passover and at Sinai (Ex. 24:5, 11).

We may say that downstream sabbath worship was in existence before the sanctuary was rebuilt. A brief expansion will help
us get a fuller grasp of this. When God created the world, He created the whole world first, and on the sixth day planted the sanctuary, setting it up as the high point and the sacramental center.
Similarly, after the Flood, God re-created the downstream situation first, and then rebuilt the sanctuary.[6] (Notice that the sanc-

---

6. For more on this pattern, see my book *Judges: God's War Against Humanism*
(Tyler, TX: Geneva Ministries, 1985), p. xvf.

tuary was built at Sinai, and then the people were allowed to go
into the new Eden: One has to go through the sanctuary to get to
the promised land.) This slow and gradual process culminated in
the placement of the ultimate New Adam, Jesus Christ, into that
sanctuary, so that He could undo Adam's sin and complete
Adam's work, the sociological effect of which was to eliminate all
exclusions and draw all men near, either for blessing or curse.

With the call of Abraham, God set apart a peculiar people
who would symbolically maintain a symbolic sanctuary, and thus
display two things. They would display over and over again what
Adam had lost when he fell, for they would themselves fall over
and over again. They would also display the privilege that would
someday come to all men, in heightened form, when the Second
Adam would renovate the world. In addition to displaying these
things, the sanctuary would, as noted above, form the re-created
environment in which the Second Adam, the Son of Man
(Adam), would engage in the work of recapitulation.

God's promise to Abraham from the start involved both
aspects of the Eden/Havilah duality. Abraham's descendants
would be great and have a great name, and would be given a
special land. At the same time, all nations would be blessed in the
blessing of Abraham (Gen. 12:1-3). In fine, the restoration of the
world would proceed from the Garden in Eden (the Temple in
Israel), even as its fall had. Abraham would be restored to Eden,
and the influences of that renewal would in certain limited ways
spread downstream to the entire world.

In terms of the Old Covenant model, this meant Abraham
needed several things. First but not necessarily foremost, he
needed land. He needed a new Eden and a new Garden, where he
would be priest to the nations. Thus, in the Abraham narratives,
we find the first mention of Jerusalem and of its priest, Melchizedek (Gen. 14:18ff.). We see right away that Abraham's priesthood
was only a figure for a greater priesthood to come. Of course,
Abraham is not given the land, but it is promised to him, and he
does acquire a downpayment of it (Gen. 23).

Second, Abraham needed seed. It was the Seed Who would
crush the serpent's head, and who would be the ultimate King and

Priest of the throne land. His descendants would be a nation of priests, who would maintain the Eden sanctuary on behalf of the all the downstream nations. Who would it be? The first candidate was Lot, but God removed his name from consideration (Gen. 13). The second candidate was Abraham's chief servant, but he was not to be the one either (Gen. 15). The third candidate was Ishmael, but he was set aside (Gen. 17). Rather, it was Isaac, the miracle-born son of the resurrected dead womb of renamed parents, who would be the seed, and whose descendants (half of them) would maintain Eden and the sanctuary.

Third, Abraham needed influence. When Pharaoh attacked him, God magnified Abraham in his eyes (Gen. 13). When Chedorlaomer and his men captured Lot, we find Abraham's influence magnified again (Gen. 14). When Abimelech attacked, God so magnified Abraham that only his intercessory prayers could avert God's curse on Philistia (Gen. 20). Here we see Abraham as a priest to the nations. Accordingly, the Philistines make covenant with Abraham (Gen. 21:22ff.), which is a sign of their conversion. Finally, we see how great Abraham became, and how great his Edenic influence, in his dealings with the Hittites in Genesis 23.

Ishmael

Now, let us trace this Eden/Havilah duality in the lives of the Patriarchs. When Ishmael was cast out, it was not because he was reprobate. In fact, Genesis 17:20-21, God promised to bless Ishmael, though the covenant would be established with Isaac. In Genesis 21:20, we read that "God was with the lad," and there are other clearly salvific promises throughout this passage. Ishmael was regenerate, elect, saved, but he was not to be the Eden sanctuary priest.[7] The covenant was not *made* with him, but with

---

7. Our presuppositions have everything to do with how we interpret texts such as these. The modern evangelical view that God saved virtually nobody during the Old Covenant period causes most evangelical commentators to assume that Jonah's Nineveh was not really converted, that Joseph's Pharaoh did not really bow the knee to God, etc. Similarly, in terms of this prejudice, the promises made to Ishmael are seen as only "common grace." This whole matter of common grace is highly problematic, since it really is only a backdoor way of reintroduc-

Isaac. Yet, he was *saved by the covenant*, by faith in it. Similarly, the Covenant of Grace was made first and foremost with Jesus Christ, and we are saved by faith in it. In that sense, it is made with us also. In a systematic theological sense, the covenant was indeed made with Ishmael, but in a redemptive historical sense it was not. The covenant was specifically made with the seed-throne people, but its benefits were extended downstream to the nations. This will become clearer as we proceed.

When Abraham was old, he took another wife, after securing the seed line by getting a replacement for Sarah. It is important to see this. Isaac takes Rebekah into Sarah's tent (Gen. 24:67). Keturah is not the replacement for Sarah, in the redemptive theological sense. The seed line is separated from Abraham, and continues on down through history. There is a new bride, and she is the bride of Isaac, not of Abraham. Isaac and Rebekah are now the maintainers of the Eden sanctuary. Abraham has bowed out.[8] He has moved downstream, and his new sons will be downstream people.

Their names are given in Genesis 25:2-4. In 25:5, we read that Abraham "gave all he had" to Isaac, but in verse 6 we read that he gave "gifts while he was still living" to his other sons. Thus, "all he had" must refer to the covenant and the Edenic throne-sanctuary privileges and blessings. There were other capital assets that Abraham could give to his other sons. In verse 6 we also

---

ing the Medieval separation of nature and grace using different terminology. See the fine discussion in Henry Van Til, *The Calvinistic Concept of Culture* (Grand Rapids: Baker, 1959), chapter 16. Biblically speaking, "common grace" is the crumbs that fall from the (wholistically sacramental) Table of the Lord. Indeed, Matthew 15:21-28 is a fine illustration of the whole thesis of this chapter, that the gentile dogs could be saved by placing trust in the benefits given to the world *through* the children of Israel.

8. The book of Genesis contains a sustained implicit critique of patriarchy, beginning in 2:24. When Isaac married, he moved away from Abraham, and he took his essential inheritance (the covenant promise) with him. Similarly, it is when Jacob is sent to procure a wife that the covenant is passed to him (Gen. 27 with 28:1-7). After that point, the text is concerned with Jacob and the covenant line, and little more is said concerning Isaac. Biblically speaking, then, a sizeable chunk of inheritance is passed on at the point of marriage; sons did not have to wait for their parents to die in order to obtain inheritance.

read that Abraham sent them away to the "land of the East." In the beginning, Adam and Eve were cast out of Eden at the east gate, and they brought sacrifices to that east gate (Gen. 3:24; 4:3, 4; with all the Tabernacle and Temple passages that connect the door with the east side). By stationing his sons to the east, Abraham was putting them in a position to receive blessing influences from the seed people, and in a position to bring their tithes and offerings to that peculiar nation of priests who maintained the sanctuary land.

Havilah is where Ishmael and his people settled, according to Genesis 25:18. It is a land directly related to Eden. Now, because of things said in the New Testament, we have the impression that Ishmael was not among those elect unto salvation. All Romans 9:6-9 says, however, is that Ishmael was not set aside to be the seed, the peculiar children of God. These verses speak of election to service, as it is usually called. The subsequent verses, dealing with Jacob and Esau, have to do with election unto eternal life, and preterition.

Similarly, in Galatians 4:21-31, Paul refers to Ishmael's "persecution" of Isaac, and from this and the rest of what is said, we draw the conclusion that the downstream, "world" peoples were in fact enemies of the Edenic, sanctuary people. Indeed, this was often if not usually the case. It was, however, not always the case. Indeed, the "persecution" spoken of took a peculiar form in Genesis 21:9, for the Hebrew text does not say that Sarah saw Ishmael "mocking," but that she saw him "laughing." Is it a sin to laugh? No, and so we are caused to look further for an understanding of the problem Sarah faced. We can take Paul's word for it that Ishmael's "laughter" demonstrated hostility, and was part of a "persecution." In calling attention only to laughter, however, the text of Genesis intends something specific.

What was the issue before Sarah? Isaac means "he laughs." This name was given him by God when Abraham laughed to hear that he would have a son by Sarah (cf. Gen. 17:17, 19; 21:3; and also 18:12-15; 21:6). The laughter of Sarah and Abraham was in response to God's surprise gift of a son to parents too old to have children. The gospel is God's great surprise in history, a surprise that destroys His enemies and delivers His friends in their darkest hour. God laughs (Ps. 2:4), and so do His people. Laughter, thus, is a preeminent blessing of the covenant. At the very least, then, Sarah is concerned that Isaac and not Ishmael inherit the laughter of the covenant. After all, God had given Isaac his name, and thus had indicated His choice.

Additionally, the fact that Isaac means "he laughs" indicates that Isaac is to be the laughter. The text of Genesis 21:9 literally says that Sarah saw Ishmael "Isaacing." In Sarah's eyes, Ishmael was a counterfeit Isaac. She saw things theologically, while Abraham saw things morally.[9] Abraham knew that Ishmael was not an evil child, and did not wish to drive him out. God, thus, assured Abraham that He would be with Ishmael. Sarah knew that regardless of whether Ishmael was bad or good, he should not remain in Eden to compete with God's new seed-laughter of redemption. He had to go, and find another position in the world. Similarly, says Paul, the question before the Church in the interval between Pentecost and Holocaust (A.D. 70) was this: Who is the True Isaac, the Jews or the Christians? When Isaac is weaned, then Ishmael will be cast out (A.D. 70).

Some observations: First, the Eden/Havilah duality does not in itself imply that those living downstream are evil. They are not the seed people, and they do not possess the covenant in the strict sense; yet they can be saved by faith in the covenant as made and maintained with the seed people. Second, because of the fall of man, the first humanity was cast out of Eden, and must remain there until regenerated by resurrection. It was a peculiar people, symbolically resurrected, who alone could live in the symbolic Eden of the Old Covenant. Those born of the "flesh," the old condition, might not enter. Ishmael, son of Sarai (Hagar) and Abram, is in this category. We have to have a miracle son, born of a resurrected womb of renamed parents. He can live in Eden, and maintain the sanctuary on behalf of all his kin. He can die for Ishmael's sins, and eventually bring all men into the sanctuary — but

---

9. Both perspectives are valid, and there is no justification for trying to run behind the statements in the text in order to psychologize and thereby criticise Sarah's perspective, or Abraham's.

that is in the New Covenant. Theologically, symbolically, Ishmael and all those living outside Eden are in the "flesh." They are in the "world" in the bad sense. They are exiled. All the same, they can be saved by the influences that flow downstream from Eden. Thus, when Paul uses Ishmael as a picture of those living under the curse because of sin, he does so in terms of the theological/symbolic aspect. He does not imply that Ishmael was unconverted in the moral/Spiritual sense.

Those who live in Havilah are to bring their tithes and offerings to Eden. Accordingly, we read of the sons of Abraham in Isaiah 60:4-9 that they will bring the wealth of all nations to the sanctuary. In verse 6 we read of Midian, Ephah, and Sheba (sons and grandsons of Keturah, Gen. 25:2-4), and in verse 7 of Kedar and Nebaioth (Ishmael's first two sons, signifying the whole of his descendants, Gen. 25:13).

Isaac, Jacob, and Joseph

As we continue, now, with the lives of the Patriarchs, there are three other passages to note. The first is Genesis 26. Here we have the story of a second threat to the seed people from the king of the nations, Abimelech. After God delivers His peculiar possession, we find a story of conflict between Isaac and the Philistines. Finally, we find that the Philistines are converted to the LORD, and make covenant with Isaac, in fulfillment of the Abrahamic promise that all nations would bless themselves in the seed. What is beautifully set out in this chapter is the relationship between Edenic water and downstream influences. The whole focus in verses 12-33 is on wells of water. Isaac's peculiar task in life is to dig wells, to provide water for others. That is what it means to be a priest to the nations. Initially, the Philistines in their depravity try to stop Isaac. They fill the wells with "dust," which is an act of killing the well (26:15 with 3:17, 19). In verses 18-22, Isaac digs two wells, which the Philistines fight over, and then finally a third well, which he enjoys in peace. This connects to the third-day resurrection theme that runs all through Scripture.[10] Then, Isaac

---

10. For a discussion of the third-day theme in Scripture, see my *Sabbath Breaking and the Death Penalty.*

sets up priestly worship (verse 25), and immediately thereafter the Philistines come to make covenant with him. The same day, another well is found (verse 32).

For some reason, modern commentators want to believe that these covenants between Abraham and the Philistines and between Isaac and the Philistines do not signify the fulfillment of the Abrahamic Covenant. The God of such commentators is a most parsimonious God, it seems. He just doesn't save gentiles. Actually, it is inconceivable that either Abraham or Isaac would form a covenantal alliance with wicked men. Moreover, in the ancient world, such covenant alliances were never "merely political," for the kind of secularism we have today did not exist then. A covenantal alliance was always religious in character.

The second story is in Genesis 33. When Jacob met Esau, the priest blessed his brother, at least with gifts (33:11). On the other hand, when Esau wanted to remain with him, Jacob insisted that he depart and take dominion over his own land (33:12-16). Esau's dominion is set out in Genesis 36, and the integrity of that land is insisted upon by God in Numbers 20:14-21 and Deuteronomy 23:7. Edom might have been a "Christian nation," living downstream from Israel, though they chose not to be. Jacob did not permit Esau to join in his priestly work, but he did help establish him in his kingly estate.

The third story shows the same principles. In Genesis 41, God destroys the pride and self-confidence of Pharaoh by interrupting his cozy world with the Word of revelation. When Joseph interprets Pharaoh's dream, we do not read that Pharaoh had Joseph driven from his presence as a religious fanatic. Rather, Pharaoh submits to the Word, and to Joseph's application of it. This is nothing other than the conversion of Pharaoh and of the Egyptians. In line with the Abrahamic promise, they choose to bless themselves in the seed. Joseph is put in charge of everything. Later, in Exodus 1, the Egyptians fall from grace, and lose the benefits of the Edenic influences — but that is later.

Here again, commentators just don't want to believe this. Partially it is because they utterly fail to do justice to the theology of Genesis and the initial fulfillments of the Abrahamic promises.

Partially it is because they are under the spell of modern secular scholarship, which maintains that there is no "evidence" of any period of grace in Egyptian history. (Humanistic scholars would doubtless refuse to see any such evidence if it did come to light. Maybe it has, and has been suppressed, or perversely misinterpreted. It does not matter; the Bible is clear.)

Joseph married the daughter of the priest of Heliopolis (Gen. 41:45). Is it reasonable that the man who fled from the presence of Potiphar's wife would marry the unconverted daughter of a heathen priest? Notice also that Pharaoh and his servants are always pictured as rejoicing at the good things that happen to Joseph and his family (45:16ff.; 47:5ff.). Indeed, in explicit fulfillment of the Abrahamic promise, we find that when Jacob was presented to Pharaoh, "Jacob blessed Pharaoh" (47:7,10).[11]

Thus we see the duality of the seed-throne people of Israel, who maintain the Edenic sanctuary as a nation of priests on behalf of all people, and the nations of the world who live outside of Eden, but who can be blessed if they will drink from the rivers that flow therefrom.

What did a "downstream priest" do? He led the people in worship, at a distance. Jethro is the Biblical example of this (Ex. 2:16; 18:12). Once the sanctuary was established, the downstream priests would particularly direct the attention of their flocks to its importance, as Jethro does (Ex. 18:12).

Circumcision

When God told Abraham to circumcise his household, He said, "This is My covenant. . . : Every male among you shall be circumcised" (Gen. 17:10). Ishmael was so circumcised (v. 25). Yet, in verse 18-19, God said that Ishmael would not hold the covenant line, but God would establish the covenant with Isaac. The thing to note here here is that *circumcision is not a sign of personal salvation. Circumcision was only for the covenant people, and they are defined*

---

11. For a fuller discussion discussion, see my essay, "Joseph's Enslavement of the Egyptians: Fair or Foul?" in *The Geneva Papers* I:36 (available for a contribution from Geneva Ministries, Box 131300, Tyler, TX 75713).

as those who maintain the throne sanctuary and hold property in Eden. The circumcision and then rejection of Ishmael forms a type of the creation and fall of man. Ishmael, the son of the "flesh," is fallen, and must be cast out.[12]

Circumcision, of course, entailed the shedding of blood, and thus was substitutionary in nature. The circumcision of the male children covered representatively for the females. Since circumcision constituted Israel as a nation of priests, and since women could not be priests, they were not circumcised in any fashion. Rather, they were saved by being connected to those who were circumcised.[13] They were saved by faith in what the blood sacrifice of circumcision entailed. Why could women not be priests? Because a priest is a guard, and Adam's task was to guard his woman. The woman is not the guarder, but the one guarded. Because this is the heart of what it means to be a priest, no woman was ever a priest.[14]

Similarly, those outside of Israel who were converted to the true religion were not circumcised, for they were not members of the priestly nation. But they were saved by putting their faith in what the circumcision of the seed meant. Ultimately, circumcision pointed to the death of Christ, the cutting off of the Seed. This was the only circumcision that ever saved anybody, and all those thus saved are saved by faith in it.

This means that there is a sociological difference between the circumcision of the Old Covenant and the water baptism of the New Covenant. We shall explore this problem in the section of this chapter dealing with the New Covenant. For now, let us get more evidence before us.

When Moses lived with Jethro, the Godly priest of Midian, he did not circumcise his sons. Commentators have puzzled over this, and generally ascribed it to sin on Moses' part. Together with this goes the presumption that Jethro was a heathen.[15] This will

---

12. In other words, Ishmael remains in the position of Noah or Shem, while Isaac is in the new position in which Abraham had been placed.
13. See my study of this in *The Law of the Covenant* (Tyler, TX: Institute for Christian Economics, 1984), Appendix F.
14. See my fuller remarks on this on pp. 44-49, above.
15. See discussion in *The Law of the Covenant*, Appendix F.

not stand up to the evidence (Ex. 18). Moses is not condemned for failing to circumcise his son in Midian, but is attacked for failing to circumcise him when he draws near the Mountain of God (Ex. 4:24-27). When he takes up his priestly role, and rejoins the priestly nation, Moses must apply the priestly sign to his son. Jethro was a descendant of Abraham (Gen. 25:2), yet circumcision was not practiced in his house. This is because Jethro's portion was not Eden but Havilah.

Similarly, Israel did not practice circumcision during the wilderness wanderings (Josh. 5:4-7). This is because Israel refused to carry out its priestly function during that period, and so circumcision was inappropriate for them. Also, they were wandering in the land of Havilah (which is located for us in Genesis 25:18). There they ate manna, which was the color of the Havilah bdellium. (The only two references to the mysterious bdellium in Scripture are Genesis 2:12 and Numbers 11:7.) There they used gold and onyx to build the Tabernacle and priestly garments, which they would then bring upstream to the Eden of Canaan (Ex. 28:9,13). As long as they were just passing through Havilah, circumcision was appropriate; but when they settled there and refused to enter the new Eden, circumcision was inappropriate.

We note that they very strictly kept the sabbath, because the sabbath was precisely a reminder that they were excluded from the fulness of priestly office. Indeed, the heart of priestly fellowship with God is to eat a meal with Him, yet it was on the sabbath day that no manna fell at all (Ex. 16). By contrast, in the New Covenant, it is precisely on the Lord's Day that we are given the heavenly Manna of the Eucharist.

Priests to the Nations

Israel was supposed to be a priest to the nations (Ex. 19:6). Her water would cause their trees to grow. This was signified to all men when Israel came out of Egypt, for "then they came to Elim, where they were twelve springs of water and seventy date palms, and they camped there beside the waters" (Ex. 15:27). Seventy is the number of the nations of the world (Gen. 10). Israel, at the Feast of Tabernacles, sacrificed seventy bulls for the nations of the world, a substitutionary atonement for them offered by the priestly nation on their behalf (Numbers 28:13-32; Haggai 2:1-9; Zechariah 14:16-21).

When Israel was reconstituted at Mount Sinai, a more elaborate system of priesthood was set up. All male Israelites continued to be priests to the nations. Thus, all were circumcised as a rite of initiation, and all dressed in special priestly garb (Num. 15:37-41). Yet, within Israel there were those who were priests to Israel; these were the Levites. And within the Levites were a closer circle of priests, the house of Aaron. And within the house of Aaron was the High Priest, with whom was the "covenant of peace" (Num. 25:12). Shall we say that because the covenant of peace was peculiarly with the High Priest, therefore there was no peace for anyone else? Not at all. Rather, peace came to them all because of their alliance with the High Priest. Similarly, blessings came to the nations because of their alliances with the priestly nation of Israel.

Each of these concentric circles of priesthood was marked by rites of initiation, special clothing, special dwelling places, and the like. Compared to the Levites, the Israelites were not priests but laymen. Compared to the Aaronic house, the Levites were not priests but laymen. Compared to the High Priest, the Aaronic house were not priests but laymen. We do not draw from this the notion that those outside a given circle were unsaved. Similarly, we may not draw the conclusion that uncircumcised gentiles could not be saved in the Old Covenant.

I want to touch on two aspects of this: the land, and the holy meal. First, concerning the land: When Israel entered the land, it was parcelled out completedly to the families of Israel (Lev. 25). Even if a family sold its land, it would revert to its original owner in the Year of Jubilee. What this means is that *no gentile could ever hold property in the land of Israel. Gentiles were excluded from proximity to the Temple, by Divine law.* Thus, the law actually reinforced the Eden/Havilah duality, by requiring converted persons who were not of the seed of Abraham to remain "strangers" in the land, or to live outside the land altogether. We shall return to this in a moment.

Second, concerning the holy meal: Only the house of Aaron might eat of the showbread in the Tabernacle/Temple (Lev. 24:9). Similarly, only they might eat certain of the sacrifices (Lev. 22:10ff.). Did this mean that they and they alone were saved? Not at all. The same kinds of provisions pertained to Israel as a nation of priests. They were not allowed to eat "unclean" beasts or anything that had died of itself (Lev. 11; Dt. 14). Yet, they might give it to strangers to eat (Dt. 14:21). Did this mean that only Israelites were saved? Not at all. The provision had to do with their priestly calling.

Now, concerning Passover: In order for a stranger to eat Passover, he had to circumcise himself and his household (Ex. 12:45-49). If he did so, he became "like a native of the *land*" (v. 48). We are so accustomed to connecting Passover with the Lord's Supper that it seems strange to consider that perhaps Passover was only for the priestly people, but such was the case. Converted gentiles were not to eat of it unless they were circumcised, and thereby were incorporated into the seed line of Abraham. Did this exclude them from salvation? No, it only excluded them from priestly duties. Did it make them second class citizens? Only in the eyes of the Pharisees. Biblically speaking, their downstream cultural labors in Havilah were just as important as Israel's sanctuary task. After all, if everyone had become an Israelite, then who would mine the gold of Havilah? Who would bring it to the sanctuary? Israel had its task, and the converted nations had theirs.

Passover was not a sign of salvation, but of *coming* salvation. Passover constituted Israel a "peculiar" people, particularly redeemed by God, and given a special priestly task. How were the gentiles related to Passover? By watching it, and putting faith in it. Someday, according to the promise of the covenant, they would be let in the House. For now, they were to stand at the doors and windows and look in. They watched the peculiar people eat the Passover, and they trusted that God would save them as well. They watched the peculiar priestly people circumcise their children, and they trusted that the benefits of that act were theirs as well.

Passover was not only a sacrifice, but a sacrament. The eating of sacrament is a sanctuary privilege. The fact that only the elders of Israel ate with God in Exodus 24:11 does not mean that the rest of Israel was unsaved; rather, all were counted as eating in the persons of their representatives. Similarly, the fact that converted gentiles did not eat Passover did not mean they were unsaved. They were counted as eating it, because their Israelite representatives ate it.

Here in elaborate form is the principle of exclusion. There are degrees of exclusion, and of inclusion, but the message of this entire system of inclusions and exclusions is this: Man rebelled, and is not fit to sit enthroned as sabbath lord, priest and king. The fact that gentiles did not eat Passover did not exclude them from eternal salvation, any more than the fact that Israel did not receive manna on the sabbath day excluded them from eternal salvation. Rather, the exclusions were pedagogical in intention.

Thus, we find no notice of circumcision's being performed on any gentile converts. Jethro was not circumcised. Naaman the Syrian was not circumcised. Jonah did not circumcise the Ninevites. In the New Testament era, the God-fearing gentiles were not circumcised (Acts 10:1,2 with 11:3). Note the two categories in Acts 13:16,26: men of Israel and sons of the family of Abraham on the one hand, and those who fear God (gentile converts) on the other.[16]

Now we can look back at the land, and raise a question: If the stranger might circumcise his household and eat of the Passover, and be counted as one born in the land, where could he dwell? All the land had been parcelled out. The answer is: in the towns (Ex. 20:10; Dt. 5:14; 14:21; etc). Just as the Levitical cities formed places of refuge for the fleeing Israelite (Num. 35), so the general towns in Israel formed places of refuge for the stranger (Dt. 23:15f.). When the High Priest died, the land was cleansed, and Israelites might leave the Levitical cities and live in the land again. Similarly, by extension, the death of Jesus Christ for the world made it possible for the stranger to return to his own land, a

---

16. See articles on "Proselytes" in standard Biblical dictionaries and encyclopedias.

refugee no longer.

Alternatively, a stranger might find an Israelite to adopt him into his clan.[17] In that case, the stranger became an Israelite, and clearly belonged at Passover. The stranger who remained in the towns, however, might not be circumcised at all. He was still under the law, and had to observe the Sabbath as well as being supported by the tithe and invited to the Feast of Tabernacles, as the verses cited in the preceding paragraph demonstrate. The word for "town" is literally "gate," and such persons came to be known as "proselytes of the gate," converted but uncircumcised.

The complex of special land, special clothing, special food, special task, is found with the Levites over against the laymen in Israel. The same complex is found with Israel over against converted laymen among the nations. There is, thus, no reason to suppose that converted gentiles had any business practising either circumcision or Passover. All this was to change radically with the coming of the New Covenant.

What emerges from all this is rather complicated. We can lay it out as a series of propositions as follows:

1. The High Priest acted as priest to the house of Aaron, the Levites, Israel, and the nations.

2. The house of Aaron, including preeminently the High Priest, acted as priests to the Levites, Israel, and the nations.

3. The Levites, including the house of Aaron and the High Priest, acted as priests to Israel and the nations.

4. Israel, including the Levites, the house of Aaron, and the High Priest, acted as priests to the other nations.

From all this we can see that the law was designed to make plain that people were always *excluded* from the sanctuary before the coming of Christ. For their own good, Adam and Eve were cast out of the Garden. Just as the Lord's Supper causes the faith-

---

17. On adoption in the Old Covenant, see Jordan, *The Law of the Covenant*, chapter 5.

less to become sick and die, so the Tree of Life would have caused Adam to die had he eaten of it. Thus, for his own good Adam was prevented from eating the sacrament.

The various laws of boundary in Exodus, Leviticus, and Numbers simultaneously show the privileges of various classes, and also the exclusion of others from these privileges. The gentile convert was excluded from living near the central sanctuary, and he was excluded from Passover, etc. The ordinary Israelite was excluded from the Temple areas. The Aaronic priests were excluded from the holy of holies. The High Priest was also excluded from the holy of holies, except for once a year.

All were excluded from the sabbath. This sounds strange, because they were commanded so strictly to keep the sabbath. The Israelite layman was not, however, permitted to draw into God's sanctuary presence, as we have just seen. The Aaronic priests, who could come close to God's presence, were forbidden to drink wine (Lev. 10:9), whereas in the New Covenant the wine of celebration is *commanded* for sabbath observance. As I have written elsewhere, "One of the most important tasks of the priesthood was to *exclude* Israel from God, to guard His holy places from defilement. The priests were like cherubim, guarding the door of Eden; and indeed, cherubim were embroidered on all the doors of the Tabernacle. The prohibition against alcohol was a sign to Israel that they had not come to sabbath in the final sense, and the inclusion of alcohol in the Lord's Supper is a sign that in the New Covenant the Church has come to that sabbath in Christ, for He has completed man's task."[18]

Thus, Israel was never *really and fully* able to serve as priests to the nations. Nor was the High Priest able really and fully to serve as priest to Israel and to the world. This whole system was inadequate due to sin, and served as an elaborate prophetic witness to the coming of the Second Adam.

With this much before us, let us go on to an examination of New Testament evidence.

---

18. Jordan, *Judges*, p. 222f. My remarks on wine and its meaning are relevant to this discussion of the sabbath, and commence on p. 221 of *Judges*.

The New Covenant

Paul deals with this duality in Romans 2 and 4. He tells us in 2:9, 10 that the order is always "Jew first, and then gentile." Salvation and/or damnation flow from Eden. When Israel functioned as a light to the nations, all the world enjoyed the blessings of salvation, but when Israel apostatized, all the world suffered darkness. Thus, judgment on the sanctuary people was always first and more intense than judgment on those living downstream.[19]

Paul goes on to say that God judges and condemns sinners according to their position. Those who sin without law are judged without law, and those who sin against the law are judged by the law (2:12). Then, Paul goes on to speak of gentiles who did not have the law, but who did the things contained in the law. The plain implication here is that such gentiles were saved (by their *faith*-full obedience). In terms of the overall Old Testament teaching we have considered, it is most likely that here Paul refers to downstream believers.

Traditionally, these verses have usually been taken to refer to moral but unregenerate gentiles. John Murray, to take a modern example of this school, takes "law" to refer to moral law revelation, which the gentiles did not have. Thus, what is in view here are "unbelieving gentiles," whose minimal moral behavior still displays the moral law as known to all men.[20] With the theology expressed by Murray we have no quarrel. Exegetically, however, Paul's concern here is with the privilege of the Jew (Rom. 3:1ff.). "Having the law" refers to their privilege as sanctuary guardians. The gentiles did not have the law in that sense, but they were

---

19. The same principle is seen in the book of Revelation. The destruction of the Great Whore (the city Jerusalem) brings with it the destruction of the beast (nations) with which she has fornicated. Because of the importance of what happened in A.D. 70 (the destruction of the first creation/covenant order), most of Revelation is concerned with it. Whether the Roman beast saw itself as dependent upon Jerusalem (Havilah upon Eden) is not important; from the Divine perspective, such was the situation, whether recognized by men or not. For a fuller discussion, see David Chilton, *The Days of Vengeance: An Exposition of the Book of Revelation* (Ft. Worth, TX: Dominion Press, 1986).

20. John Murray, *The Epistle to the Romans* (Grand Rapids: Eerdmans, 1959).

taught it by Israel, and if they lived in faith, they were saved. Cranfield is on safer ground in referring, with Augustine, these verses to converted gentiles.[21] He takes them as New Testament converts, however.

Returning to Paul, we find that the Jews were supposed to be guides to the gentiles (Rom. 2:19). We find that because of the sin of Jews, the gentiles were led astray (v. 24). Paul summarizes by saying that, Spiritually speaking, the Jew who sins is going to be treated as uncircumcised, while the gentile who obeys in faith is going to be counted as and treated as circumcised (vv. 25-29). We should note that Paul is *not* in this passage concerned with the union of Jew and gentile into one new man in Christ. He is referring to the Old Covenant situation.

This becomes clearer in Romans 4. Abraham's faith was reckoned to him as righteousness while he was yet uncircumcised, says Paul (4:10). As a result, Abraham was the father both of the circumcised and of the uncircumcised (vv. 11-12). He was the father of neither camp, if it was unfaithful, but he was the father of both camps provided they were faithful (John 8:31-47). The law was given to the Jews for a particular reason, but not as a means of salvation (4:13-15, with 3:1ff.). There is no reason to take the two groups here as Old Testament Jews and New Testament gentile Christians. That simply is not in the horizon of the passage. Rather, we have here a reference to the Eden/Havilah duality. Abraham was the father of the faithful in both groups.

Now, Paul's ultimate point is that the purpose of the law and of circumcision, of the seed-sanctuary people in other words, was limited and has now been fulfilled in Christ. The Pharisees were wrong to think that only Jews were saved, and so were their Judaizing followers. Israel had a distinctive and important purpose to play in the plan of God, but not as the only saved people in the Old Covenant world. There is no more need for Israel, for Christ has fulfilled the purposes they symbolized. He is the Seed. His circumcision now saves all the faithful. Israel's purpose having been

---

21. C. E. B. Cranfield, *The Epistle to the Romans* (Edinburgh: T. & T. Clark, 1975).

fulfilled, the duality between Eden and Havilah, between saved Jew and saved gentile, is obliterated. What remains is the righteousness of faith, which always undergirded both faithful Jew and faithful gentile.

We must now look at Ephesians 2. The horizon of discourse differs here. Paul is not concerned with the interplay between faithful Jew and faithful gentile in the Old Covenant. Rather, he speaks of the gentile as a stranger to the commonwealth of Israel, as without God, and without hope (Eph. 2:12). We should expect him to argue from this that now the gentiles get to be included in Israel. The wall is broken down, so now gentiles can get in. That, however, is not the argument. Rather, Paul states that the gospel transformed both gentile and Jew into one new man. Both needed reconciliation (2:16). Both needed to be preached to (v. 17). A new building has commenced in Christ. Both Israel and the nations have been set aside.

In Ephesians 2:12, Paul uses language to describe the gentiles that is true from one perspective, but hyperbolic from another. It is true that the Old Covenant gentiles were "separated" from Christ, but to a lesser degree so were the Jews. It is true that they were "alienated from the commonwealth of Israel [that is, Eden]," but this does not mean that they could not be saved at all. It is true that they were "strangers to the covenant of promise," but this does not mean that they could not be saved, only that they were not the bearers of the covenant line. And it is true, from one perspective, that they were "without hope and without God in the world," but again this statement must be read in terms of everything else the Bible says about the salvation of gentiles in the Old Covenant. Compared to the Jew, they were "without God and without hope," for they lived not in Israel but "in the world." Such language, however, is always relative.[22]

Paul's use of quasi-hyperbolic language for the sake of effect is also seen in Galatians 4:5, where he speaks as if the Jews themselves were wholly bereft of God. He says that the Jews were in

---

22. See Appendix B on three New Testament perspectives on the Old Covenant world arrangement.

need of redemption. They were like slaves (4:7). Compared to the New Covenant believer, they were like Ishmaelites (4:21ff.). In spite of his very real privileges, the Jew was still essentially *excluded* under the Old Covenant. New Covenant believers are now *included* and restored to the privileges of being guardians of the Garden (given the keys to the gate of the Garden, the keys of the Kingdom.)

Thus, the Pauline perspective is this: Under the Old Covenant all men were saved by faith. Yet within the category of those saved by faith, sons of Abraham, there was a division of labor and privilege. Some were of the circumcision, and some of the uncircumcision. Those of the circumcision had greater privilege, and their position displayed the nature of salvation. Thus, salvation came to the gentile by virtue of his faith in the Seed of the circumcised line. When we get to the New Covenant, we do not find that gentiles are now incorporated fully into Israel. Rather, we find that the entire system is done away, and a new creation comes.

There is more we have to say about this, but let us ask a couple of questions here. Was Israel the church of the Old Covenant? Yes and no. Yes in the sense that it was the heart and core, the *focus* of the church. Yes in the sense that it was *definitively* the church. Yes in the sense that it was *centrally* (in a very literal, geographical sense) the church. But no in the sense that the population of circumcised Israel was the outer limit of the community of the redeemed.

Did the church begin at Pentecost? In the New Testament sense of "one new man," yes. In the sense of the community of the redeemed, no.

The New Creation

To understand the sociological arrangement of the new creation in Christ, we have to remind ourselves of man's original task, which our Lord in essence completed. It was to overcome all barriers in the world by glorifying all of it. The world would go from Garden/Eden/Downstream to being all "New Jerusalem" throughout (cf. Rev. 21:22). All the dualities in the world would be "overcome" by glorification, leaving only the first duality of heaven and earth. Finally, that duality would also be overcome when the world was transfigured, and man would have a new Spiritual body capable of movement in both heaven and earth.[23] In Christ, all of this came to pass. For that reason, there is no longer any separate earthly sanctuary, for all the earth has been cleansed so as to become possible sanctuary contact-points. This may not be visibly true yet, but it is *officially* the case. What is the sanctuary for earth? It is heaven.[24]

This means that there is no place on earth for us to go to worship God. Thus, we have to go into heaven to worship Him. And that is just what we do.

In the Old Creation, there was a duality between the High Priest and all the other priests. The same duality existed between Israel as a nation of priests, and the "priesthood of all believers" possessed by believers living downstream. Where is that duality today? It is the duality that exists between Christ and the rest of us priests, as follows:

1. Christ is living totally in the sanctuary land of heaven. We live in an "already but not yet" sanctuary on earth, both downstream and in sanctuary. In worship, however, we are enabled to join Christ in the fulness of sanctuary.

2. Christ is living in perpetual sabbath rest and joy. We live in an "already but not yet" perpetual sabbath on earth, given full rest in Christ but still having our own work to do. In worship, however, we are enabled to join Christ in the fulness of sabbath rest.

---

23. This motif of the progressive "coalescence of culture and cultus" has received attention throughout church history. Of particular usefulness is Klaas Schilder, *Heaven: What Is It?*, trans. and condensed by Marian M. Schoolland (Grand Rapids: Eerdmans, 1950). Schilder reflects at length upon the duality of heaven and earth, and the eschatological joining of the two in the new heavens and earth. He also points to the transfigured "perpetual sabbath" as another example of the merging of work and worship.

24. For liturgical and social reasons it is important that certain places be set apart as sanctuaries, for worship and for refuge. The point is that *any* place may be thus set apart, at the decision of men, because *all* places have judicially been declared sanctuaries by God.

3. In His person, Christ exists in a transfigured, Spiritual body; which is the same thing as saying that as our priest He wears special clothing. He is a member of a different race, being the Only-begotten of the Father. By adoption, however, we have joined the family, and in baptism we have been invested with the robe of transfigured glory — judicially — though the full outworking of that investiture is still to come.

This, thus, is the new duality that has overcome and replaced all the others.

The great demonstration of this change in the New Testament is the destruction of Jerusalem in A.D. 70.[25] In Matthew 23:35, Jesus states that the destruction of Jerusalem in His generation would avenge "all the righteous blood shed upon the earth, from the blood of righteous Abel unto the blood of Zechariah the son of Berechiah." Note: from *Abel* forward. The destruction of Jerusalem was the end not of the Mosaic nor of the Abrahamic arrangement, but of the whole first creation as cursed. It put to an end the entire system of restrictions and exclusions that began when Adam was cast out of Eden. It also signalized that the Garden was no longer needed as a central sanctuary on the earth. (The outflow from Jerusalem in Acts corresponds to the movement from the Garden downstream to Havilah. When Paul arrives in Rome, the outflow is complete, because the "head" of the world has been in essence conquered by the establishment of the Kingdom there. Thus, the old Garden, earthly Jerusalem, can be eliminated.)

---

25. The reader is directed to the following studies on this subject:

David Chilton, *Paradise Restored: An Eschatology of Dominion* (Tyler, TX: Reconstruction Press, 1985).

David Chilton, *The Days of Vengeance: An Exposition of the Book of Revelation* (Fort Worth, TX: Dominion Press, 1986).

Marcellus Kik, *An Eschatology of Victory* (Phillipsburg, NJ: Presbyterian & Reformed, 1971).

Roderick Campbell, *Israel and the New Covenant* (Tyler, TX: Geneva Ministries, 1981).

With great reservations because he goes too far, Max King, *The Spirit of Prophecy* (privately published, but available from Trinity Book Service, Box

Let us look again at three of the primary features of the first creation, this time in more detail.[26] There was the duality of one central sanctuary and downstream lands, with a middle wall of partition between the two. There was but one Throne of God on the earth: the Tree of Life, the Tabernacle, the Temple. Second, there was the flesh of Adam, and the consequent principle of genealogy by blood. To show that this blood was defiled by sin, the foreskin of the organ of generation had to be cut off of all male members of the Seed line. All the same, genealogical records were of central importance in demonstrating continuity in the old creation. Third, there was the sabbath day, a token that someday the first creation would mature and be transfigured into a new creation.

The coming of the New Covenant does *not* restore the original world. Rather, we find that the work of Christ brings the first creation to its fulfillment, and inaugurates a new one. The arrangement of space in a duality of sanctuary and land is set aside, and one new "land" comes in its place. That "land" is the community that exists in the sphere of the Spirit, which is nothing other than heaven itself.[27] The first man is of the earth, but the new man is in the sphere of the Spirit (1 Cor. 15:47). That is, the first man was made of earth (Gen. 2:7), and there was a tie between man and the earth, such that when man fell, the world was affected by this and became cursed. Salvation removes man from this essential tie to the land, and places him essentially in the eschatological sphere

---

131300, Tyler, TX 75713).

James B. Jordan, "Interaction Tapes on the A.D. 70 Question," being replies and criticisms to the book by Max King (mentioned above), and to J. Stuart Russell's book, *The Parousia* (Grand Rapids: Baker, 1983). These tapes are available from Geneva Ministries, Box 131300, Tyler, TX 75713 for $14.00 (four lectures).

James B. Jordan, Lectures on Matthew 24, available from Geneva Ministries (address above) for $35.00 (eleven lectures).

26. The careful reader will realize that I am presenting this material in spiral form, discussing the same basic subjects over and over, but adding more each time. It seemed to me to be the best way to present my thesis.

27. On this idea of a community in the Spirit, the reader should read two seminal works. The first is R. B. Gaffin, *The Centrality of the Resurrection* (Grand Rapids: Baker, 1978). The second is Meredith G. Kline, *Images of the Spirit* (Baker, 1980). The reader who is unfamiliar with these ideas is advised to read these two books in this order.

of the Spirit. Yet, man is still in some ways tied to the land, and thus influences from the sphere of the Spirit are mediated through redeemed man to the earth. In this way, the salvation of men guarantees the redemption of the original cosmos, and its eventual maturation (cf. Rom. 8:19ff.).[28]

There is no longer a central, Edenic sanctuary. Instead, "where two or three are gathered together in My Name, there am I in their midst" (Matt. 18:20). The sanctuary is in heaven. Man is sacramentally incorporated into this heaven by baptism. In baptism, the water showers down from the glory cloud, bringing heaven to the person baptized, and thereby uniting him to heaven sacramentally.[29] Thus, the baptized person is admitted to the heavenly sanctuary by the sprinkling of water. In terms of this, it should be obvious that baptism by immersion is a grotesquely inappropriate practice, for it can only signify a reinsertion into the old, fallen cosmos.[30]

Similarly, the flesh of Adam is replaced by the flesh of Jesus Christ. The new genealogical principle is not union with Adam, but union with Christ's body in the sacrament of His flesh and blood. Apostolic succession, in the true sense of the continuity of the church and her ordinances, replaces the fleshly succession of Adam. The new man exists in union with the *resurrected* flesh of Jesus Christ.

Finally, the sabbath day is transformed. Indeed, to continue to observe the sabbath in the old way is to deny that Christ has finished Adam's work. It is to deny that the new creation has come (Col. 2:16f.).

Sabbath

As creation ordinances, God established two different but non-competitive times for worship. The first was regulated by

---

28. For more on the relationship of man to the ground, see my comments on the avenger of blood in *The Law of the Covenant*, pp. 97ff. On the eschatological Spiritual environment for man, see my monograph, *Sabbath Breaking and the Death Penalty*, chapter 1.

29. Compare the observations in footnotes 3 and 5, earlier in this chapter. In the new creation, the water comes from heaven, not from the primordial sea.

30. For a thorough Biblical demonstration that baptism must be performed by water falling from above, see Duane E. Spencer, *Holy Baptism: Word Keys Which Unlock the Covenant* (Tyler, TX: Geneva Ministries, 1984).

heavenly clocks: Genesis 1:14 says that the lights in the heavens govern signs and *seasons*, which should be translated "appointed times." (There is a different Hebrew word for seasons of the natural year.) From reading the Old Testament, we see worship meetings taking place on the new moons of each month, as well as at seven special festive times during the year (Lev. 23). The second system of worship was the weekly sabbath.

After man was cast out of Eden, worship was crippled. What man was excluded from was not the right to hear God's Word and to offer Him praise. Rather, he was excluded from the sacrament of the Tree of Life. As we have seen, in various ways certain people were set apart for the occasional privilege of eating the sacrament, but most continued to be excluded. In Israel, weekly sabbath worship was non-sacramental, while Passover among the annual feasts was sacramental. Synaxis and eucharist were segregated in synagogue and Temple. All of this shows the exclusion of man from the fulness of worship because of sin.

In the New Covenant, these segregations are replaced. Worship still has non-sacramental (synaxis) and sacramental (eucharist) elements, but both are conducted together at the same *time,* in terms of both a weekly and an annual cycle. Both are conducted at every place, so that every *place* becomes potentially a central sanctuary. There is no longer a distinction between priests and non-priests; rather, every man and every woman is a *priest.*

This points to that final coalescence of culture and cult, of heaven and earth, which will be the characteristic of the New Covenant in its final (eternal) phase. Today it is still necessary for us to distinguish between special and ordinary times, and to hold sacramental worship at the special times, called Lord's Days (or Days of the Lord). Today it is still necessary for us to distinguish between special and ordinary places, the special place being the environment created around the special sacramental Presence. Indeed, in a developed Christian culture, the church building forms a sanctuary for the accused and the oppressed. And today, even though all are priests, yet there are still some set apart by the laying on of hands to be elders, special officers in the church. They and they alone have oversight of the sacraments.

This arrangement is necessary because the duality of heaven and earth still exists. There is a "distance" between the heavenly Priest and earthly priests. The officers in the church are not priests who minister on behalf of an excluded people; rather, they are "elders and overseers" who *conduct* the people into the presence and ministry of the One High Priest. As His representatives, the officers (servant priests) appoint times and places, and minister to His people. Unlike the Aaronic priests in Israel, church officers possess no privileges not enjoyed by all members.

There is also this difference between the dualities of the Old Covenant, even before Adam's fall, and that of the New: In the Old Covenant, during the childhood of humanity, God Himself appointed one central sanctuary; God Himself appointed the times of worship; and God Himself appointed various concentric circles of priests. Men had no say. The dualities were absolutely fixed, and in twisted form these became the "holy versus profane" oppositions found in all pagan religions.[31]

In the New Covenant, man is regarded as mature (Gal. 3:23 - 4:11; Heb. 5:11 - 6:2), and is called upon to set aside places for worship.[32] There is little debate about this among the churches of the Reformation, though dispensationalists wrongly suppose that the land of Canaan is still special, and Roman Catholicism treats some places as having "holiness" bound up in them because some miracle happened there. Second, man is called upon to set aside those who will be special priests, by election and the laying on of hands. There is no real debate about this either, since the Urim and Thummim are no longer with us. (Though here again, we run across people who claim that God set them apart by special visionary revelation, even though they have been recognized by no human church.) Third, man is called upon to establish the special

---

31. See virtually any study by Mircea Eliade, but particularly *The Sacred and the Profane: The Nature of Religion*, trans. by Willard R. Trask (New York: Harcourt Brace Jovanovich, 1959).

32. On the subject of human maturation and the New Covenant, see James B. Jordan, "Rebellion, Tyranny, and Dominion in the Book of Genesis," in Gary North, ed., *Tactics of Christian Resistance*. Christianity and Civilization No. 3 (Tyler, TX: Geneva Ministries, 1983).

times for special worship. This point is greatly debated, since the Puritan parties in the various churches have always maintained that the sabbath appointment of the Old Covenant is simply transferred to the New Covenant. For that reason we have to devote a little more space to the sabbath question.

Paul is quite clear that the sabbaths and annual festivals of the Old Covenant are cancelled in the New (Col. 2:16; Gal. 4:10f.; Rom. 14:5). They are part of the "elementary principles," the foundational ordinances of the First Creation order. To do justice to the concerns of the Puritan parties, we have to say that the pattern of New Covenant worship is definitely sabbatical and festive, and that the Lord's Day on the first day of the *week* (1 Cor. 16:2; Acts 20:7; Rev. 1:10) indicates a continuity of pattern. To do justice to the Church Fathers and to the Reformers (all of whom were non-sabbatarian), we have to note that in the New Covenant, "the Son of Man is Lord of the sabbath" (Mark 2:28). The phrase "son of Man" means Second Adam, and is used to refer to office-bearers of the Old Covenant (throughout Ezekiel primarily), as well as to officers of the New. Jesus' illustration demonstrates this. The decision to eat the consecrated bread, which was unlawful, was made by the two office-bearers David and Abiathar.[33] They had the right to make "adjustments" in the basic pattern set up by God, *applying* the law to new situations.[34] While this is tremendously exceptional in the Old Covenant, it is a foundational characteristic of the New Covenant: The officers of the church determine the times and places of meetings. In times of persecution, they may designate times other than the first day of the week for meetings, if that is necessary.

There is a sense in which the new creation has come, and a sense in which it has not. We still live in pre-resurrection, Adamic

---

33. Jesus' example of sabbath "breaking" is the eating of the Tabernacle showbread. Not an example that would readily come to our minds! Apparently we are to regard the Tabernacle as existing in perpetual sabbath time, and its bread as a perpetual sacrament. Thus, any layperson entering that space was also entering sabbath time. Here we see again the connection among land, time, and genealogy that existed in the Old Covenant.

34. On the need to make such applications, based on general wisdom derived from internalizing the Law, see my book *The Law of the Covenant*.

bodies. We still need to rest one day in seven. We still need places
to meet for worship, and these are thrones of God upon the earth.
We still need special officers. Yet in essence, if not in manifestation, the new creation has come.

Land

We have discussed briefly the change in the arrangement of
time and its implications (Temple and synagogue joined, sacramental worship every Lord's Day, freedom to develop a new
Christian annual cycle). Let us now discuss briefly the change in
the arrangement of space. In the New Covenant, the sanctuary is
located in heaven. By virtue of the Spirit's making Christ present
to us, heaven can become manifested on earth anywhere "two or
three are gathered" in His Name. We are no longer told precisely
how our houses of worship are to be built, but the pattern remains. Thus, a study of the Old Covenant Tabernacle and Temple has value for church architecture. There are special places,
and they should be glorious and beautiful, just as the houses of
God were in the Old Covenant.

We noted that under the Old Covenant, men could not get
back into the land of Eden without going through the sanctuary
(Garden). In one sense, we saw, the promised land was the land of
Eden, which the Israelites could enter because they were permitted into the sanctuary. To the extent that their sanctuary privileges were limited and provisional, to that extent their enjoyment
of a new Eden was also limited. Culture flows from cult.

The full opening of the heavenly sanctuary in the New Covenant carries with it a pledge that man can move back into an
Edenic home. The movement is no longer cursedly eastward,
away from Eden through the back door of the sanctuary. Rather,
the movement is westward. In the New Covenant, man can not
only draw near to the door of the sanctuary (westward movement), he can also go into the sanctuary, and out the other side
into Eden.[35] Thus, the fallen world is drawn through the sanc-

---

35. Thus the orientation in New Covenant churches is exactly the opposite of
that under the Old Covenant. The "east wall" is the front of the church, where

tuary into a reestablishment as Eden. The sanctuary through which the fallen world is drawn is heaven, which can be anywhere public worship is established. Thus the multiplication of earthly sanctuary contact-points (churches) guarantees the transformation and restoration of the world. Cult restores culture.

In the original creation, the Garden of Eden was a permanent sanctuary that served as Eden's sanctuary, but also would have remained preeminent among all the sanctuaries later built in Havilah, Cush, etc. Adam, living in Eden and maintaining the Garden, would be an earthly head over all the nations that later came from his loins. In the new creation, this situation has changed. True, the gospel originally went forth geographically from the central sanctuary in Jerusalem, and to the Jew first. With the destruction of Jerusalem and the Temple, however, there was no longer any central sanctuary on earth, to which all other subsequently-erected sanctuaries might relate. Rather, the center of the church and the original sanctuary is now in heaven.

Thus, if missionaries from the church (sanctuary) in America go to Zaire and plant a church (sanctuary) there, the new church (sanctuary) is not to view itself as dependent upon the church (sanctuary) in America, but to relate itself directly to the foundational sanctuary in heaven. Similarly, the notion that all the particular churches in the world must be related to one central earthly one, such as the Vatican, is an Old Covenant notion. The central sanctuary, from which all earthly manifestations proceed, is in heaven. (Note the diagram on the page following.)

Priests (Seed)

Finally, let us discuss briefly the change in priests. First, Christ alone is our Priest now, in the sense of representing us in a holy place for which we are not yet fitted. He does have special representatives on earth, however. Just as the God-designated special officers of the Old Covenant were invested with garments

---

altar-table and pulpit are found, and the "west wall" is the door. Coming to church involves a movement from the west to the east, on the assumption that we are now dwelling in Eden, no longer in the downstream lands.

Old Creation

New Creation

of glory and beauty, so should the officers of the New. Away with "business suits," which make the officers look just like everyone else while they perform God's special office!

Second, the sign of Israel's sanctuary priesthood was circumcision. The New Covenant sign of general priesthood is Holy Baptism. It is not the same thing as circumcision, yet the pattern is the same. The principle of infant circumcision has been extended in two ways. It extends to females, and to gentiles. There are no longer any concentric circles of priests (High Priest, Aaronic priests, Levites, Israelites, Spiritual leaders among the gentiles). Rather, men are either God's priests or they are His enemies.

Thus, all believers are to be baptized, along the lines of households as the New Testament makes clear.

Third, the genealogical principle is still sound, but is transformed. It is union with the flesh of Christ, not with the flesh of Adam, that is determinative. The order of regeneration, however, follows the order of generation. Insertion into the body of Christ by baptism, and continuance in that body by eating the flesh and drinking the blood of Christ, is for believers and their seed. The theological ground of infant baptism is not that they are the children of believers, for all they can inherit from their parents is original sin (John 1:13; 3:6). We baptize them because the order of regeneration follows the order of generation. Salvation restores the whole fabric of life, including the genealogical principle. Each new infant is to be placed by baptism into the covenant, into the church.[36]

Summary

In the new creation, under the New Covenant, the duality of Eden and Havilah, of Jew and gentile, has gone. All believers now are priests. All are Levites. All indeed are High Priests. In fact, all transcend the privileges of the Aaronic High Priest, in that they are united with One who is after the order of Melchizedek, and can approach the throne of God anytime, not just once a year (Heb. 7-10).

At the same time, all have the cultural, downstream tasks to perform. The distinction between cultic and cultural duties, between sanctuary maintenance and dominion labor, is no longer maintained in terms of racial callings. Instead, it is a matter of personal calling to some extent, and of apportioning one's time.

Thus, in the New Covenant the distinction between the church (as people of God) and the world is much simpler. Converted people are in the church, and have all privileges. Unconverted people are in the world. Under the Old Covenant, the mat-

36. On this see James B. Jordan, ed., *The Failure of the American Baptist Culture.* Christianity and Civilization No. 1 (Tyler, TX: Geneva Ministries, 1982).

ter was much more complicated. Whether someone was in the "world" or not depended on whether he was "downstream" from you. From Aaron's standpoint, everyone else was in the world, and he alone had the privileges of being fully in the church — but Aaron was painfully aware that he was excluded from the greatest privilege of continual dwelling in the Presence, and of drinking wine with the King of kings. From the standpoint of an Israelite, all gentiles, even converted ones, were in the world.

The principle of outflow is, of course, still in force. We no longer have an outflow from an earthly Garden to the four corners of the world. Nor do we have an outflow from the Temple into Jerusalem, Judaea, and to the uttermost parts of the earth. Rather, we have an outflow from heaven to earth. When heaven is set up on earth for a temporary period during worship, the people of God are briefly transfigured, like Moses on the Mount. When they come out of heaven to earth, they bring the demon-destroying, world-transforming glory of God with them (Matt. 17:1-20). Having drunk of Christ, now living water flows out of them into the world (John 7:37-38), water that will not stop its work until all has been transformed (Ezekiel 47).

I should like to close this essay with a few remarks about covenant theology and dispensationalism. What we may call the covenant theology perspective sees the church as being the same in all ages. From the covenant theology perspective, circumcision for Israel is the same as baptism for the New Covenant, and is simply the mark of inclusion in the church. One problem with traditional covenant theology is that it is unable to explain the phenomenon of uncircumcised but clearly converted gentiles. The major problem with traditional covenant theology is that it does not do justice to the radical nature of the New Covenant, and its discontinuity with the Old. Traditional covenant theology subsumes both Old and New Covenants under one overarching "covenant of grace." In fact, however, the New Covenant is simply the Old Covenant dead, resurrected, and transfigured. Christ, born under the Law, became the embodiment of the Law, and in His death on the cross, the Law and the Old Covenant died. In His resurrection, these came to life again, but in transfigured form. Traditional covenant theology simply does not do justice to this radical transformation in the Covenant.[37] In the New Covenant, the gentiles did not simply "join" the church; rather, Jew and gentile were together transformed into one new man.

The dispensational theology perspective fails at exactly this same point. A failure to understand the dualities inherent in the Old Covenant and how these are done away in Christ leads dispensational theology to posit that these dualities (priest/people; Jew/Gentile) are simply set aside for the Church Age, and then reinstituted for the Millennium. Such a view actually minimizes the greatness of the transition from Old to New Covenant, in that it regards them merely as "plan A" and "plan B." God simply shifts back and forth from one to the other, but there is no theological ground in the death and resurrection of Christ for this change in administration. Dispensationalism fails also to see that the New Covenant is the Old Covenant in transfigured form. Because of this, even though dispensational theology has the potential to do a great deal with the duality of Israel and the nations, that potential has not been realized.

It is my hope that this essay can challenge both camps to rethink some of the fundamental presuppositions that they have in common. I believe that the best insights of both schools of thought can be preserved thereby, while the dross of each can be identified and purged.

---

37. I have discussed this transformation and its implications at somewhat greater length in *The Law of the Covenant.*

Part II

THOUGHTS ON MODERN PROTESTANTISM

The word 'protestant' is commonly misunderstood to mean 'someone who protests.' Because of this, it is easy to think of protestants as "catholics in exile." Protestants were once within the catholic church, it is held, but because of serious errors in her midst, protestants had to protest or complain against the hierarchy, and thus left the catholic church. If the catholic church were to shape up, then protestants could go back into it.[1]

While there are doubtless protestant theologians who think and write this way, such a construction misses the mark of what protestantism is all about. As Peter Toon has written, the word 'Protestant' comes from Latin and "means first of all 'to declare something formally in public, to testify, to make a solemn declaration.' The connotation of 'protesting against error' is only a secondary meaning."[2] Toon goes on to show that the original use of 'protestant' by the Reformers had reference to "a powerful declaration of faithfulness to the gospel of our Lord Jesus Christ. . . ."[3] The protestant Reformers did not claim to be in exile from the Roman Catholic Church; rather, they claimed that they were perpetuating the true catholic church against the Italo-Papal hege-

---

1. Thus, William H. Cleary writes, "Historically, the homeland of all Protestants is, after all, the Catholic Church. Protestant theologian George Lindbeck ten years ago compared Protestants to liberation fighters in voluntary exile from their homeland — to which they hoped to return, some day, bringing more freedom." See "Undocumented Protestants," *The Christian Century* 102 (1985): 736f.

2. Peter Toon, *Protestants and Catholics: A Guide to Understanding the Differences among Christians* (Ann Arbor: Servant Books, 1983), p. 13.

3. *Ibid.*

mony that was corrupting her. For the Reformers, it was really the Roman Church that was in exile from her true Head.

There is an important difference between the ecclesiology of the Roman Catholic Church and all other churches at just this point. While the earthly head of the church in the Old Covenant was located in earthly Jerusalem, in the New Covenant the Head of the Church is located in heavenly Jerusalem, and He is manifested whenever and wherever a local assembly draws into heaven for worship. Our Head is visible to us in the mystery of bread and wine. Accordingly, the seven churches of Asia Minor are shown in Revelation 1-3 as seven separate lampstands, not as branches of one stand. Christ is in their midst, but there is no necessary political union among them.

Writing of Eastern Orthodoxy, which has preserved the view of the early church, Timothy Ware states, "For Rome the unifying principle in the Church is the Pope whose jurisdiction extends over the whole body, whereas Orthodox do not believe any bishop to be endowed with universal jurisdiction. What then holds the Church together? Orthodox answer, the act of communion in the sacraments."[4] There are several Eastern churches, each "autocephalous" (having its own head), that are in fellowship with one another and with the Ecumenical Patriarch in Constantinople. Although there are differences over how this works out in practice, the principle held by the Eastern churches is the same as that held by the protestant.

The Fringe

People who look only on the outward, sociological appearance tend to think of small, conservative denominations as on the "fringe" of the church. Nothing could be farther from the truth. It is true that such a denomination as the Association of Reformation Churches, to which I belong, is on the fringe of the heretical, gnostic, modernist "mainline" churches in America, but it is also true that the ARC is smack-dab in the center of historic catholic

---

4. Timothy Ware, *The Orthodox Church* (Middlesex: Penguin Books, rev. ed. 1983), p. 250.

orthodoxy. It is the "mainline" churches, with their blatant denial of the fundamental articles of the faith, that are on the fringe of the historic church. (It rather prejudices the discussion, doesn't it, to refer to these groups as "mainline"?)

But what about the fine liturgies in these churches? Isn't that in the middle of historic orthodoxy? Not at all. The mere performance of outward rites is not a criterion of orthodoxy or catholicity. The gnostics of the ancient world had really nice liturgies, and so do modern gnostics. Gnostics use a lot of language in common with true Christians. It is only to the superficial eye that gnostics appear to have a connection with the historic church.[5]

In fact, the performance of the *cultus* of worship for its own sake is the essence of mystery cult religion.[6] In Christianity, it is Truth that calls men together to worship. Worship is a response to Truth. Thus, the meagre "widow's mite" worship of an evangelical church is acceptable in God's eyes, while the glories of a gnostic cult only add to the damnation of its participants. This is no reason, of course, not to work to enhance the glory of true Christian worship, but we must not forget that liturgical splendor is in itself no criterion for the selection of a church—Thomas Howard to the contrary![7]

Thus, while liturgically the humble evangelical church may appear on the fringe, it is not, for Truth rather than glory is the first criterion of catholic orthodoxy.

The True Church Syndrome

The fact that visible orthodoxy is seriously impaired in "mainline" churches, as well as in the Roman Catholic and Eastern

---

5. Gnosticism is the great counterfeit of Christianity. Gnosticism replaces the *facts* of the history of creation and redemption with *philosophical ideas*. The Apostles' Creed, in that it simply recounts history, is the premier anti-gnostic document of the church. The most famous modern gnostic was Karl Barth, and his followers are legion.

6. On this, see Alexander Schmemann, *Introduction to Liturgical Theology* (New York: St. Vladimir's Seminary Press, 1966), and my essay on "Christian Piety: Deformed and Reformed," *The Geneva Papers* (New Series), No. 1.

7. In a recent *Christianity Today* interview, Howard explained that his basic reason for joining the Roman Catholic Church was its institutional and liturgical glory and fulness.

Orthodox, is sufficient in my opinion to invalidate their claims to be in the center of the faith. To the extent that they deny Christ in confession or in practice, they are on the fringe. Note: "to the extent" — that is important. Revelation 2 and 3 describe churches in a variety of conditions. My point, again, is this: It is ridiculous for Sardis to claim that it is more faithful than Philadelphia just because it is older or bigger!

There is another avenue of approach to this problem that yields the same conclusion. The title of Robert Webber's latest book, *Evangelicals on the Canterbury Trail*,[8] is revealing: There is a tremendous interest on the part of evangelicals today in the historic forms of the church, both governmental and liturgical. This wonderful and healthy interest in historic orthodoxy is translating, unfortunately, into a naive belief that one or another modern "mainline" church is the reservoir of that orthodoxy. Thus, one hears that we ought to go into the Protestant Episcopal church and work within, or to Rome, or to Eastern Orthodoxy.

One man says we should all join the Protestant Episcopal church, since it was the original church and has "apostolic succession," though it seceded from Rome a few centuries back. Well, (1) Rome has never granted that that secession was lawful. (2) The Protestant Episcopal church may be the original one in England, but hardly in America. Maybe we all are obligated to become Puritan Congregationalists, if mere historical age is what matters! (3) All churches have apostolic succession, because that succession does not take place in the servant priesthood (ordained clergy) but in the royal priesthood (all believers).[9]

Of course, for another man, the Protestant Episcopal church is suspect. He hears the call of Louis Bouyer, former Lutheran pastor, that we need to join Rome. Rome is the True Church. Jesus prayed for unity, and we need to get away from this fragmentation of protestantism.

---

8. (Waco, TX: Word Books, 1985).

9. On "apostolic succession" see the marvelous discussion in Geddes Mac-Gregor, *Corpus Christi* (Philadelphia: Westminster Press, 1958), pp. 210ff.

Ah, says a third man, but Rome is herself schismatic, adding *filioque* to the Creed without the agreement of the whole East. Only Eastern Orthodoxy has preserved the faith of the Seven Councils without addition. Anyone interested in the historic, unified Church must go East!

But why stop here? There are churches alive today, such as the Coptic and the Armenian, who did not go along with all seven Councils. In their eyes, Eastern Orthodoxy is schismatic. Moreover, Armenia was the first nation to convert to the faith. Thus, it stands to reason that we must all join the Armenian church!

Now, it may be offensive to some that I have written this *reductio ad absurdum*, but it cannot be helped. The fact is that this line of argument is absurd. It must be supplemented with arguments about truth. That is, are the doctrinal positions of Rome, or of Eastern Orthodoxy, correct or not? Once we are into this discussion, however, we are willy-nilly on "protestant ground," because we'll have to measure things by the Bible. The true churches will be those who preserve the Biblical faith.

It is possible to expand the discussion of this issue by calling attention to the fact that the ascended Christ has sent gifts to His church, which gifts are gifted men (apostles, prophets, evangelists, pastors & teachers). Thus, it is important that our church be in the true tradition of gifted men God has given to the church for her guidance. To despise that tradition, as something real but secondary to the Bible, would be to despise the Spirit.

True. But the best scholars today universally admit that neither Anglicanism, nor Rome, nor the East has preserved that tradition well. Russian Orthodox scholar Alexander Schmemann's *Introduction to Liturgical Theology* well shows the corrupting influence of mysteriological piety on the post-Constantinian church. Roman Catholic scholar Louis Bouyer readily admits throughout his writings that the protestant Reformation was a movement sorely needed because of the ethical and liturgical corruption in the medieval church. Bouyer also points out that the liturgy of the Anglican *Book of Common Prayer* is less catholic in its view of the Supper than was the Form of Prayers of John Knox![10]

---

10. Bouyer, *Eucharist* (Notre Dame: U. of Notre Dame Press, 1968), pp. 419ff.

This point is worth expanding upon. Churches using the *Book of Common Prayer* are strapped with prayers that are more Zwinglian than Calvinian, and thus farther removed both from the early church and from the great tradition than John Knox's original formulary. Moreover, the service of Holy Communion in the Prayer Book removes the Gloria in Excelsis from its place after the Kyrie, and puts it at the end of the service. In the 1928 Prayer Book, the word "holy" is unaccountably dropped from the Nicene Creed, in the phrase "one holy catholic and Apostolic Church." The Sanctus is chopped in half, and the Agnus Dei is dropped. This is a radical alteration of the historic service, an alteration that the Lutherans, for instance, did not make.

My point is not that such alterations are sinful, or that there is something wrong with such groups as the Reformed Episcopalians or the United Episcopalians, to mention two orthodox bodies. My point rather is that with such alterations in its liturgy, the Anglican church's claim to historical continuity does not measure up very well next to the claims of others. The Puritans had a more catholic understanding of the Eucharist. Lutherans have preserved the traditional structure of worship better.

Thus, measured by tradition, who is the True Church? Who indeed! Our worship at Westminster Presbyterian Church in Tyler follows the historic structure of Western worship. Our understanding of the Eucharist is Calvinian and thus catholic. Measured by tradition, we are at the heart of the true church!

Tradition, however, is not the proper measure.

The Facts

The reason, in my opinion, for confusion over these issues is that men have a hard time admitting to the *Truth* of the *Facts* of the *Message* of the gospel. I want in this section to set out what I regard as three incontrovertable *Facts* that men tend to ignore.

1. It is a fact that we live in a theocracy in America. Christ is King of America today. His laws are in force, and anyone who violates these laws receives punishment from the King in this life. Anyone who does not believe this is simply insane, because it is

what the New Testament clearly teaches. We live in a country that is little better than an insane asylum, because most people go around pretending that Christ is not King, and that they can break His laws with impunity. Such people are crazy. They are not adjusted to the truth about the real world in which they live. Our goal is to persuade men of this truth, so that they will stop suppressing the truth in unrighteousness. They need to recognize the fact that Christ is King, and bow the knee. When that happens, the judgments of the Kingdom will turn to blessings. We don't make Christ King; we recognize that He is already King.

2. It is a fact that the church of Jesus Christ is unified. Jesus prayed the Father in John 17 that we might be one, and the Father does not deny the petitions of the Son. Therefore, we are one. We eat of one Christ. We hearken to one Word. There is one Lord, one faith, one baptism, etc. Anyone who denies this is insane, not adjusted to reality. Thus, we cannot unite the church, and church unity is not a problem, any more than we can make America a theocracy. What we need is for people to stop pretending that the church is not united, because such a pretense is a denial of the truth. When men recognize the truth, and stop being fooled by vain appearances, then the judgment upon the church will be turned to blessing.

To recognize the truth of church unity means to grant prima facie recognition to the orders and government of all other Trinitarian churches, even to the church in Sardis. It means allowing to communion any baptized person who has not been excommunicated and who is a member of a local body. We cannot make the church united by negotiation. Rather, we must simply confess that the church is in truth one, and act accordingly.[11]

---

11. What if a man is wrongfully excommunicated? Suppose a man applies for membership in our church who has been excommunicated by a baptist church. He claims that he was excommunicated unlawfully because he had come to believe in predestination and infant baptism. In that case, we should grant prima facie recognition to the decision of the baptist church, and talk with the pastor to make sure there was not some other reason for the excommunication. If, in fact, the man had been wrongfully excommunicated, and things could not be worked out, then we would simply have to refuse recognition of this one particular action. That would not require us, however, to declare the church totally apostate. Nowadays, of course, the opposite is true. If a man is declared excommunicate,

3. It is a fact that the church is brought into being by the work of the Spirit, who proceeds from eternity into time at every moment of time. Thus, it is not historical succession that matters, but Spiritual procession. This explains how churches with a long history can apostatize, and new churches arise. Ultimately it is faithfulness, not history, that counts. The Bible tells us that the new birth is not by blood (historical succession) but by the will of God (the Spirit). Now, because God's plan involves historical maturation, historical succession has a real, though secondary, importance. We baptize our children, confessing that they are outside the Kingdom by birth, but that God is placing them into the Kingdom by baptism. This creates an apparent historical succession, but a succession in which there are a continual series of complete breaks. Each new generation is born dead in trespasses and sins. Each new generation must be brought into the Kingdom, by baptism initially and by perseverance thereafter. Thus, succession is only a visible effect, not a cause. Spiritual procession is the cause.

Claims of apostolic succession by themselves, then, are not only meaningless, they can easily become idolatrous, substituting temporal continuity for the discontinuous new-creating work of the Spirit. According to the Creed, only the Spirit is the "Lord and Giver of life."

Thus, we should not be surprised when it turns out to be relatively new churches that are the true heirs of the wealth of the past. It is what we should expect, when we realize that our God "makes all things new."[12]

---

he goes to another church, and the new church gleefully rejoices in the opportunity to shaft her sister and takes the man in without making any investigation whatsoever.

12. It might be objected that the analogy between the needed new birth of each new generation of men and the "making new" of the church is a questionable analogy. In fact, though, there is no such thing as "church" apart from God and people. The word "church" refers to people under the aspect of a certain quality. Thus, the measure of a given church is in terms of what its people are, as in Revelation 2 and 3. If the people are not born again, the church is dead, and Christ has departed. Thus, the principle of historical discontinuity (death and resurrection) applies both to individuals and to churches, as I have set it forth.

Failure to keep these facts, these truths, in mind leads to per-versions in practice. Failure to keep in mind that Christ is already King leads "New Christian Right" activists to place too much em-phasis on political activity as a way of making America Christian. Failure to keep in mind that the church is already one leads con-versative ecumenists to place too much emphasis on negotiated unions. Failure to keep in mind that the church is constantly be-ing re-created leads to looking for the true church in historical in-stitutions rather than in places where truth and life are found. We should have political action; we should labor to make our unity more visible; and we should appreciate the historical heritage of the church; but we must only do so out of a firm understanding of the secondary nature of these things.

Encouraging Words

We find a lot of encouraging words coming from some quar-ters of Eastern Orthodoxy, Roman Catholicism, and "mainline" protestantism today. There does seem, here and there, to be new life in some places. Some remarkable and very "Reformed" books have been written by such men as Alexander Schmemann (East-ern Orthodox), Louis Bouyer (Roman Catholic), and others. Bible believing Christians find themselves marching against abor-tion shoulder to shoulder with Roman Catholics, while many Bible believing friends refuse to do anything. As a result, we live in a time of sifting and change.

At the same time, the fact that there are a few good men in the Roman church, and the fact that there are Bible studies springing up in many places, does not mean that the Roman church repre-sents the ideal of catholic orthodoxy. In fact, the Roman church is still pervaded by superstition and heresy, a fact obscured in France, England, and America because of the heavy protestant influences there. Face to face with revolutionary atheism, and in-heriting a tradition of Huguenots and Jansenists, French Roman Catholic thinkers have moved in a very "protestant" direction dur-ing the last century. That is not the case in Spain, Latin America, Poland, etc. Face to face with communism, some Russian Orthodox theologians have moved in a "protestant" direction, but that is not true in Greek Orthodoxy.

By and large, Roman Catholicism today presents its people with a choice between bleeding statues and revolutionary Marxism. Would that this were not so, and maybe it will change. Or, maybe such men as Bouyer and his kin will be driven out of Rome eventually. (And I should point out that in spite of many good things in some areas, Bouyer's writings are thoroughly corrupted with JEDP views of how the Bible came to be written.)

Thus, why should I leave my church, which clearly witnesses to catholic orthodoxy, to join a Sardis-like church in which that witness is almost totally obscured? To do so would be to move from the center to the fringe. Yes, the Roman church has a powerful witness, but it is a witness that is 10% gospel and 90% error. Hopefully that is changing, but it has not changed yet. A few encouraging words from a handful of Roman theologians does not indicate that Rome has moved very far from the fringe yet. I'd rather stay in the catholic center.

David's Band

The true churches today are not in positions of outward leadership and glory. In all the "mainline" churches Saul is presently on the throne, because men have put him there. Biblical churches, working for renewal, are in exile, but not an exile to the fringe! David is anointed king, and we are with him. Year by year, David's band is growing as true churches, dispossessed by Saul's armies, are joining it. In a few more years, Saul will pass away, and it will be made manifest who are the true heirs of the historic church. Until that day I'd personally rather be with David than with Saul.

After all, Saul is no longer interested in fighting Philistines or Amalekites, or in driving Jebusites and Pornites from the citadel of Zion. If you want to be involved in fighting Geshurites, Girzites, and Abortionites you need to be at the center of things in Ziklag Bivouac with David (1 Sam. 27). Saul and his men are too busy out on the fringe in Endor consulting the spirits with necromancer Bishop Pike to be effective for the Kingdom (1 Sam. 28).

The Kingdom starts small, like a mustard seed. The denomination of which I am a part, the Association of Reformation Churches, is tiny. So are other faithful denominations. We live in a time of re-creation, and so we start small. We are not to despise the day of small things.

The Problem

The problem is that most conservative protestants today do not act like catholics. That is, they don't act as true protestants should act. They tend to act more like sectarians, condemning those who differ with them, undermining other congregations, refusing to recognize the discipline of other churches, and so forth.

The essays in this section are devoted to certain aspects of this problem. Chapter 4 deals with the sectarian, statist, and catholic aspects of the historic Reformation churches. Chapter 5 takes up a particular sociological problem centered particularly in youth ministries. Chapter 6 is a satire on how protestants tend to treat one another. The next two chapters deal with issues currently widespread in American Christianity. Chapter 7 is designed to point to a catholic "middle way" among the factions in the dispute over miracles today, while Chapter 8 deals with the heresy of Christian Zionism that currently plagues the church in the United States. Chapter 9 deals with present state-church conflicts.

4

THE THREE FACES OF PROTESTANTISM

It is commonplace nowadays to say that the protestant Reformation had two branches. These are called the "magisterial" and the "anabaptist" branches. What is meant by this is that some of the Reformers (the "magisterial" ones) looked to the newly emergent nation states of Europe to promote the Reformation against the Catholic Church, while others (the anabaptists) were opposed to the state as well as to the Roman Church.

This way of looking at the Reformation sees it in terms of church-state relations. Some Reformers wanted to put the church under the state, while others wanted to drop out of society. Because the issue of church-state relations is so important in our own time, we should consider whether or not these are the only two options available to us.

In fact, this model of the Reformation is not correct, and is very misleading. From an anabaptist perspective (which is more and more common nowadays), it might be useful to divide the Reformers into "anabaptists and everyone else," but looking at the problem historically, such a perspective is of little value.

In fact, there were three major trends in the protestant reformation, if we look at it in terms of "sociology." It is the purpose of this all-too-brief essay to set out these three trends, and to show why it is important for the church today to reflect on this matter.

The three faces of Protestantism were, and are, the imperial or nationalistic face, the sectarian or drop-out face, and the catholic face. The Reformers can fairly easily, though roughly, be divided into these three groups. There were drop-out anabaptists;

137

there were those who looked to the state for reformation; and there were those who sought to reform the church in a catholic manner, apart from the state. In brief, the Lutherans and the Anglicans tended to be magisterial in their approach, setting the prince or the king over against the Pope of Rome. Calvin and Bucer, along with some of the other Swiss Reformers, focussed more on a reformation of the Catholic church, and avoided nationalism.

These three faces of the Protestant movement were not new in the church; rather, they continued trends that had their origin much earlier in history. Let us, then, briefly survey the history of church-state relations in the Middle Ages.

Church and State in the Middle Ages

As our first guide, we shall use Brian Tierney's valuable book, *The Crisis of Church and State, 1050-1300*.[1] Tierney begins by pointing out that in pagan cultures, society is ruled by a king who is also the chief priest of the people. Social order cannot be maintained by sheer force, so "the most common solution has been to endow the ruler who controls the physical apparatus of state coercion with a sacral role also as head and symbol of the people's religion" (p. 1). Christianity, however, shattered this unity, and Tierney comments, "The very existence of two power structures competing for men's allegiance instead of only one compelling obedience greatly enhanced the possibilities for human freedom" (p. 2).

When Christianity invaded Europe, the customary social arrangement was that of paganism, with a priest-king at the head of society. The church claimed, however, that there were two powers on earth, and that Christ had committed to the state the power of the sword, and to the church the power of the sacraments (excommunication). As Ambrose of Milan put it, "Palaces belong to the emperor, churches to the priesthood." And when summoned to appear before an imperial council, Ambrose said, "Where matters of faith are concerned it is the custom for bishops to judge Chris-

---

1. (Englewood Cliffs, NJ: Prentice-Hall, 1964)

tian emperors, not for emperors to judge bishops" (p. 9). In fact, "in 390, Ambrose went so far as to excommunicate the emperor Theodosius himself, and Theodosius eventually acknowledged his faults and performed a public penance in the cathedral of Milan before being readmitted to communion" (p. 9). Later on, this same type of battle had to be fought with the rulers of the tribes of northern Europe.

It became very easy, during the Middle Ages, for the rulers to northern Europe to pretend that the issue was not church and state, but rather a cultural battle between southern and northern Europe. The Pope rules in Italy, they maintained, and he wants to bring us under his yoke as well. By stirring up hatred for the Papal court, the kings of Europe concealed their real motive, which was to dominate the church in their lands.

During the distressing years after the death of Charlemagne and the rise of the civilization of the high middle ages, the traditional pagan culture of northern Europe made many inroads into dominating the church. "All previously established institutions suffered, not least the church. In every part of Europe ecclesiastical lands and offices fell under the control of lay lords" (p. 24). It was easy for the civil powers to point out the crimes of the clergy, real or invented, as a pretext for taking over the churches — while the civil rulers themselves lived even more wicked lives!

Gradually, both church and state recovered from the years of turmoil, and right away there was a tremendous conflict over who would control the churches of northern Europe. The conflict reached its first climax in the battle between Henry IV and Pope Gregory VII. "Henry could not give up the right of appointing bishops without abandoning all hope of welding Germany into a united monarchy" (p. 45). In other words, it was a purely statist goal that led the imperial forces to try to control the church. After all, why on earth should Germany be united as one big powerful state? The existing confederacy could join hands to repel invaders, so it was just plain statism that motivated the imperial court's opposition to "Rome" and "Papacy." Imperial theologians defended the right of the king to rule the church, while church theologians argued for the integrity of church government, and the separation of church and state.

During all these centuries there were scores of drop-out movements. Some of these remained within the church, but argued that the church should avoid the "world" and especially that the church should "follow Christ's example and live in poverty." The imperial theologians found it very convenient to support the theology of the sects, for an impoverished and powerless church was exactly what the kings of northern Europe wanted. They wanted no earthly institution to compete with their own.[2]

In the later Middle Ages, unfortunately, the Papacy came to function more and more like an imperial monarchy. The ideal had always been a universal, catholic church with its headquarters in Rome. It was harder and harder for people to believe in this vision when the Papacy was acting more and more like a state in itself. Naturally, the imperial and statist thinkers of the North (and in Italy, too) took every opportunity to point out Roman inconsistencies, and to maintain that their struggle was not with the "pure" church but with the Papal perversion of it.

Ernst Kantorowicz has described the shift in catholic thought that accompanied the drift into Papal statism.[3] In the early church and in the early Middle Ages, the *corpus mysticum* or "mystical Body" was the sacrament of the Lord's Supper, around which the church was gathered. The center of the church's earthly dominion was the sacrament, which she administered in Christ's name. Christ was the head of the church, and He made Himself present and active through proclamation and sacrament. The church's earthly power was the power to excommunicate from Christ. The church was *corpus Christi,* the body of Christ, centered around His mystical body.

The first shift away from this early and biblical way of thinking came when the term *corpus mysticum* (mystical body) came to be used for the church instead of for the sacrament. In a subtle

---

2. The drama of these three forces: catholic, imperial, and sectarian is described cogently in the recent celebrated novel by Umberto Eco, *The Name of the Rose*—a fascinating book.

3. Ernst Kantorowicz, *The King's Two Bodies: A Study in Medieval Political Theory* (Princeton: Princeton University Press, 1957), pp. 193ff.

kind of way, the transcendent power that created the church came to be identified with the church herself. Instead of being dependent upon the mystical body of Christ for her life, the church began to see herself (partly) as the mystical body of Christ. This terminological shift by itself would not seem to mean very much, but the mass of ideas and associations that went along with it were powerful. The church began to hold what I call a "deposit" view of grace, the idea that grace has been deposited in the church and the church manages and dispenses grace. This "deposit" view of grace works against a "receptionist" view, which says that the church is nothing in herself, and must get everything from her Lord. Back when *corpus mysticum* referred to the sacrament, the church clearly knew that she got everything she had from Christ; now, however, it seemed that the church had power in her own right. Indeed, for some the sacrament got its efficacy from the church—a reversal of the true order.

The third and final shift came when the phrase "mystical body of Christ" began to give way to "mystical body of the church." Of course, theologians such as Aquinas did not stop talking about the sacrament and how Christ creates the church; nor did they stop speaking of the church as the mystical body of Christ. The shift was this: The political aspect of the church was separated off, to a great extent, from the sacraments. The political aspect of the church, the "mystical body of the church," was centered on the Pope as its political, earthly head. Because these ideas are strange to us, putting it simplistically may be of help—so think of it this way: The "spiritual" church is the body of Christ gathered around the Eucharist; but the "earthly" political church is a political body gathered around the Pope. Thus Papal theologians could say, "the church compares with a political congregation of men, and the pope is like to a king in his realm on account of his plenitude of power."[4] As Kantorowicz goes on to say, "it was a long way from the liturgy and the sacramental *corpus mysticum* to the mystical polity headed by the Pope."[5]

---

4. *Ibid.*, p. 203.
5. *Ibid.*, p. 205.

Thus, the "international" catholic church began indeed to take upon itself the trappings of a civil empire. And at the same time "the secular state itself — starting, as it were, from the opposite end — strove for its own exaltation and quasi-religious glorification."[6] Thus, imperial thinkers began to speak of the *corpus reipublicae mysticum*, the "mystical body of the commonweal." This mystical body of the state was gathered into the person of the King, just as the (political) mystical body of the church was gathered into the person of the Pope.

The result, at the end of the Middle Ages, was that there were two statist orders in competition with one another. There was the largely statist order of the Papal Monarchy, which also controlled the church catholic, and there were the statist orders of the kings of Northern Europe, who claimed religious prerogatives. Into this mess came the Protestant Reformation.

The Reformation

Luther provided a convenient way for the princes of Germany to do what they had always wanted to do: take over the visible power of the church. Luther so stressed the personal and charismatic aspect of the gospel, over against the institutional side, that his movement fitted nicely with the designs of the princes. At the same time, from a political point of view, Luther and his followers needed the help of "godly princes" in order to protect them from Papal threats.

Conflicts in Germany over the reformation eventually led to the formulation *cuius regio, eius religio*: whoever reigns, his religion. The faith of a given region would be determined by the religion of the ruling prince. At this point, Lutheranism in Germany had become pretty much wholly statist in character, in terms of any real independent power for the church. Lutheran acquiescence in the power of the state has continued to be a problem for Christianity in Germany down to the present day, and accounts for the passivity of the Lutheran churches in the face of Nazism.

---

6. *Ibid.*, p. 207.

Another magisterial reformation took place in England. Everybody knows that Henry VIII had less than pure motives in "reforming" the English church. It is noteworthy that the first "reforming" act of the new church was the elimination of two feast days from the Medieval calendar: the feast of the martyrdom of Thomas Becket, and the day observed to memorialize the public penance performed by Henry II, who had been responsible for Becket's death. Becket had stood against the power of the state, and for the integrity of church government. The magisterial reformation in England clearly set its face against any true church government.

In spite of Cranmer's greatness in so many other areas, the great flaw in his thinking lay just in this area: He was thoroughly committed to the idea that the king should rule over the church. A church that is completely tied in with political authorities is a church that cannot exercise any kind of discipline. And of course, to this day one of the hallmarks of Anglicanism and Episcopalianism is that virtually no one is ever excommunicated from it.

If these two major branches of the Reformation fell into the trap of statism, so that religion became little more than a department of state, the Swiss reformers Calvin and Bucer did not. Once again, these reformers needed the protection of the Swiss cities against the Papacy, but they insisted on and strove for the integrity of separate church government. In this respect, Calvin and Bucer and their associates sought to transcend the war of the two imperial forces, and create a Reformed Catholic Church in Europe.

It is for this reason that Bucer especially spent himself in one meeting after another, colloquy upon colloquy, with Anabaptists, Lutherans, and Roman Catholics, striving to prevent the splitting and fragmentation of Christ's church. One, holy, catholic, "international" church was the dream of Bucer and of Calvin, but it was not to be. Thus, there are no churches named for Bucer or for Calvin, for their work and thought has gone out into the church catholic at large.

Walker's comments on Calvin are most appropriate: "Catholicism and Calvinism, according to Hume Brown (*John Knox,* 1895), are the only two absolute types of Christianity. It would be more accurate to say that there are two types of catholicity, one Roman, one Reformed. They stand in fundamental opposition because of a certain fundamental likeness, for Geneva offered to Rome an alternative that was ultimate and in itself complete. A partial synthesis was indeed achieved by Canterbury, but at the price of creating parties that finally sundered the religious unity of England. And the Anglican genius is rather of the Byzantine type; primarily a way of worship, of *orthee doxa*, it can become almost a department of the state. Calvin stood closer to the Latin tradition of churchmanship, and on the formal basis of *sola Scriptura,* he sought to realize at least some ideals of the great medieval popes."[7]

An example of how the catholic Reformed viewpoint was co-opted by northern European statism is the history of the Heidelberg Catechism. The original version of the Catechism does not contain the present Question 80, condemning the Mass. At the insistence of the *political* authorities, Q. 80 was added, setting out the difference between the Roman mass and the Reformed view of the Lord's Supper. Not satisfied, the political authorities demanded a third edition, which called the mass an "accursed idolatry." It should be obvious that the religious leaders of the Reformation were still hoping for a catholic reformation, but the political leaders were looking for a tool to use in their political struggle against the Papal monarchy.

How convenient it is to insist that the Papacy is "the man of sin, the antichrist" and so forth — convenient for the statist! It is politically useful to programme people into thinking that an "international" catholic church is evil, and that nationalistic churches are good. Like the imperials of the middle ages, the princes of early modern Europe were interested in only two kinds of churches: ones they could run, or drop-out sects that were no threat to them. The greatest danger, after the Roman Catholic Church, was a Reformed Catholic Church. Such was the very last thing they wanted!

---

7. G. S. M. Walker, "Calvin and the Church," from McKim, ed., *Readings in Calvin's Theology* (Grand Rapids: Baker, 1984), p. 230.

Post-Reformation Developments

Because of the failure of the Reformed Catholic movement of Bucer and Calvin, protestantism was very quickly identified with nationalism. The war to free the Netherlands from Spain was all tied up with the conflict between Reformational and Roman Catholic theology. The struggle of Scotland to maintain independence from England was all mixed up with theological and ecclesiastical concerns. Instead of one international catholic church, the protestant churches came to be nationalistic churches, and the result was low morals and a low spiritual life. Baalism (religious nationalism) seemed to be engulfing the Reform.

As it happened, there were reactions against this. In Germany, the "Pietist" movement arose to protest the dead orthodoxy of statist religion. In England, the "Puritan" movement did the same. Anglican liturgist and theologian Dom Gregory Dix has this penetrating remark to make about the Puritans: "The incipient presbyterian and congregationalist movements under Cartwright and Browne did express, however awkwardly and inadequately, a desire for a less bureaucratic and above all a more *religious* organisation and life of the church *qua* church. They had a real sense that the church is not, and ought not to appear, a department of the state but a divine society with a supernatural life of its own. In their own ways they were 'high church' movements."[8]

In short, to some extent, the Puritan movement was a catholic movement, away from northern European statism, and toward the historic Medieval church tradition. Sadly, Puritanism was also largely a sectarian movement, ignoring the history and development of the church, and shooting for "New Testament" ideals while generally overlooking the wisdom of the historic church. In this respect, Puritanism was no heir of Calvin and Bucer. For protestantism by this time had come to associate "catholic" with "Papal," and the abuses of the late medieval papacy at that. The ideals of Bucer and Calvin were lost in a sea of reaction. The early Puritans still retained much of the vision of the "Reformed Catho-

---

8. Gregory Dix, *The Shape of the Liturgy* (Westminster, England: Dacre Press, 1945), p. 684.

lics," but their later heirs were mostly sectaries in their thought.

This is as good a place as any to point out that catholic, nationalistic, and sectarian tendencies can be found in any of the churches of the Reformation. Except for extreme Anabaptist sectaries and extreme Erastian nationalists, all three faces of protestantism can be found within any particular church in any land. What we can notice, however, is that in protestantism as a whole, the catholic impulse tends to be lost in a battle between sectarian and nationalistic tendencies. In both Scotland and in Holland, for instance, there were numerous church splits, yet each little splinter group maintained that it was the true national church, and thus entitled to receive a dole from the state!

In protestant lands, it seemed as if Catholicity were impossible. "Catholic" meant bad. The early church was ignored, and the great gains of the medieval period were all viewed as evils "produced by antichrist." Unthinking protestants gave away the governmental power of the church to the state, and the result was that protestants had only two choices: either the church was ruled by the state, or else the church was a drop-out sect that made no claim to be an alternative government on the earth. The sects emphasized preaching, and the governmental side of the church disappeared. What protestant church today has law courts, or a law school? Where are the protestant texts on church law? Where are protestant canon lawyers? To ask such questions is to expose the sad truth that the protestant churches have given away the great gains made the by early and medieval churches. The result is rampant statism everywhere.

The Catholic Reformers in Switzerland did not capture the day. Had they won out, there would have been a Reformed Catholic Church. There would have been weekly communion, so that the threat of excommunication would have meant something real. There would have been Reformed church courts, with elders and ministers sitting as real judges over matters pertaining to the spiritual government of the church. The statism that has led to so many wars in Europe over the past several centuries would have been restrained. There would have been no extreme Puritan movements that threw the baby out with the bathwater in the areas of worship and of church government.

In fact, however, the vision of an international Reformed catholic church died with the first reformers. There was something of a revival of it at the Synod of Dordt, and catholicity has never wholly been absent from protestant thinking, but it has been a weak and minority position.

America

After the War for Independence, the various states began to disestablish their churches, and soon there were no established churches in America. The result was that all the churches became sects. A strange thing then happened: Groups of immigrants brought over their churches with them, but where these churches had (often) been nationalistic in the mother country, in the new world they were "denominations." A denomination is nothing but a large sect.

The churches in America have not functioned in any kind of catholic or Biblical fashion as regards government. After all, the government of the church only exists by recognition, because the church does not wield a sword to force its will upon anyone. But what happens if a man is excommunicated from a Baptist church? He just goes down the street and joins a Methodist one. The churches do not recognize one another's government. And how convenient this is for empire-building sectarian churchmen! By despising all the other churches, they can build their own.

The American churches have been afflicted with a curious mixture of nationalism and sectarianism. We have just noted how sectarian they all are, and how they work to despise one another in practice. Let us also for a moment recall just how nationalistic (Baalistic) American churches tend to be. Go into most American churches and you will see an American flag displayed down front. What is it doing there? Your guess is as good as mine, but one thing is for sure: It has no business there.

Another simple and obvious illustration comes from the Civil War. Virtually every "denomination" in America split during the

war. Why? The Catholic church existed for centuries, through all
the wars of Europe, without splitting into various nationalistic
churches, but the American churches could not endure one century without splitting along purely nationalistic lines. Frankly, it
is disgusting to think about. (I'm not trying to say who was at fault
in any situation, I'm just talking about how corrupt the protestant
churches have been in this area, due to their basic mentality.)

One of the saddest things in recent years is that the more conservative a protestant group is, the more sectarian it is. Instead of
linking conservatism and Biblicism with the historic and catholic
posture of the true church as a whole, each tiny protestant group
assumes that it has all the truth, and despises the rest. This is even
true within denominations. A man excommunicated from one
congregation of the Presbyterian Church in America (in Birming-
ham) just went down the street and was welcomed at another
PCA church. Such is the situation: No mutual recognition; no
catholicity; just a bunch of sects warring among themselves.

Of course, even in America, and even in American presbyterianism there have been those who sought for a more catholic view
of the church. I think, right off the top of my head, of Charles
Hodge, who so appreciated the catholic labors of the Reformed
thinker and historian Philip Schaff, and who authored his own
book on the Constitutional History of the Presbyterian Church.
Hodge took a dim view of sectarianism, as his assessment of
George Whitefield indicates.[9] Hodge has some nice things to say
about Whitefield, but his basic catholicity was offended by Whitefield's anarchism.

Conclusion

Clearly, the imperial/nationalistic notion of the church is
gravely wrong, for the church is not a department of state. We
also hold that the sectarian notion is wrong, for the church must
have an institutional, governmental presence in the world. Part of

---

9. See the citation of Hodge's comments in James B. Jordan, ed., *The Reconstruction of the Church*. Christianity and Civilization No. 4 (Tyler, TX: Geneva
Ministries, 1985), pp. 7ff.

the calling of the church is to stand against the monolithic state.

The vision of a true, catholic church is needed in America in our time. The church must recover herself as a government. Local churches must begin recognizing one another's discipline, and this night of anarchy and of undercutting one another must end. Protestants must shake themselves loose from the mindless sectarian stupidity of kneejerk reactions against everything that "smacks of Rome," for we Reformed Catholics are the true heirs of the early church and of the greatness of the Medieval church. Conservative protestants must also begin to read the writings of people outside their own immediate circles, for there is much wisdom to be learned from Christian thinkers in other traditions.

This was the vision of the first Geneva, of Bucer and Calvin. It must be our vision today.

5

CONVERSION

My purpose in this essay is not to provide a complete theology of conversion, but to comment on an experience I had in the summer of 1984. I was invited to speak at a conservative Presbyterian church. I spoke in the morning, and in addition to the regular congregation I found I was speaking to a group of bright-eyed college students, who were in the area for the summer. As part of a basically Campus Crusade oriented ministry, this group of students was working at earning money for tuition during the week, attending Bible classes in the evenings, and doing beach evangelism on the weekends. This kind of thing is very common, and I was personally pleased to meet these young people. I was also happy to see that this conservative Presbyterian church had become their home for the summer, welcoming them into its fellowship.

As I said above, I spoke in the morning. The evening service was put on by the students, it being their last Sunday in the area. They had formed a chorus, and sang some of the modern post-Jesus Movement songs that are the standard (and sadly superficial) fare among these groups. They also gave testimonies, and one of them preached to the congregation.

As I listened to the testimonies, and to the little sermonette, I realized that there was a time when this kind of thing would have moved me, but that it no longer seemed very relevant. Was this because my own faith had grown cold? I hope not. Was this because their method of presenting the gospel was so grossly off-base as to be unacceptable? Well, this is sometimes asserted in "hard-core Reformed" circles, and I once felt this way myself. But

151

as I thought about it, I came to a different conclusion, and this essay is the result.

Let me encapsulate one of the testimonies I heard. A young woman got up and said something like this: "When I went to college, I thought I was a good Christian. I didn't use dope, and I'd grown up in a good Christian home and had been active in a good Christian church. But I found out that I wasn't *really* a Christian. I had to break some idols in my heart, and meet Jesus *personally*.

"There was this boy, you see. We'd been dating seriously, but he was not a Christian. I didn't want to give him up. I found myself in more and more tension over this, and finally I got down and prayed that Jesus would just take over. I was finally willing to give up this boy. And you know what? We broke it off, and I've never missed him since. I've found something more wonderful to live for. I hope you do to."

Now remember, the people she was addressing with this testimony were mostly well over 30 years of age. Many were over 50. I could tell that they were delighted that she had found Christ, but I could also tell that they did not really connect up with her experience readily.

Now, the testimony I just rehearsed for you is a standard testimony ritual. Impressionable young people take up the forms and attitudes of influential older people who minister to them, and this kind of testimony ritual is standard in campus ministries. Point 1: I thought I was already a Christian. Point 2: I realized I was not, because I had not given *all* to Him. Point 3: I gave it all to Him, and found peace. Point 4: You can too.

Now, is there something *wrong* with all this? Well, clearly not, in one sense, but in another sense there is something wrong. What is wrong is that there is an erroneous understanding of conversion operating here.

What is Conversion?

Conversion is a turning from sin to Christ. Now, let's think about that. Does conversion happen only once in a lifetime, or does it happen many times? That is the question, I believe, that needs answering.

From my experience, and from my understanding of the Bible and of Christianity, there are four kinds of conversion experiences. First, for a person totally outside the faith, there is an initial conversion experience when that person comes to Christ for the first time. This kind of conversion has become the norm for everyone, unfortunately, even though it applies to relatively few Christian people.

Secondly, there is daily conversion. Each day, and many times during the day, we have to turn from sinful tendencies, and turn back to Christ. These "little turnings" are so many daily conversions. By magnifying the initial conversion experience, modern evangelism does not say enough about daily conversion.

Third, there are what I call "crisis conversions." There are crisis points in every Christian's life. At these crisis points, the Christian needs to reaffirm his or her faith by making a major break with some problem that has crept up, and make a major turn toward Christ.

Fourth, there are what I called "stage conversions." By this I don't mean conversions that are merely put on for show. Rather, I mean that God brings Christians through various stages of growth and maturity, and at each stage it is necessary for the Christian to come to a fuller understanding of what it means to be a Christian.

Now, I don't think enough justice is done to this matter of stages of life. As a person grows, his understanding of himself, of the world, and of God will change, because he is himself changing. His understanding grows wider, and embraces more factors of life. He becomes aware of things he was not aware of before. Moreover, his understanding grows deeper, and more profound. Learning to adjust to a spouse, and then to children; learning to adjust to authorities on the job, and learning how to relate to subordinates; learning how to manage money; etc. — all of these things cause a person to deepen and widen his understanding. Hopefully, they cause a person to become more and more wise and stable.

These changes of understanding happen slowly and gradually, without our being aware of them. One day, however, we wake up and realize that we have changed. I am not the same person I was ten years ago, I realize. And my understanding of God and of His ways, of what it means to be a Christian, had better change too. My faith needs to deepen and broaden. Once again, I need to give *all* to Him, because my understanding of "all" has expanded.

This means that the kind of Christian experience I may have had in college is not the norm for my entire life. This is the important point. The college-type Christian conversion experience may be a very important and necessary *stage* in my Christian development, but it would be wrong (even perverse) for me to try continually to keep up that kind of "lighthearted" Christian experience in the midst of a mature adult world, with all its cares, responsibilities, and tribulations.

This is why the kind of testimonies these college students were making before the Presbyterian congregation seemed off base to me. They were not really relevant to my stage of life as a 34-year old family man. I could appreciate and rejoice in what the Lord was doing with them, but I also saw that He was not doing quite the same thing with me.

Between my senior year of high school and my freshman year of college, I too was "converted." I read Billy Graham's *World Aflame*, and I came to understand for the first time that I had to be justified apart from any of my own works and intentions. I accepted Christ into my heart, and for a month I was on a kind of "honeymoon" with the Lord. For years, I told people that I had not been a Christian before, only a "good churchgoer." I now no longer tell people that.

Was I not a Christian before? Was the young woman whose testimony I reproduced above not really a Christian before she went to college? I think I was, and I think she was, too. What happened was that we came to a new stage of maturity, a stage at which we needed to understand in a new, more profound way, what the Christian faith entails. We went through a crisis, and experienced a conversion.

I believed in Jesus when I was little, and I'm sure she did to. We were both loyal to Him. We kept His rules. We went to His church. We sang hymns to Him. We had the kind of faith appropriate for the childish stage of life. When we got to age 17, however, we needed to deepen our faith. We went through a crisis. We had a conversion.

Now, the problem comes in the notion that this experience is *the one and only conversion for one's whole life*. If we think that way, we always look backwards to that conversion. We want to recapture the simplicity of that initial warm experience of the love and acceptance of God, and this is a mistake. It freezes faith at an immature level, and prevents us from pressing on to maturity. People influenced by this way of thinking tend to want to recover the experiences of their late teen years.

(To take a parallel example, we see this most commonly in the way people retain a strong, often binding affection for whatever kind of music they listened to in their late teens. People who danced to Lawrence Welk's "champagne music" were horrified when their teenagers liked the Beatles. Now the Beatles generation has its own children, and they are horrified at modern punk rock. The beatnik generation, which came in between, still clings to the sounds of off-beat folk music. There is nothing necessarily wrong with some of this music, and there is nothing wrong with an occasional nostalgia for childhood, but there can be a real problem when this nostalgia becomes an intransigent refusal to mature.

(Continuing this parenthesis: America is a strange culture. It glorifies youth, and it provides most people with the means to surround themselves with youthful fictions. Women at 30 years of age, after bearing children, want to be as slim and weightless as they were at age 18, a manifest impossibility. Similarly, the phonograph record and the cassette tape enable people to continue the experience of late teen years via music. Thus, that this kind of intransigent nostalgia is present in the area of faith is no surprise, but it is regrettable. We are called to press on to maturity — in every area of life.)

Thus, I appreciate the "Campus Crusade" type of college conversion experience. I think it is healthy for many young people, and I don't think it harms anyone. (After all, if the reprobate don't persevere in the faith, that is their fault.) The problem is in making this kind of youthful experience the norm for mature Christian faith.

The Abundant Life

The youthful campus evangelists who addressed us in church that Sunday evening were very concerned that we come to know the "more abundant life that earth can never give." I got the impression that these young people suspected that we stodgy old folks just were not experiencing the abundant life!

Scripture clearly tells us that Christ offers a more abundant life. The question, however, is this: Abundant in terms of what? What a teenager *perceives* as the abundant life may not be (and should not be) the same as what a 35 year old homemaker or laborer perceives as abundant living. First of all, the glandular/emotional quality of life at 18 is not the same as it is at 35. So, how we *feel* about Christ when we are 18 is not likely to be the same as how we feel about Him when we are 35, or 70.

Second, as mentioned above, we mature as we get older (hopefully). Maturity includes an expanded horizon of awareness of the world and life. It includes an expanded sense of time, and of how much time it takes to accomplish some matters (even many generations of time). It includes a more profound awareness of pain and suffering. All these grow with age.

Moreover, at about age 30, we begin to become much more aware of debilitation and death. We begin to realize that in fact not all our goals are going to be met. The golden dreams of youth have become tarnished. All the problems are not going to be overcome. Thus, as we get older we begin to appreciate more and more that this life is transitory. It is a trial run. What we accomplish here is indeed important, but none of us is going to accomplish anywhere near all we set out to accomplish. And, we begin to realize that there is much pain and weakness that will not be overcome in this life, and we shall simply have to endure it. This is a much more sober outlook on life than that of the college student.

Young people should dream dreams, and I am glad for the brand of "abundant life" I experienced in college. In fact, however, I am older now, and that kind of Christian experience is not for me. The mature brand of the abundant life is more serious (and in fact, it is more abundant!).

Reactions

Let us return now to the matter of conversion experiences. The neo-Puritan movement reacted strongly against "easy believism." From my experience, they tended to substitute "hard believism" for it. The neo-Puritans complained that the campus conversion experience is too superficial: People aren't warned about hell, about the suffering that Christians will face, about predestination, etc.

My problem with the neo-Puritan critique of campus conversion experiences is the same as my problem with campus conversionism. Both groups act as if some big crisis or decision were necessary to come into the faith. Both groups ignore the reality of the faith of young children. (In fact, both groups are heavily Baptist, thus typically American, in orientation; the neo-Puritans being almost to a man Reformed Baptists.) Both groups put too much stress on an initial conversion experience. The neo-Puritans don't like the soft-sell "easy" conversion; they want a hard-sell gospel with all the hard facts brought out first. They seem to want to manipulate "true conversions," and eliminate "stony ground and thorny ground" conversions. This, however, I do not think is Biblical. The Sower sowed the stony and the thorny ground, and did not object to the plants that sprang up from his "easy and free" sowing. Not all persevered, however, a fact that the Sower also recognized (Matt. 13:4-9, 18-23).

Perseverance is the real issue here. There is no need to react against simple evangelistic methods, such as the "Four Spiritual Laws." The issue is not initial conversion. Rather, the issue is perseverance. Once people are brought into the faith, they need to be shepherded into maturity.

The Four Spiritual Laws

After all, what is so terribly wrong with the "Four Spiritual Laws"? The Bible says that God created man good, and offered him a wonderful plan. That's law one, and it is exactly where the Bible begins. The Bible says that man rebelled, and came under God's wrath, and thus cannot know God's wonderful plan. That's law two, and I cannot fault it either.[1] The Bible says that the sacrifice of Jesus Christ as a substitute for us is the only way of salvation: One Way. That's law three, and who wants to question this? The Bible finally says we have to appropriate the gift of eternal life by faith in Christ, and persevere in that faith until the end. That's law four, and it is true also.

Most "four law" type booklets warn the reader not to rest on experiences. "Observe this train diagram," they read. The engine (God) pulls the train. The coal car (personal faith and trust) provides the fuel. The caboose, the most attractive car (emotional experiences), comes last. The train can run with or without the caboose. It's nice, but not necessary. So also with emotional feelings: They are nice, but not absolutely necessary. Trust in God, and let your emotions get in line as they will.

The neo-Puritan critique of "four law" evangelism generally runs along two lines. First, it is objected by some (not all) that God does not elect everybody, so we ought not say that God offers a wonderful plan to everybody. The problem with this is that puts us in God's place. Election is His business; evangelism is ours. God does offer salvation to all men, covenantally speaking.

Second, it is objected that we cannot say "God loves you" and "Christ died for you" to all men. This, however, is a linguistic error. In one sense, the full heavy theological sense, it is true that God does not *love* all men, and that Christ did not die *for* all men; but in ordinary language, which is the level at which evangelism takes place, it certainly is true that God has a love for all men, and that the death of Christ brings benefits for all men.[2]

Now I once tried real, real hard to be a neo-Puritan, but try as

---

1. The serious problem I see with "law two" in most booklets is the diagram showing men trying to reach God through ethics, good works, philosophy, other religions, etc. This is completely false. The purpose of ethics, etc., according to Romans 1 is to help man escape God and suppress all knowledge of Him. Rebellious man never tries to reach God.

2. For a thoroughly Reformed and Calvinistic discussion of these matters, see Norman Shepherd, "The Covenant Context for Evangelism," in John Skilton, ed., *The New Testament Student and Theology* (Phillipsburg, NJ: Presbyterian & Reformed, 1976); and the interaction on this matter in the pages of the *Banner of Truth* magazine, issues 166/167 and 170.

I might, I just could not get real excited about the horrors of "four law" evangelism. It seems to me that the problem is not with the evangelism, but with the follow-up: Independent evangelistic organizations tend to replace the sacramental fellowship of the church. That, however, I do not think is something to criticize them heavily for. Let the church get to work and do the evangelism, and we shall see the "withering away" of independent organizations. Until that time, I think most of them do good work.

(There is, clearly, a place for theological inspection of "easy believism," and there is much value in the criticisms produced by the neo-Puritans. But I have come to think that some of them at least are throwing the baby out with the bath.)

The Sacramental System

Effective pastoral care helps people progress to maturity. Historically, the Christian church worked out the sacramental system to assist people with the various conversions of life. While we Protestants believe in only two sacraments, it is helpful for us to look at the sacramental system, because there is some wisdom in it.

As a young person begins to approach maturity, his understanding undergoes a shift (called puberty nowadays). To harness this change, and minister the needed "stage conversion," the church has used the rite of confirmation. Youth are told that they now must become "soldiers of Christ." The military imagery helps them harnass their new drives, and channels them toward productive things. Protestant churches that do not practise confirmation tend to have equivalent things, such as catechism classes, or teen-age youth groups. Everybody understands that this is a crisis-stage in life, and youth need help in converting through it.

Marriage is another crisis. Generally, people are so happy to get married that they do not recognize that there are going to be problems, and that some conversions are going to be needed. The old sacrament of Matrimony was designed to ask for God's special blessing on the couple getting married, and while protestants don't call it a sacrament (rightly), they do the same kind of thing.

Sickness is a crisis that generally causes people to reassess their lives — leading to what we are calling conversions (renewed faith in Christ). The sacrament of Unction was designed to provide a place for pastoral ministration in this time of need. While protestants again don't call this a sacrament, protestants do often obey James 5:15 and anoint the sick.

But how about the daily conversions, and the crises that come from time to time, and the hidden "stage" changes that we undergo? The old church set up the confessional to provide pastoral care for this: the sacrament of Penance. People would come to the pastor and talk over their problems in the confessional box. It is a little enough known fact, but the Protestant Reformers tried to retain the practice of confession in the church, because they saw it as a healthy way to minister to the people (see James 5:16). Protestants generally have not worked out a good way to deal with this, but the rise of the modern counselling movement in protestant circles is an attempt to help people with the crises and needed conversions of life.

Food for thought? I think so.

Along these same lines, one protestant substitute for the confessional, in America at least, has been the rededication service. By having a week of special meetings annually, the Baptistic churches provide an opportunity for persons in crisis, or who have moved to a new stage of maturity, to externalize this crisis in a ritual of rededication to Christ. Unfortunately, the Baptist theology of conversion often comes into play here, and people tend to think that they were not "really" Christians until the day they "walked the aisle." All the same, this is another way in which the church has provided opportunities for people to handle the crises and changes of life.

Rather than ridicule these customs (Catholic and Baptist), we Reformed Christians ought to ask whether or not there is something to be learned from them. What regular means do we provide in our churches for people to approach, *with ease*, their pastors and ask for serious counselling? Both the confession box and the rededication service provide situations wherein people can feel free to discuss their problems and change their lives. Until we have worked out something along these lines, I don't think we are really doing our jobs. Counselling cases pile up precisely because our churches do not have regular ways of handling problems before they come up.

The sacramental system in the Roman Catholic Church is hardly perfect, but the way protestants have come to handle the crises and "conversions" of life has not proven adequate either. It should be on our agenda to give serious consideration to reforming our teaching and practice in this area.

6

THE EFFECTIVE CHURCH SPLITTER'S GUIDE

You're a pastor, and you've just left your latest church. It is blown up, and in shreds—but who can blame you for that? You tried, but the people just weren't holy enough. Now you've gone to another town, and joined a local church. You're temporarily out of the ministry. Your work is ahead of you.

You've got to be careful at this point. Discernment is needed. In your new church there are bound to be some areas of sin and looseness that you can exploit. The task before you is to be judicious in selecting just which issues to make noise about. And you have to do it fast, else when you leave you will not have credibility.

Maybe some of the people, even leaders, of this new church smoke. Of course, maybe you smoked back in your old church, so a frontal attack on smoking would not be a good tactic to use. You might wind up embarrassed. You have to discern quickly whether it will or won't be credible to say that "the people here smoke too much." Of course, who knows how much "too much" is? That's the beauty of vague, generalized discontent.

Let's look at some things you might select to express "grief" over, shortly after you first arrive. Do people go to see "too many" movies? Do they have "too many" parties and get-togethers? Or, equally juicy, do they "not have enough" fellowship? Do the elders visit the people "enough"? Is there "too light" or "too serious" an attitude among the people? Are they "too loose" or "too intolerant" on the sabbath? (This is an especially good one, for every church on earth is either too loose or too intolerant on the sabbath. You can have a grand time exploiting this one.)

163

Other issues you might notice are: Are the elders high enough grade? (Remember, to lead a successful split, you have to outshine at least some of them.) Is there "too loose" an attitude about popular music, or about Roman Catholicism? Either of these is good to exploit. Are some of the people a bit weird, off into strange political movements like survivalism? You can make hay with this, if you are careful.

Another great issue for you is this one: church discipline. Every church on earth is either too harsh, unloving, and intolerant, or else too loose and tolerant of sin. You can make any church out to be wrong one way or another. You have to decide, however, and decide fast, which course to pursue in your new church. Maybe you can go with both approaches at once (though the novice church splitter might not try this until he has had a bit of experience): too loose on movies or tobacco, and too strict on adultery. This works well with solid, Reformed churches.

Finally, you can always win by saying that you sometimes feel a little like *maybe* the elders are lording it over the people just a *wee* bit. That's all you need to say. And in every church, there are people who want to believe just this very thing, since their *pure sensibilities* in the areas of *piety* and *true holiness* are *grieved* by the leadership.

Now you've arrived, and you are already beginning to sense some of the items you might select to make trouble over. You will find that if you judiciously leak out some of your dissatisfactions, some people will come to you and express theirs to you. After all, you are cutting a "most holy" image. Where the church is "extreme," you counsel "moderation." Where the church is "compromised," you advocate "faithfulness." Where the church is "harsh," you advocate a "loving spirit." Where the church is "too tolerant and longsuffering," you advocate a "firmer hand." You will find people who want to hear just this kind of talk. Keep them in mind for the future.

Chances are the rulers of your new church are not used to people like you. If they have had experience with church splitters before, they may set up some roadblocks. We'll deal with them soon. First, let's deal with the simple scenario—the one you are most likely to encounter.

In either scenario (simple or tough), you need to make a practice of spending some time with the church's rulers. Give them advice. Try to find areas of "looseness" or "harshness" where the rulers already have strong opinions, and advise them to change their ways. They won't heed you, and this is fodder for the future. You can then *honestly* say that you *tried to work things out*, but it was just *impossible*.

Another benefit of spending time advising the elders is that it makes you look like one of the boys. You look like a leader in the eyes of the people, and soon you will have a group for which you can be spokesman.

In time (about a year to eighteen months), you should be in a position to make a move (this is simple scenario). You simply bring your malcontent group with you, and tell the rulers that these people and you don't think that the church is doing right, and that they want to start a new church, and they have, surprisingly, chosen you as the leader. If the elders are wise, they may just let you go. They don't want malcontents in their midst either. If the elders are less experienced (which we assume here), they may be very angry. They'll accuse you of "sheep stealing" and other bad things. You need to be able to say with a "clear conscience" that you never sought this honor; rather, these poor unloved people sought you out.

Now, the elders will realize and be angry that you have sprung this on them overnight. You need to be able to say "I warned you about such and such a problem." That's why you need to spend time with the elders beforehand, "warning" them about the problems that you have perceived (and are stimulating) in their nice, warm, cozy church.

No church splits without hostility, because people feel betrayed, and because a church covenant is kind of like a marriage covenant. All the same, now is the time for you to put on the mature act, and admonish everyone to "separate in peace." That may be a farce, but you want it to look as if you were the peaceloving one.

Now let's go to the tougher scenario. In this church the elders have had experience with guys like you before. As you chafe against them, they may admonish you. Be sure to come right back with a counter-admonition. This will be your list of all the "unrighteous" things in the church. Hopefully this confrontation will not come until you have been there for a year or so.

As you can see, *providence* may *force* you to leave the church and start your own. At the same time, it is important to have an appearance of legitimacy about what you do. If you can, contact another denomination and get them to come in and sponsor you. They'll be only too happy to do so, since the heart and soul of conservative American evangelicalism is the art of backstabbing. Get this all arranged before taking the sheep out of your church. If it comes suddenly, there will be nothing the elders can do. After all, they don't want to fight with the other denomination.

Once you are out, and have your own church going again, you can always split from the denomination that sponsored you. While it looks better to be in fellowship with other churches, you know that you will personally brook no interference with your ministry. Thus, if it looks as if you need to get free, I suggest you simply begin teaching something or doing something you know that the new denomination will not tolerate. In time, they'll cut you off; you get to be a martyr for "the truth."

Now, it is important, once you have your own church going, that you "extend the right hand of fellowship" and offer "fraternal relations" to the church you just shafted. If they refuse, it makes them look bad; if they accept, you don't lose anything. If they refuse close relations with you, then it proves what you said all along, that they are "unloving."

One other scenario, and the most complex, is this. Suppose the elders of the church are really onto you. You know you won't win against them, because they already know your tricks. You can still force them to checkmate, however. First, after you've been there for a year or so, and you've had a confrontation with the elders, just leave the church and transfer peacefully to another church in town. This is, of course, a temporary move. It is totally lawful, and makes you look good. And, you might get some sheep from this new church also.

Keep in close, personal touch with known malcontents in the

church you just left. Never offer to start a new church. Try to work it around so that one of them suggests it. Remember, when it finally happens, it will be "the leading of the Lord." At that point, get with the denomination you have already contacted, and get your church underway.

When soliciting sheep from the old church, never come right out blatantly and invite them to go with you. Instead, just give them a lot of pious brother-talk: "I just phoned to let you know, brother, that some of us are starting a new work, brother, and I just wanted you to hear it from me rather than from someone else, brother." This kind of indirect solicitation works best, and nobody can complain against it. Who dares accuse you of stealing sheep!

The reason for going through all the legalities is that you want your "transition" to be "peaceful." You could just go out and start a new church, and ignore an excommunication from the old one. That puts you under a cloud, however. Make it peaceful, and legal, even if it takes a little longer.

Now you have gotten all the really holy people out of the false church. These are the real seekers after truth, the truly inflexible people of God. Now the fun begins, because at last you have a real, godly church.

Or do you?

At any rate, it is really fun being a wolf.

7

PROPOSITIONS ON PENTECOSTALISM

The following propositions are offered in the interest of providing a catholic and Reformed assessment of the use of the "gift of tongues" in the 20th century charismatic movement. They are not offered as an attack on Christian brethren, but in the interest of enabling all of us better to "reason together."

1. The gift of tongues was a special form of prophecy that ceased in A.D. 70.

    1.1. Tongues were a sign to the Old Covenant church of the judgment of Israel and the internationalization of the church (Is. 28:11; 1 Cor. 14:21).

        1.1.1. The tongues resembled drunken speech, which Israel preferred to hear rather than the Word of God (Is. 28:7-11; Acts 2:13).

        1.1.2. The foreign speech indicated that the locus of Divine salvific activity had shifted from Israel to the nations (Gen. 9:27; Deut. 32:21; Jonah 1-4; Rom. 11; Acts 2).

        1.1.3. Jews were always present when tongues were spoken (Acts 2; 8:14ff.; 10:44ff.; 18:7; 19:1-6).

            1.1.3.1. These same passages disclose a progressive withdrawal from Israel to the gentiles, climaxed in Acts 28.

    1.2. Tongues were translatable languages (see scriptures cited above, and 1 Cor. 14:5, *et passim*).

    1.3. The final judgment against the Old Covenant in A.D. 70 rendered the lesser sign of tongues unnecessary.

    1.4. The revelation of the New Covenant gospel in non-

Hebraic tongues continues in inscripturated form in the very fact that the New Testament is written *not* in Hebrew but in a foreign tongue (Hebraized Koine Greek).

1.4.1. The prophecy of Isaiah that Israel would have to hear the gospel in a foreign language received an Old Covenant "shadow fulfillment" in the fact that the good news of the rebuilding of the Temple was published in Aramaic, not Hebrew, in the book of Ezra, and in that much of Daniel is also written in Aramaic.

1.4.1.1. Daniel 2:4 - 7:28 are in Aramaic. These passages record the conversion of the gentile Kings Nebuchadnezzar and Darius to the true faith, a prophecy of the conversion of the world in the New Covenant. Daniel 7 pictures the coming of the New Covenant, when Israel will be set aside, a message that troubled Daniel (7:15, 28). The fact that these passage are written in "tongues" rather than in Hebrew simply reinforces their prophetic character.

1.4.1.2. Ezra 4:8 - 6:18 and 7:12-26 are in Aramaic. The initial fulfillment of the promises of restoration and of the conversion of the gentiles is seen in the post-exilic history of Israel. It was the gentile kings of the world who were most concerned that prayer and sacrifice be restored at Jerusalem, for they realized that the world would fall apart without that restoration. The letters from these kings, guaranteeing the security of the restoration project, are written in "tongues," not in Hebrew. The good news came in other tongues.

2. The cessation of the sign-gift of tongues does not prevent the eternally active God from working true language miracles in our day.

2.1. The penetration of the gospel into new parts, such as early medieval Europe and on the mission field today, is often accompanied by miraculous actions designed to confirm the messengers. This has included language miracles.

3. Glossolalia, modern tongues-speaking, is not a foreign language, but a natural reflex or capacity of the human body, like

weeping, laughter, or hysteria.

3.1. Therefore, glossolalia is a God-given gift to man, which can be used for good, but which can also be abused.

3.2. Like any other human action, the practice of glossolalia should be directed as a thank offering to God.

3.2.1. The use of glossolalia in prayer is no more problematic in principle than the use of laughter or weeping in prayer.

3.3. Any gift may be abused, and glossolalia may be used as a "tripping device," analogous to drug taking.

3.3.1. Pagan religions worldwide use glossolalia in this manner.

3.3.2. Modern pentecostalism, which so often focuses on entertainment, often also abuses glossolalia this way. (The swiftness with which charismatics have moved into the entertainment fields of recorded music and cable television shows all too clearly how thoroughly oriented toward entertainment many of them are.)

3.4. The erroneous assumption that glossolalia is the same thing as the New Testament gift of tongues has brought confusion and bondage to much of the church.

4. The modern pentecostal movement is an irrationalistic reaction against an overly rationalistic culture and church.

4.1. The Reformation produced an overly rationalistic church.

4.1.1. The refusal to cultivate emotional richness in worship produced an intellect-centered worship.

4.1.1.1. Churches descended from the Calvinistic wing of the Reformation have tended to take the Regulative Principle — worship is to be regulated by Scripture — in a wrongful, minimalist sense, because of a failure to understand the difference between the Old and New Covenants on this point.

4.1.1.1.1. Fear characterized Old Covenant worship to a great extent, because man was still excluded from Eden, under pain of death. Men feared to transgress the boundaries set up by a holy God.

4.1.1.1.2. Joy and freedom characterize New

Covenant worship, because man is now *included*. While the moral boundaries still exist, they have to be interpreted in a different light. Alexander Schmemann has written concerning the beauty of the liturgy "which has so often been denounced as unnecessary and even sinful":

"Unnecessary it is indeed, for we are beyond the categories of the 'necessary.' Beauty is never 'necessary,' 'functional,' or 'useful.' And when, expecting someone whom we love, we put a beautiful tablecloth on the table and decorate it with candles and flowers, we do all this not out of necessity, but out of love. And the church is love, expectation, and joy. It is heaven on earth, according to our Orthodox tradition; it is the joy of recovered childhood, that free, unconditioned, and disinterested joy that alone is capable of transforming the world. In our adult, serious piety we ask for definitions and justifications, and they are rooted in fear — fear of corruption, deviation, 'pagan influences,' and whatnot. But 'he that feareth is not made perfect in love' (1 John 4:18). As long as Christians will *love* the Kingdom of God, and not only discuss it, they will 'represent' it and signify it in art and beauty."[1]

4.1.2. The failure to maintain the Real Presence in the sacraments, and to keep the Eucharist at the center of weekly worship, also served to de-mystify and overly intellectualize Christian experience.

4.1.2.1. The Eucharist is the normal weekly miracle of the faith. Failure to keep that miracle at the center of religion has led to a general depreciation of miracle throughout traditional evangelicalism, and thus in these circles a strong reaction against miracles (real or supposed) in pentecostalism.

4.1.3. The catechisms produced in Reformed churches to train youth concern the definitions of doctrinal terms, and bear no resemblance to the whole-life orientation of that Biblical catechism, the Book of Proverbs.

4.2. Thus, the churches descended from the Calvinistic wing of the Reformation have been haunted by revivalism as an

---

1. Alexander Schmemann, *For the Life of the World* (New York: St. Vladimir's Seminary Press, 1973), p. 30.

irrational counterpart to their primacy-of-the-intellect form of worship.

4.2.1. It is not an accident that revivalism sprang out of the incredibly infrequent communion seasons of the Scottish and Puritan churches.

4.3. The Newtonian world-view, adopted in Reformation lands, and used in apologetics, is mechanistic and overly rationalistic.[2]

4.4. Rationalism can be used for good or for ill.

4.4.1. The development of doctrine in the Reformed church has been a good.

4.4.2. The tendency of the Reformed churches historically to slip into Amyraldianism, Arminianism, Unitarianism, and Liberalism has been an ill.

4.5. Irrationalism can also be used for good or for ill.

4.5.1. The renewed life in the churches after revivals has been a good.

4.5.2. The sexual and other emotional-type sins produced by revivalism and pentecostalism have been ills.[3]

5. The modern pentecostal movement has produced much good and much ill.

5.1. Good things include breaking down intellectualism and extreme rationalism among conservative churches, breaking down rationalistic liberalism in large denominations, renewed love for and study of Scripture in many circles, renewed concern for the trans-rational aspects of the faith.

5.2. Bad things include sexual and other forms of moral license, downgrading of Scriptural authority in favor of enthusiasm, increase in demonic activity in many circles, and a general orientation toward entertainment that goes so far as to see

---

2. The works of Cornelius Van Til sounded the deathknell for traditional rationalistic and evidentialistic apologetics. The intellectual (though not personal) hostility to Van Til has been so great throughout evangelicalism that he is generally either ignored or accused of not believing in apologetics at all.

3. See Gary North, "Revival: True and False," in *Biblical Economics Today* 8:6 (Oct./Nov., 1985).

worship itself almost wholly in terms of stimulation.

5.3. General evaluation: Depending on the persons involved, the charismatic experience can result in Christian renewal, or it can result in apostasy into cultic pantheism of one sort or another. The numerous anti-Trinitarian pentecostal cults in America (the United Pentecostal Church, the Children of God, etc.), and all over Latin America, testify to the latter.

6. Some hopes for the future.

6.1. We need to repudiate the historic protestant stoic and intellectualistic interpretations of worship (of the regulative principle), and reintroduce cultivated musical and artistic beauty in worship.

6.2. We need to repudiate worship by proxy, and train people for active participation in worship.

6.3. We need to reintroduce the mystery of the Eucharist as Christ's Real Presence in our midst, as the center of special worship, weekly, with our children not excluded.

6.4. A renewed committment to conjoining Word and Mystery should greatly resolve the rational-irrational tension in the Reformation churches.

8

CHRISTIAN ZIONISM
AND MESSIANIC JUDAISM

One of the most grotesque aspects of the sociology of modern American protestantism is the phenomenon of Christian Zionism. While related to the theology of dispensationalism, Christian Zionism is actually something altogether different theologically. The purpose of this chapter is to explore this movement, and in particular to point out its grievously heretical theoretical basis. To facilitate discussion, we shall interact with the expressed beliefs of a Christian Zionist, Jerry Falwell. We close with a brief note on Messianic Judaism.

Zionism

Zionism is a political movement built on the belief that the Jewish people deserve by right to possess the land of Palestine as their own. During the last part of the 19th and first part of the 20th centuries, Zionism gained support throughout the Christian West. This was due to two factors: the influence that Jewish wealth could purchase among politicians, and the emotional support that the history of Jewish tribulation could elicit from a Christianized public conscience.[1]

With this support, Zionist guerillas succeeded in throwing Palestine into havoc during the late 1940s, and eventually took over that land. The result was the disenfranchisement of the people who had historically dwelt there. The Moslem Palestinians

---

1. On the former aspect, see Ronald Sanders, *The High Walls of Jerusalem: A History of the Balfour Declaration and the Birth of the British Mandate for Palestine* (New York: Holt, Rinehart, & Winston, 1984).

were formally disenfranchised, and the Palestinian Jews were effectively disenfranchised as a result of being swamped by larger numbers of European Jews who immigrated to the new State of Israel.

It is important to realize that the most conservative Jews were anti-Zionists, believing that Palestine was not to become a Jewish land until made so by the coming of the Messiah. (This viewpoint was dramatized in the recent and rewarding film, *The Chosen*.) Much of the most severe criticism of the political Zionist movement has come from anti-Zionist Jews, the most noted being Alfred M. Lilienthal.[2]

Spurious criticisms of Zionism abound on the right. I have no wish to be associated with these, and so at the outset I want to critique them before dealing with the heresy of Christian Zionism. First of all, we hear from some rightist sources that it is a myth that 6,000,000 Jews were slaughtered by the National Socialists. It is argued that there were not that many Jews in Europe, that it would be impossible logistically to do away with that many people given the time and facilities that the Nazis had, and so forth. This may be true; I have absolutely no way of knowing. The argument, however, seems to be that virtually no Jews were slaughtered by Nazis, and this is nonsense. Even if the number is 600,000 rather than six million, the event is still a moral horror of astonishing magnitude. Even if only one man were killed simply because he was a Jew, this would be a moral horror. And there can be no doubt but that many, many Jews were slaughtered.

Of course, a blasphemous theology has been erected upon this in some Jewish circles, which is the notion that the Nazi persecutions fulfill the prophecy of Isaiah 53, and that the Jews suffered for the sins of the world. As Christians we can only abominate such a construction, and we must call it what it is: a Satanic lie. Still, it is not necessary to deny the event itself in order to argue against an evil theological construction put upon the event.

Perhaps more common is the assertion that most modern Jews

---

2. Lilienthal has authored several books on this subject. His magnum opus is *The Zionist Connection* (New York: Dodd, Mead, & Co., 1978).

are not Jews at all: They are Khazars.[3] The Khazari race seems to lie behind the Ashkenazik Jews of Eastern Europe. This kind of assertion can, of course, be debated. The real problem in the discussion is the notion that Jewishness is a blood or racial phenomenon. It is not.

Biblically speaking, a Jew is someone who is covenanted into the people of the Jews by circumcision, for better or for worse. When Abraham was commanded to circumcise, he was told to circumcise his entire household, including his 318 fighting men and his other domestic servants (Gen. 14:14; 17:10-14). Competent scholars imagine that Sheik Abraham's household probably included at the very least 3000 persons. These servants multiplied as the years went by, and Jacob inherited them all (Gen. 27:37). Although only 70 from the loins of Jacob went down into Egypt, so many servants went along that they had to be given the whole land of Goshen in which to live.

All these people were Jews, but only a small fraction actually had any of Abraham's blood in them. Later on we see many other people joining the Jews; indeed, the lists of David's men include many foreigners, of whom Uriah the *Hittite* is but the best known. What this demonstrates is that covenant, not race, has always been the defining mark of a Jew (as it also is of a Christian). Genealogical records were kept for the immediate family, of course, since the Messiah had to be of the actual blood of Abraham, and later of David; but this could not have applied to more than a fraction of the total number of people.

Thus, the Jews are those who claim to be Jews, who are covenanted with the Jews. The Khazari converted to Judaism in the Middle Ages, and they are Jews, British-Israelite rightist nonsense to the contrary.[4] (Of course, modern Zionists do not under-

---

3. On the Khazars, see Arthur Koestler, *The Thirteenth Tribe* (New York: Random House, 1976.)

4. British-Israelitism claims that the Anglo Saxon people are the true Jews, and thus inherit the covenant promises by means of race alone. This weird, stupid idea is promoted by the Armstrong cult, but also crops up in right wing Christian circles. For a fine analysis and refutation of this viewpoint, see Louis F. DeBoer, *The New Phariseeism* (Columbus, NJ: The American Presbyterian Press, 1978).

stand this religious principle any more than do their British-Israelite critics. Both conceive of everything in terms of blood and race.)

So then, it is spurious to criticize Zionism on the grounds that "Jews really didn't suffer during World War II," or "Who knows who the real Jews are?" It is pretty obvious who the Jews are, and they are, as always, a force to be reckoned with.

The third line of criticism against Zionism concerns the rightness or wrongness of its invasion and conquest of Palestine. We can listen to arguments to the effect that the Jews stole the land from its inhabitants, that they have persecuted the Palestinians, that they committed horrors during their guerilla campaign, and the like. Then we can listen to arguments that say that the Jews in Palestine were mistreated under Moslem rule, that the Palestinians are better off today under enlightened Jewish government than they formerly were, that the Jews have exercised dominion over the land and the Moslems did not, thereby forfeiting their right to it, and the like.

Actually, none of this is any of our direct concern as Christians. As Christians we see both Jews and Moslems as groups that have rejected Christ as Messiah, and who have opposed the true faith. If they want to convert, we rejoice. If they want to kill each other off, then that is too bad, but let them have at it—there's nothing we can do about it.

But then, that brings us to the issue: Are Bible-believing Christians supposed to support a Jewish State, for theological reasons? Such is the assertion of Jerry Falwell, and of the heresy of Christian Zionism. Let us turn to this doctrine.

Orthodox Dispensationalism versus Christian Zionism

During the nineteenth century, a peculiar doctrinal notion known as "dispensationalism" arose. Its leading lights were Darby and Scofield; its Bible was the Scofield Reference Bible; and in recent years its primary headquarters has been Dallas Theological Seminary. Technically, dispensationalism teaches that God has two peoples in the history of the world: Israel and the "Church."

We presently live in the "Church Age," and God's people today are Christians, the Church. At the present time, the Jews are apostate enemies of God and of Christ, and are under God's judgment until they repent.

Someday soon (It's always soon!), Christ will return to earth invisibly and snatch away all the Church-Christians (this is called the "Rapture" of the saints). At that point, God will go back to dealing with Israel. There will be a seven-year period called "The Tribulation," and during that period, apostate Jewry will form an anti-God alliance with the Beast, but God will begin to convert the Jews, and in time the Beast will turn and begin to persecute these converted Jews. Just when things look hopeless, Christ will return and inaugurate the Millennium.

One other point to note: There are absolutely no signs that the Rapture of the Church is near. It will come "as a thief in the night."

Now, this entire scheme, though popular in recent years, has no roots in historic Christian interpretation of the Scriptures, and at present it is collapsing under the weight of criticism from Bible-believing scholars of a more historically orthodox persuasion. All the same, there are several things to note.

First, by teaching that there are no signs that precede the Rapture, dispensationalism clearly implies that the modern State of Israel has nothing to do with Bible prophecy. If Israel collapsed tomorrow, it would make no difference. The existence of the State of Israel, while it may encourage dispensationalists to believe that the Rapture is near, is of no theologically prophetic importance.

Second, dispensationalism teaches that Jews of today, and even into the Tribulation period, are apostate, and this certainly implies that they are under the wrath and judgment of God. Christians should minister to them, and try to convert them, and show them all kindness as fellow human beings; but Christians should understand that *during the Church Age, the Jews are not the people of God.* Rather, the Church is the people of God today.

Third, by teaching that Israel is "set aside" during the Church Age, dispensationalism clearly implies that the promises made to Israel are also "set aside" during that period. The land promise, and the promise "those who bless you, I will bless," have been set aside, until we re-enter "prophetic time." Thus, the Jews have no right to the land during the Church Age, and also there is no particular blessing for Gentiles who treat the Jews with especial favor.

Fourth, dispensational theologians are most strict on the point that the Church is a "new people," composed as one body in Christ of both Jew and Gentile. During the Church Age, the distinction between these two is not to be felt in the Church. Thus, dispensational theology is, by implication, opposed to the kind of standpoint articulated in many "Messianic Jewish" groups.

What I am setting forth is standard, consistent dispensationalism. As far as I am concerned, dispensationalism is sorely wrong in its prophetic view, but it is at least orthodox in its view of salvation and blessing. Blessing comes to the Jews when they repent and accept Christ; until then, they are under God's curse. How can it be otherwise? All blessings are in Christ. This is the teaching of orthodox Christianity, and Darby and the early dispensationalists were orthodox Christians on this point, as far as I can tell.

Jerry Falwell and Christian Zionism

My description of dispensationalism may seem rather strange, because this is not the teaching of Hal Lindsey, of the modern Dallas Theological Seminary, or of other modern dispensationalists. I call these people "pop-dispies," for short. In contrast to the dispensational system, these people hold that God *presently* has two peoples on the earth: the Church and Israel. The consistent dispensational system teaches that there are no prophecies whose fulfillment takes place during the Church Age, because the Church exists outside of prophetic time, but modern pop-dispies teach that the reestablishment of the nation of Israel in 1948 was a fulfillment of prophecy.

Consistent dispensationalism teaches that God is dealing with His "heavenly" people today (the Church), and that during the Church Age, God has "set aside" His apostate "earthly" people (Israel). Pop-dispies, on the contrary, hold that *even though apostate,*

Israel still must be regarded as being under God's present blessing. They hold the heretical notion that the Jews do not need to repent in order to obtain the blessings of God's covenant. They hold the un-Biblical notion that apostate Jewry is not today under the wrath of God.

A well-known advocate of this unfortunate position is the Rev. Jerry Falwell. A modern Zionist, Merrill Simon, has recognized this fact, and has written a book, *Jerry Falwell and the Jews.*[5] This book is a series of interviews with Rev. Falwell, designed to present him as a friend of Zionism, and to alleviate suspicions that liberal Zionist Jews naturally have when it comes to a supposedly orthodox, fundamental Christian preacher.

I should like to cite some quotations from this book, and make some appropriate comments. The books says, however, "No part of this book may be reproduced in any manner without prior written consent from the publishers," which rather cramps my style. You'll just have to believe me, as I summarize Falwell's comments. You can always go to your local library and look it up for yourself.

On page 13, Falwell is asked if he considers the destruction of Jerusalem in A.D. 70 as a sign of God's rejection of Israel. Falwell answers by saying that he surely does not believe a "vengeful" God brought the Roman army to Jerusalem to destroy the Jews. Falwell ascribes the event rather to anti-Semitism.

Now let's hear what the Bible says about it. We needn't quote Leviticus 26 and Deuteronomy 28 in their entirety. Read them at your leisure, and ask this question: Do we see an angry, "vengeful" God here threatening to bring horrors upon Israel if they apostatize? Also read Psalm 69:21 and ask Whom this refers to, and then continue reading until the end of the Psalm, remembering that the Romans surrounded Jerusalem at Passover time. Notice Psalm 69:25 speaks of the "desolation" of Jerusalem, and consider that in connection with Jesus' pronouncement of the desolation of Jerusalem in Matthew 23:38. Falwell is completely out of line with Scripture on this point.

On page 25, Falwell says that he believes anti-Semitism is in-

---

5. Middle Village, NY: Jonathon David Publishers, Inc., 1984.

spired exclusively by Satan, as part of his opposition to God. Against this, read Job chapters 1 and 2. Here we find that Satan is never allowed to do anything without God's permission. Moreover, we find from the rest of the Bible that God frequently raises up enemies against His people, as scourges to punish them. Read the Book of Judges. Read Kings and Chronicles about Assyria and Babylon. Read Habakkuk. This is not some minor point tucked away in some obscure passage. Rather, this truth pervades the entire Scriptures.

It is true that anti-Jewish feelings are not part of the Christian message, and that Christians should be as considerate toward Jews as they are toward all other men. It is also true, however, that it is God Who stirs up the Babylonians and Assyrians. Until the Jews repent and convert (as Romans 11 promises that someday they shall), they remain God's enemies, and He does stir up pagans against them. Anti-Jewishness has been part and parcel of secular humanism from the time of Frederick II, through the Renaissance, down to today. The Christian church protected the Jews throughout the Middle Ages, and has continued to do so.[6]

On page 55, Falwell says that Jews and Christian may differ at some points, but they have a common heritage in the Old Testament. Would Falwell be willing to say the same to a Moslem? At any rate, the statement is incorrect. Judaism looks to the Talmud, not to the Bible, as its law. It shows extreme ignorance of Judaism, medieval or modern, to think that Christians can appeal to the Old Testament as common ground. Judaism never approaches the Bible except through the Talmud.

On page 62, Falwell says that the future of the State of Israel is more important than any other political question. He says that the Jews have a theological, historical, and legal right to Palestine. He affirms his personal committment to Zionism, and says that he learned Zionism from the Old Testament.

The Bible teaches us that when Adam and Eve rebelled, they

---

6. On the church's protection of the Jews, see Harold J. Berman (himself a Jew), *Law and Revolution: The Formation of the Western Legal Tradition* (Cambridge: Harvard U. Press, 1983), pp. 90, 222.

lost their right to the Garden, and God cast them out. God used the very same principle with Israel, giving them the land, but warning them over and over again that if they rebelled, they would be cast out. It is beyond me how Falwell can read the Old Testament Scriptures and fail to see this. Modern apostate Jews have absolutely no theological, and therefore no historical and legal right to the land of Palestine.

The church of all ages has always taught that the New Testament equivalent of the "land" is the whole world, in Christ, and ultimately the New Earth. God's people, Christ-confessors, are given the whole earth, in principle, and progressively will take dominion over it in time. Even if dispensationalism were correct in its assertion that someday the land of Palestine will be given back to the Jews, we should still have to say that they must convert to Christ first!

On page 68, Falwell says that one thing in modern Israel disturbs him. It is that Christians do not have the liberty to evangelize for the gospel. In other words, *Falwell is aware that Christians are being persecuted in Israel today, but he still supports Israel!* If this is not a betrayal of the faith, what is?

Finally, on p. 145, Falwell is asked about abortion, since modern Jews advocate abortion. Simon asks him whether or not the death penalty should be used against a woman who has an abortion, and her physician. Falwell replies that he has never thought about this before, and that he thinks any action against the woman would be wrong.

Well, there we see it. Mr. Simon knows what the issues really are, but Rev. Falwell is so confused, befuddled, and blind that he cannot see them. Obviously, if abortion is murder, then we have to advocate the death penalty for it! Of course, Falwell here sounds just like most of the rest of the modern anti-abortion movement: They've never even thought about some of the most basic, elementary issues involved. "Abortion is murder," they cry. "Reinstitute the death penalty for murder," says the Moral Majority (Falwell's political group). Anybody with an IQ over 25 can figure out the implications of these two statements, but apparently Falwell has never thought of this before. We live in sorry times, when such a novice is the spokesman for the New Christian Right!

Christian Zionism is blasphemy. It is a heresy. Christians have no theological stake whatsoever in the modern State of Israel. It is an anti-God, anti-Christ nation. Until it repents and says "blessed is He Who comes in the Name of the Lord," it will continue to be under the wrath of God. The modern State of Israel permits the persecution of Christians and Christian missionaries. We must pray that God will change the hearts of Jews, as of all other pagans, to receive Christ. But to support the enemies of the Gospel is not the mark of a Gospel minister, but of an anti-Christ.

I've been pretty hard on Jerry. Somebody needs to be. This kind of thing is inexcusable, and needs to be repented of. A couple of years ago I wrote an essay defending Falwell against a somewhat liberal critic.[7] What I have said here does not change what I wrote then, because Falwell's critic was wrong; but I have certainly come to take a dimmer view of Mr. Falwell since. His trumpet is giving forth an uncertain sound. He needs to clean it out.

Messianic Judaism

In recent years, a large number of Jewish young people have turned to Jesus Christ as their Lord and Savior. Many of these young people have formed "Messianic Synagogues," and have articulated here and there various theologies of "Messianic Judaism." For many, Messianic Judaism is simply a way of keeping some Jewish cultural traditions while becoming Christian, and there is nothing wrong with this. It is proper for Christians of various tribes and tongues to give expression to the faith in a variety of cultural forms.

Unfortunately, for some, Messianic Judaism is seen as an alternative to historic Christianity. This is due to the influence of pop-dispyism. After all, if the Millennium is right around the corner, and Jewish culture will be imperialistically triumphant dur-

---

7. See my essay, "The Moral Majority: An Anabaptist Critique?", in James B. Jordan, ed. *The Failure of the American Baptist Culture*. Christianity and Civilization No. 1 (Tyler, TX: Geneva Ministries, 1982).

ing the Millennium, then even today Jewish practices anticipate that superiority. In fact, some Messianic Jews apparently believe that they can claim unlimited financial support from Gentile Christians, because of this preeminence.[8]

Most of what I have written regarding Christian Zionism above applies to this group of Messianic Jews. I should like, however, to call attention to another facet of the matter. These Messianic Jews believe wrongly that Gentile Christianity (the historic church) departed from Biblical forms in the early days of the church. They see as their mission a restoration of these customs, which they believe they have preserved.

In fact, this is completely false. Anyone who has seen a presentation of "Christ in the Passover" is amazed at the number of non-Biblical rites that are discussed and exhibited (the use of eggs, bread broken in three pieces and hidden in cloth, etc.). These customs arose after the birth of the church, and do not preserve Old Testament ritual at all. Moreover, to try to place a Christian interpretation on the various features of these rituals is most misguided and artificial. Clever as such presentations are, they are grossly misleading.

As a matter of fact, the leading features of Temple and Synagogue worship were brought straight into the church, as she spoiled the new enemies of God: apostate Jewry. The period of this spoiling was A.D. 30 to A.D. 70. Once the church had completed her integration of the spoils of the Old Covenant into her new, transfigured body, God destroyed the remnants of the Old Covenant completely. Modern Jewish rituals and music owe far more to racial/cultural inheritance from the peoples of Eastern Europe than they do to the Old Covenant.[9]

---

8. See Gary North, "Some Problems with 'Messianic Judaism,'" in *Biblical Economics Today* 7:3 (Apr./May, 1984).

9. Louis Bouyer has shown at considerable length that the eucharistic prayer of the early church was a modification of the prayers of the synagogue and Temple. See Bouyer, *Eucharist* (Notre Dame: U. of Notre Dame Press, 1968). Similarly, Eric Werner has shown that the plainchant of the Christian church preserves the style of music known among the Jews of the Old Testament period. See Werner, *The Sacred Bridge* (Columbia U. Press, 1959; the paperback by Schocken only reproduces the first half of this important study).

Thus, while there is nothing wrong with converted Jews maintaining a cultural continuity with their past, there are no grounds for the assumption that post-Christian Jewry has preserved the musical and liturgical forms of the Bible. Those forms were preserved in the church, and in her alone. Jews who wish to recover their heritage would do well to study the early Church, not the traditions of Eastern European cultures.

9

SHOULD CHURCHES INCORPORATE?

In our day, the state increasingly demands that the church come before it and request "incorporation." Well meaning Christian leaders have, from time to time, advocated that the churches go along with this. I believe, on the contrary, that the church should resist this trend as much as possible, and should refuse "incorporation."

The Christian doctrine of "incorporation" is sacramental. It is the sacramental body of Jesus Christ that creates the oneness of the church on earth, and that makes her one "body," one "corpus," incorporated into Christ and into one another. Thus the sacramental body of the church has a life of its own, and continues down through generations. The church as a sacramental corporation has given a perspective of continuity to men, and thus men have analogously set up other corporations that provide continuity for their works.

Non-Christian Forms of Incorporation

Pagans also have notions of incorporation that provide continuity over generations. In paganism, the primary form of incorporation is either familistic or statist. Pagan familism sees the patriarch as head of a clan consisting of all the sons (and maybe daughters also) and their wives and children. Thus the family is granted continuity over the generations, and the family (or clan) becomes a visible power on the earth in this sense.

Such a philosophy flies directly in the face of the command of Genesis 2:24, "For this cause a man shall *leave his father and mother*

187

and cleave to his wife." The Christian position is that each new marriage starts a new family, separate from the old one. When we read the book of Genesis, we find this command carried out literally, for Isaac did not live near Abraham, nor did Jacob live near Isaac (though they visited one another from time to time). Patriarchal familism is one of the pagan forms of incorporation, for it makes the family the primary place of incorporated continuity and power. It is true that the family has a corporate aspect, an aspect of succession, but in Christianity that aspect of the family is greatly diminished when compared to patriarchal familism. The older "corpus" or body is cut off when the son or daughter leaves and cleaves. The family, thus, is incorporated for only one generation.

This is the more the case because, theologically, the line of generations from Adam was corrupted by the fall. Thus, that old line is cut off. The genealogies of Scripture lead to the Second Adam, but not beyond. All those genealogies were completely destroyed by God when He visited His wrath upon Jerusalem in A.D. 70. The family of Adam has been replaced by the family of the Second Adam, and the line of generations is no longer through the blood of Adam via procreation, but through the blood of Jesus via sacrament. The family as an institution is, of course *reestablished* through grace, but the primary family is no longer the natural one, but the Spiritual one, which is the church.

The second form of pagan incorporation, most common today, is statism. For Aristotle, as for virtually all sophisticated pagan thinkers, man is a "political animal." Man's ultimate reference point is the *polis* or state-community. We live with this today. "Incorporation" today is something granted by the state. That is the common meaning of the term, and of the concept embraced by the term. Since this is that case, churches ought not to "incorporate," since to do so is to sue for a license from the state.

The church is already a true corporation. She is so by virtue of the sacramental presence of Christ's body in her midst and at her heart. She does not need to "obtain incorporation" from any earthly power.

The Corporate Church

The church is a unique institution on the earth. There is nothing like it in paganism. Religious ritual in paganism is either a form of ancestor worship (familism) or state worship (statism) or both (usually). In paganism, there is no concept of an institution that makes visible in concentrated form the presence of God upon the earth, and the presence of men in heaven before His throne.

In the Christian faith, the church is not only one institution among several (state, family, business), she is also the primary institution among all of them, in one sense. This is because the life of the church encapsulates all the rest of life. She is the nursery of the Kingdom. Her courts are the foundation of all other courts. Her laws are the foundation of all other laws. Her discipline of excommunication is the most terrible of all punishments, of which execution by the state (frightening as it is) is but a shadow by comparison. Her ritual sets the tone for all of life.

Briefly, to make the point clear, let us look at this last point about ritual. The central ritual of the church is the action of Holy Communion. Jesus *took* bread, *gave thanks*, *broke* it, *distributed* it, and they all *tasted* (evaluated) it, and *ate* it. This six-fold action (taking, thanking, restructuring, sharing, evaluating, enjoying) is the key to the Christian life in every area. An artist takes raw material, thanks God for it, creates his art and distributes it (playing a concert, exhibiting a painting), and evaluates and enjoys it in fellowship with others. A businessman takes raw material, thanks God for it, works with it and shares it by means of the free market (exchanges it for a share of someone else's goods), and then evaluates and enjoys it in fellowship with others. This is the Christian life, and it finds it most concentrated expression in the liturgy of the sacrament.[1]

Once upon a time, it was understood that the sacramental body of the church was the primary form of "incorporation" on the

---

1. I have written on this at some length in my essay, "Christian Piety: Deformed and Reformed," *The Geneva Papers* (New Series), No. 1 (1985); available from Geneva Ministries, Box 131300, Tyler, TX 75713.

earth, and that all other corporations were secondary in comparison to the church. The church performed marriages, maintained marriage certificates and birth records, granted divorces, etc., thus showing that the corporation of the family is an extension of the life of Christ and the Blessed Trinity in the world. The church ordained kings, showing that the corporation of the state is an extension of the work of Christ in the world (*i.e.,* His work of vengeance and wrath).

If that is what some well meaning Christian leaders mean by incorporation, I am with them. Let the state come to the church and request incorporation! Sadly, of course, that is not what is in view.

Mere Notification or Something More?

It has been argued that formerly "the incorporation of a church or Christian agency of any kind was simply a legal formality notifying the state of the existence of such a body and its immunity from statist controls." I seriously question if this was ever the case. Granted that such a legal notification is desirable, I do not think that incorporation has ever been the means for it. In the state of Virginia even to this day churches are not permitted to seek incorporation at the bequest of the state. Rather, churches who wish to can simply create a trust document and deposit a copy of it in the records of the county or state. This is notification enough. The state is obliged to file all such records submitted to it, but such a procedure does not entail any request for permission.

Some have argued that "the matter can be compared to filing a birth certificate." That is true of a trust document, but not of incorporation papers. There can be no question of the fact that at the present time a grant of incorporation by the state is a grant of privilege, and makes the church beholden to the state.

Even simply filing a trust document can be dangerous. After all, who will adjudicate the trust? Moreover, if we say (rightly) that God the Holy Spirit is the Author/Originator of the trust (the church), that God the Father is the Beneficiary of the trust (1 Cor. 15:28), and that God the Son, in the persons of His representatives (elders), is the Administrator of the trust—well, will the modern, pagan state accept such a trust as valid? I doubt it.

If the church is truly *sui generis* (that is, of her own kind, unique, having no foundation in any other human institution), then the church is under no *obligation* to make any notification to the state at all. Westminster Presbyterian Church of Tyler, Texas, of which I am a member, is neither incorporated nor set up as a trust, yet it holds property, does business, etc. Under common law the church is recognized not as a corporation, nor as a trust, but as the church, a unique institution on the earth.

As a courtesy, a church may notify the state that it has been formed. This would be particularly true in a Christian land. Today, when the state stands as an enemy against the church (at least at the point of jurisdiction), there is no need to invite trouble by having any more to do with the state than we absolutely have to. But, if we are going to do anything, a trust rather than incorporation is the way to go.

The jurisdictional aspect of the church was lost in Protestant lands centuries ago. Church buildings are no longer physical sanctuaries. Once upon a time, the Emperor Justinian did not dare send his soldiers into the Church of St. Lawrence to remove condemned criminals who had been given sanctuary; but today the sheriff of Cass County, Nebraska, does not hesitate to bring his storm troopers into the midst of a religious meeting and forcibly haul out scores of ordained clergymen. We've come a long way, and today the state is engaged in little more than a mopping up exercise when it comes to taking over the church. Relatively speaking, the battle was lost long ago. In our society, the church is nothing more than a religious club. It exercises no dominical power for good in society.

Is the Church Vulnerable?

Why incorporate then? What conceivable benefit accrues to the church, which is already incorporated in Christ, if she goes and obtains a second incorporation from the state? One writer has stated, "Given the vulnerability of the church as an incorporated legal entity to statist controls, we should not forget the total vulnerability with disincorporation. In some court cases, the results are proving to be especially disastrous." Frankly, I cannot imagine what this means. It seems clear to me that an unlicensed church, which has not sought or been granted incorporation by the state, is in a much better position than a church that has applied to the state for some benefit, real or imagined. We may ask what any Christian church is doing in a state court anyway? Does the state now judge the church?

It seems to me that we need to fight this battle at a much deeper level. No church should heed a summons to appear before the court of the state. Church officers may and should appear as a courtesy, by "special appearance," but not as if the church herself is on trial. If the church and her officers are put on trial (by the sheer brute force of the state), the church has already lost the primary battle, the battle of jurisdiction. The church, her laws, her ordinances, her decrees, her property, etc., are simply not under the inspection of the state. We must not grant any such claim.

To be sure, when they have a gun to your head, you give them your wallet. If the state refuses to honor the principle of jurisdiction and threatens to close down a given local church, she may choose to pay a bribe to state officials (for instance, property taxes, as discussed later in this essay). We know that eventually the church will emerge victorious, as she always has. Two thousand years from now, when the United States of America has but a paragraph in world history books, the church of Jesus Christ will still have true incorporation in Christ, and will still have her own courts, laws, and property. We can afford to be "wise as a serpent, and harmless as a dove," for we know in Whose hands the victory already lies.

This has been the tactic of the Roman Catholic Church for centuries. She maintains lawyers and gives outward compliance to all laws, pretending deceptively to be under the rule of the state. The Roman Catholic Church expects to be around when the modern state has faded from the collective memory of mankind. The Roman Catholic Church is patient. We as Protestants (Reformed Catholics) may well take our cue from this.

At the same time, if a church finds herself paying a property tax, or a social security tax, or in court before a secular judge, this is not because the church recognizes the legal jurisdiction of the state over the church. It is not because the church has obtained incorporation from the state. It is only because the church recognizes that God has given temporary raw power into the hands of Babylonians, to chastise His true Israel, for a season, and we recognize that we must submit to His smarting rod, even as our Lord did.

Even so, when we stand before Caesar's governors, we must say, as He did, "The Kingdom of the church is not of this world. You do not have authority over it. You have power only because it has been granted you from On High, and we submit to your power, but not to your authority. As citizens and individuals, we are under your government, but as the church of Jesus Christ, we are under His government alone."[2]

Is the church totally vulnerable if she disincorporates? Hardly. As a minor point, we can note that the immunities of the church are recognized in common law. While in a general sense the church lost the battle for jurisdiction long ago, yet in specific cases she may still win. Moreover, maintaining the rights of Christ's Kingdom before the magistrates of this age is a time-honored form of evangelism. Also, few states are as vindictive as Nebraska, and few local judges have the guts to behave as Judge Ronald Reagan (Yes, that's his name!) in Nebraska has, putting pastors into jail for months on end, denying them paper to write on, etc. It is possible to win local battles, in other words. But this is not the major point.

The Awesome Power of the Church

The major point was made by Jesus when He said, "Be not afraid of them that kill the body, and after that have no more that they can do. But I will forewarn you Whom ye shall fear: Fear

---

2. I have dealt at some length with the differences between submission to legal authority and submission to raw power in my essay, "Rebellion, Tyranny, and Dominion in the Book of Genesis," in Gary North, ed., *Tactics of Christian Resistance.* Christianity & Civilization No. 3 (Tyler, TX: Geneva Ministries, 1983). This essay also deals at length with the question of deceiving tyrants.

Him which after He hath killed has power to cast into hell; yea, I say unto you, Fear Him" (Luke 12:4-5). What is the ultimate power of the state? It is the power to kill. What is the ultimate power committed to the church? It is the tremendous power to excommunicate, and to place a curse upon the wicked, as discussed below in Chapter 13.

Are we vulnerable, then? Does the modern pagan state want to pit its pitiful "incorporation" against the omnipotent incorporation of the church into the very body of Christ, the King of kings and Lord of lords? Let us see who wins such a contest!

From what I can see, however, such a contest is usually unnecessary. No state requires churches to incorporate, and all states (except Louisiana, I understand, which is under the Code of Napoleon on this point) continue to grant implicit recognition to the church as a *sui generis* institution. We need not give this privilege away.

The fact that I disagree with some fine Christian leaders on this one point should not be blown out of proportion. If incorporation were only what they say it should be (a mere notification to the state, out of politeness), I should agree with them. From what I can tell, however, that is not what incorporation means in our society, and I think that it is best for churches to stay out of the way of the state as much as possible; and certainly I think it best for them not to incorporate.

Do we go to the stake for this? No. If officers of the state are really going to close down the church, or if non-compliance with pressures to incorporate is going to result in a severe crippling of the church's ministry, then clearly it is better to go ahead and go along with their nonsense. The church will outlast them. We draw the line at the point of the central matters, such as preaching and the sacraments. To return to a paradigm we used earlier in this book, we should fight to protect the shell, but only die to protect the very heart of the church.

Property Taxes

With this in mind, a given local church may decide to go ahead and, for instance, pay property taxes. This is indeed what we had to decide to do, in Tyler, Texas. A change in law enabled the state to require property taxes of the churches. We could have applied for an exemption, but to do so meant filling out a long form, telling the state all about our various ministries. This we were unwilling to do. We contested the matter for well over a year, but without success. We could have fought the measure further, but we almost certainly would have lost, costing us much time and money that we thought, before God, had better go for more productive things. We therefore adopted a time honored compromise measure, which has been used before in the history of the church.

In France, the clergy used to vote a "free gift" to the king, which they were bound by force and custom to do. They refused to call it a "tax," since the church is not subject to taxation from earthly kings. The state thought they were taxing the church, but the church knew that they were merely giving a free bribe.[3] With this in mind, the church of which I am a member decided to enter the following official statement into her minutes:

Official Statement of Westminster Presbyterian Church

Whereas, certain civil taxing authorities have notified Westminster Presbyterian Church that the church owes the payment of certain monies which they term "property taxes," "penalty & interest," and "collection penalty"; and,

Whereas, the church cannot be faithful to the Lord Jesus Christ and willingly pay tithe money in taxes to Caesar; and,

Whereas, the State of Texas presently claims the coercive power to lay property taxes on the property owned by the church of Jesus Christ; and,

Whereas, Westminster Presbyterian Church has not been given the resources to mount an assault on this practice of taxation (Luke 14:28-32); and,

Whereas, the sons of the Kingdom are exempt from earthly taxation, so that Jesus Christ Himself was willing to contribute [give] money rather than give offense, thereby establishing a

---

3. My source for this point is a brief reference in Henri de Lubac, *The Mystery of the Supernatural* (English edition; New York: Herder & Herder, 1967), p. 97.

principle that we may give equal money as a contribution [gift] without recognizing the legitimacy of taxing authority; and,

Whereas, the church administers the tithe as the earthly representatives of Jesus Christ, and He was willing to make this contribution [gift], thus setting a pattern for His church;

Therefore, Westminster Presbyterian Church resolves the following:

1. To send to these taxing authorities money equal to what they have demanded.

2. To send with this money a letter explaining our position, that our beliefs will not permit us to recognize them as a taxing authority over the church, but that we are willing to make a voluntary contribution in the amount they have stated we owe, so as not to give offense; and we ask them to receive this in good faith.

The letter we regularly send along with these "contributions" reads as follows:

Letter to: [Appropriate Taxing Authority]
To Whom It May Concern:

Enclosed is a check in the amount of $xxx. Please regard this as a contribution from Westminster Presbyterian Church to cover the payments you require as noted on the forms enclosed.

It is the position of Westminster Presbyterian Church that Jesus Christ alone is Lord of the church, and that He has sole jurisdiction over the tithes and property held in trust for Him by the officers of His church. We believe that the church as a Spiritual institution governed by Christ is not subject to the jurisdiction of any earthly power, and thus not subject to any secular taxing authority. It is also our position, however, that God would not have us to give offense, but to give over such money as is required, so as to live at peace with all men.

Therefore, in making this contribution, Westminster Presbyterian Church is not recognizing in principle the right of any civil authority to tax the church or her property. Rather, we are freely making a contribution to the civil taxing authorities. We ask that you receive this contribution in good faith, and that you keep this letter on file as a statement of our position.

I am happy to report that the taxing authorities have accepted this subterfuge, at least thus far. This is an unhappy thing to have to do, of course. The point is that we should resist the encroachments of the state as much as possible, but it is not wrong outwardly to capitulate rather than have one's ministry destroyed.

Of course, there are places where we would have to fight. If the state ordered the church to serve the sacraments to a heathen, or to an excommunicated person, we could not do so. If the state ordered us to stop preaching, we could not do so. If the state subpoenaed the minutes and financial records of the church, it would be a good idea to "lose" them accidentally, or have someone "break in and steal" them, rather than permit the state to inspect the inner workings of the church.

Won't Compromise Hurt our Witness?

I don't think so. Rather, judicious compromise is *part* of our witness. It was Jesus Who told us not to try to sack a city if we lack the troops. Suppose they called me, as a church elder, into court and said, "Because you paid over this tax money, you granted us jurisdiction, so we now demand to see your books"? How would I reply? I would just say, "No, we never granted you any jurisdiction. We just paid you a bribe, because you extorted it from us."

Suppose they said, "Because you compromised, we judge that you are not really serious Christians"? I would reply, "It is not your place to judge. You have nothing to say about it."

The state can think what it wants about our actions. The fact is that the modern secular state is dying, and will soon be gone. What matters is what God thinks of us.

Part III

RETHINKING WORSHIP: SOME OBSERVATIONS

A tremendous liturgical awakening has begun in the 1980s among the evangelical and Reformed churches. Publishers have found a ready market for such books as *O Come, Let Us Worship* by Robert G. Rayburn of Covenant Theological Seminary,[1] and two studies by Robert G. Webber of Wheaton College.[2] I find myself in complete sympathy with this movement toward the restoration of formal public worship, as should be obvious from my remarks in chapter 1 of this book. Evangelical Christians are the true heirs of the catholic heritage, and should begin taking full advantage of it.

There have been three liturgical movements in the Western church. The first was the Reformation. At the time of the Reformation, the primitive rites of the church had become almost totally obscured with overlays of devotional piety that were too often superstitious. Moreover, there was absolutely no congregational participation in worship. The service was said silently or mumbled under the breath by the priest.[3] What was said was in Latin, and was thus incomprehensible. There was no proclamation of the Word in the liturgy. The people seldom if ever communicated, and then children were excluded, and all the people

---

1. (Grand Rapids: Baker, 1980).
2. *Worship: Old and New* (Grand Rapids: Zondervan, 1982); and *Worship is a Verb* (Waco, TX: Word, 1985).
3. On the rule that the service be said in silence, see Louis Bouyer, *Eucharist* (Notre Dame: Notre Dame University Press, 1968), pp. 371ff.

were excluded from the cup. Psalmody had disappeared.[4]

The Reformers did the best they could to restore the original catholic rites, though they did not possess the scholarly tools we have today, and thus did not always make the best decisions.[5] They reintroduced psalmody. They wrote prayerbooks in the vernacular so the people could participate. They restored the cup to the laity, though unfortunately they did not restore communion to children. The overwhelming power of Medieval tradition, however, worked against them, and in a short time the churches of the Reformation were back to annual or at best quarterly communion, and congregation participation rapidly shrank to a minimum.

The second liturgical movement took place in the 19th century. As Shands has written, "it must be understood against the background of interest in both medieval and classical civilization which that century produced. We must see it as a part of the medievalism that produced Sir Walter Scott's novels and the revival of Gothic architecture." Shands goes on to say that "the concern was much more romantic than based on the needs of men." This movement, he writes, "was characterized by its historicism, its churchiness, its romanticism, its lack of touch with society, and its passionate desire to revive the fullness of the Christian tradition."[6] This neo-medieval movement gave rise to "high church Anglicanism," in which the congregation remained basically a spectator, though there was a more beautiful spectacle to watch and hear!

The third liturgical movement began within the Roman Catholic Church. It can be dated from a "speech which the great Dom Lambert Beauduin made in Malines in 1909 in which he proposed

---

4. For a Roman Catholic admission of the gravity of the situation, and a generally positive discussion of the efforts of the Reformers, see Bouyer, *ibid.*, pp. 381ff.

5. Bouyer, *ibid.*, is overly severe on the Reformers for this. He does not sufficiently appreciate the liturgical magnitude of taking the liturgy from Latin into the vernacular. Moreover, Bouyer finds the theologies of the Reformers to be more eucharistic (thanksgiving-oriented) than the rites they composed, but his criticisms of these liturgies fail to take into account that the theology of the Reformers was *preached* to the people as *part of* the worship service.

6. Alfred R. Shands, *The Liturgical Movement and the Local Church* (London: SCM Press, 1959), p.21f.

what was to become the basis of the Belgian liturgical revival. The proposals stated that the liturgy is not something which we are meant to see and hear alone, but rather is something in which we all take part, bringing to God 'the whole individual man in the whole Christian community.' "[7] Though beginning within the Roman church, the 20th century liturgical movement early attracted protestants to its ranks, because it was seen that what was being advocated was thoroughly protestant in character. For the Bible believing evangelical, there is a gold mine of information in the writings of the liturgical movement, and in that it represents a "back to the Fathers, back to the Bible" trend in the Roman church, this movement is one of the most hopeful signs of reawakening within that communion.[8] In his helpful book, Shands summarizes the viewpoint of the liturgical movement as follows: "The basic idea in liturgy is action, and a very practical action at that. Further, it is an action for the sake of others or another. This key thought behind liturgy was, it seems, precisely the notion which the early Church held about worship. The characteristic word they used was, of course, 'eucharist' or 'thanksgiving'—the action of *giving* thanks. Obedience to the commandment, 'Do this in remembrance of me,' meant for the early Church both an interior and an exterior action of taking, blessing, breaking, and distributing the Bread which was Christ.[9] The interior action was the self-offering of each member through the action of Christ.

"Liturgy is the most expressive word of the worship of Christians because it is centred in the union between Christ and ourselves—the Body. It expresses the fact that we can give no acceptable worship to God apart from Christ. We are able to worship only inasmuch as He is worshipping the Father in us. In spite of our own personal inadequacy to worship the Father, we must of

---

7. *Ibid.*, p. 22. Detailed discussions of the history of this movement are found in Louis Bouyer, *Liturgical Piety* (Notre Dame, Indiana: Notre Dame University Press, 1955); and in Bouyer, *Rite and Man* (Notre Dame: Notre Dame University Press, 1963).

8. Generally speaking, the writings of Louis Bouyer, mentioned above, are the best place to start in coming to grips with this Roman awakening.

9. To which I would add "appreciation, and resting"; see my discussion in chapter one, pp. 35-36.

course offer our own worship, yet it is Christ who makes it adequate. Secondly, liturgy expresses the fact that Christian worship is communal worship with other members of the Body. There is a sense in which worship of the Father through the Son is incomplete unless *all* the members of the Body are participating: In the early Church, the Sacrament was taken to all those who for some reason were unable to be present at the Eucharist. Though there is much scope for individual prayer, there is no room for individualism in this norm of Christian worship. It stresses the organic union of all the members too clearly."[10]

The fruits of the liturgical movement are finding their way into American evangelical and Reformed circles, and that is as it should be. At the same time, from my point of view as a presuppositionalist, not every aspect of liturgical renewal is above criticism. One fears, for instance, that the stoic barrenness of American evangelical worship is simply driving some young people into an uncritical, emotional adoption of liturgical forms for their own sake, rather along the lines of the romantic Oxford Movement of the 19th century. For these people, we have moved from seeking emotional fulfillment in "relevant, modern, contemporary" formulas to seeking emotional fulfillment in nostalgia and tradition. To this extent, the liturgical movement in evangelicalism is but a part of the overall conservative trend in our society.

This is a trend to be welcomed, of course. The Bible teaches us to respect age, and it is high time that the stupid perversity of American California-youth culture came to an end. (I wait earnestly for evangelical radio stations to outgrow the gooey youth pop trash they presently pollute the air with, and begin to play the great Christian music of the past.) Still, simply forsaking be-bop share-group worship in favor of an awareness of the solemnity of majesty is in and of itself a vain action, if the motivation for it is simply emotional fulfillment. Rather, we need a Biblical and theological grounding for worship.

Because of our democratic background, we Americans do not have a good feel for when to be formal and when to be informal.

---

10. Shands, p. 19f.

Americans tend to try to make everything informal, and then find formality awkward. In fact, God is both Abba, Father, and also the God of Hosts, the King of Kings. There are times to approach Him informally, as a child crawls into its father's lap; and there are times to approach Him formally, making a public presentation before the King. A healthy church life requires a balance of both approaches. Americans have no trouble calling each other by their first names; rather, we have trouble being formal. Other cultures have the opposite problem.

A second general difficulty I find in some of the new evangelical appreciation of formal worship is the theological error of incarnationalism. It is assumed that the physical incarnation of Jesus Christ is what validates the physical, earthly creation and its consequent use in worship. This puts the cart before the horse. It is the goodness of God's original creation that made possible the incarnation. The same kind of error crops up more perniciously when certain evangelicals speak of salvation. They write as if it is our incorporation into Christ's incarnation that saves us, and that the church is a continuation of that incarnation. This is fundamentally wrong. Our salvation comes in the death and resurrection (transfiguration) of Christ. His incarnation was merely the necessary prelude to His work. It is not the incarnation but the resurrection that transforms men and the creation.

Incarnationalist language seems the rage in some quarters of evangelicalism today, but it is very dangerous. Writing on the festival of the nativity from within the Roman Catholic liturgical movement, Father Louis Bouyer warns against identifying our new birth with Christ's incarnation: "Nothing could be more foreign to the whole teaching of St. Paul and St. John than such an idea of participation in Christ's birth. It is *on the Cross*, in the Blood and water flowing from His side, that the Church is *born* of Christ . . . as Eve was born of Adam. This is the teaching of St. Augustine and of all the Fathers. . . . To the mind of the Fathers, the Incarnation can only be called redemptive in one very definite sense: in the sense that it was an incarnation in a flesh which must undergo death, so that the death of Adam should die in the death of Christ."[11]

---

11. Bouyer, *Liturgical Piety*, p. 201f. All italics his.

Similarly, Presbyterian Geddes MacGregor warns: "It is easy to see that the slightest tendency towards Monophysitism in christology makes it exceedingly dangerous to develop an ecclesiological theory that would make the Church in any way a 'new Incarnation' or an 'extension of the Incarnation.' Such a christology suggests to anyone engaged in such ecclesiological speculation that God and humanity are somehow mysteriously fused together in the Church; even, indeed, that the mystery of the Church consists in their fusion." MacGregor goes on to say that "the Church is not only not to be identified with the divine nature of Christ; it is not even to be wholly identified with His human nature. Christ, in His human frailty, stumbled under the weight of the Cross He carried to Calvary; yet His stumbling was sinless. The Church, in its human frailty, stumbles sinfully, the redemptive process notwithstanding."[12]

It is thus confusing to read such statements as this: "The doctrine of the Incarnation is the focal point for a theology of form. In the Incarnation the eternal Word was enfleshed in a human person. . . . God used creation (the body of His Son) as the instrument of salvation. Consequently, the physical creation (including the body as well) has a place in worship."[13] Rather, we should say that the creation has a place in worship because it is created good, and for that purpose. Moreover, it is not the Incarnation as such, but the resurrection of Jesus in a transfigured body, and His ascension into the sanctuary of heaven, that makes it appropriate to bring the creation before the throne of God once again.

At its best, incarnationalist language is confusing. At its worst it moves in a direction of seeing salvation as incorporation into Christ's sinless Adamic body, making the cross theologically unnecessary. We must ever affirm clearly, however, that it is only in-

---

12. Geddes MacGregor, *Corpus Christi: The Nature of the Church According to the Reformed Tradition* (Philadelphia: Westminster Press, 1958), pp. 150, 152.

13. Webber, *Worship Old and New*, p. 112. I can endorse virtually everything in Robert Webber's two books on worship except for this strand in his presentation, and he is not unique in this misplaced emphasis on the incarnation. I should note that Webber also grounds the use of the creation in worship upon the surer bases of creation and revelation.

corporation into His transfigured body, on the other side of His death as payment for our sins, that is our restoration. The emphasis must be on resurrection from the dead, not on incarnation as such.

A third general difficulty with the current liturgical movement is that there is sometimes not enough respect paid to the regulative principle of worship. We are to worship God only in the ways He has "commanded" us. As evangelicals come to appreciate their catholic heritage, they need to assess that heritage from the standpoint of the Bible. The Bible has things to say on such subjects as the placement of visual images in the environment of worship, the use of vestments, the use of incense, the value of an ecclesiastical calendar, preferable forms of architecture, the use of musical instruments, and so forth. The essays in this section are devoted to exegetical investigations of some of these matters.

10

HOW BIBLICAL IS PROTESTANT WORSHIP?

The goal of the Protestant Reformation was, in part, the purification of worship from pagan accretions. Principally, the Reformers believed, rightly, that the worship of saints, relics, and Blessed Mary Ever Virgin was superstitious. They also noted that the performance of worship (the mass) in Latin excluded congregational participation. Thus, their twin goals were to restore congregational participation, and to reform worship according to the standards of the Bible.

Inevitably, however, this reforming movement was corrupted by reaction. Anything that "smacked of Rome" was to be rejected. In part, this reaction was justified. To use an analogy: We know that there is no sin in the moderate use of alcohol. If a man is a drunkard, however, it may be necessary for him to fast from alcohol altogether (except in Holy Communion) for a period, until he acquires the maturity to handle it correctly. The danger is that he will develop a false understanding of why he is avoiding alcohol. Instead of seeing it as a temporary fast, he may come to see it as something evil in itself. This is, in fact, a common viewpoint in American fundamentalism: Alcohol is regarded as evil in itself. This perspective is fundamentally demonic and manichaean, ascribing evil to God's good creation (1 Tim. 4:1-5).

Similar errors cropped up in Protestantism. If Roman Catholics kneel for prayer, Protestants will refuse to do so. If Roman Catholics celebrate the grace of God manifested in His gifts to the church (saints and martyrs), Protestants will refuse to do so. If Roman Catholicism has a perverted theology of Mary, Protestants will take no notice at all of her. If Roman Catholics chant the psalms in precise translations, Protestants will either versify the psalms (losing much in the process), or stop singing psalms altogether.[1] If Roman Catholics keep Christ nailed to the cross, Protestants will war against the cross as a symbol altogether. If Roman Catholics have processions and street dancing, Protestants will reject all bodily expression in worship. If Roman Catholics ritually sanctify wedding rings during the "sacrament of matrimony," then Protestants (the Puritans and Anabaptists at least) will say it is sinful to wear a wedding band at all. And so it goes.

This is not Biblical fasting from an abuse. It is a perversion. Instead of getting their theology and practice from Scripture, Protestants have too often gotten them from reacting against Rome. As a result, many of the things that the Bible teaches about true worship have been lost in many Protestant churches.

The Regulative Principle

The Reformers taught that "nothing should be introduced or performed in the churches of Christ for which no probable reason can be given from the Word of God."[2] The general rule on this is that we must have Biblical warrant for what we do in special worship — warrant consisting of principle, precept, or example. Rather rapidly, however, this sound and salutary principle was reduced to the slogan "whatever is not commanded is forbidden," a simplistic formula that is a long way from the principles of the protestant Reformers. There is a lot of difference between Bucer's "probable reason" and "commanded."

This simplistic version of the regulative principle is hard to apply. First of all, no one is able to apply it without modifying it, because we find no Biblical *command* for church buildings, pews, etc. Second, in its simplistic form the principle is almost always

---

1. Of course, singing versified psalms in the vernacular is a vast improvement over listening to them sung in incomprehensible Latin.

2. Martin Bucer, *Censura*, trans. by E. C. Whitaker in *Martin Bucer and the Book of Common Prayer*. Alcuin Club Collections No. 55 (London: SPCK, 1974), p. 42f.

applied dispensationally, as if only the New Testament were allowed to teach us about worship. Another problem, which is obvious when one reads the literature coming out of such circles, is that the principle often leads straight to a form of legalism. Instead of finding the large, overarching principles of worship in Scripture and noting particulars in that context (as the Reformers did), we are enjoined to find explicit detail statements to back up every little thing.

The "Puritan" approaches the Bible with preconceived ideas of what constitutes evidence and what constitutes proof. He does not get his hermeneutics from the Bible, but from modern rationalism. If the Bible indicates something "indirectly," or by way of example, this is not as good as if the Bible comes right out and says something "directly," in terms of what modern man thinks is "direct." Thus, for traditional Puritanism and Presbyterianism, the fact that the New Testament books nowhere explicitly command the use of musical instruments in worship, proves (for them) that it is forbidden to use musical instruments in worship. This is in spite of the overwhelming Biblical evidence in both Old and New Testaments that God wants musical instruments used in His worship. The point here is that the Puritan and Presbyterian traditions bring arbitrary and rationalistic canons of proof to the Word of God, and demand that the Bible submit to these modern notions of logic and proof.[3]

For instance, the Bible nowhere commands us to keep a feast of the Incarnation at the Winter Solstice; therefore, we are forbidden to do so. People who argue this way do not have a problem with Wednesday night prayer meetings, even though these are nowhere commanded in Scripture either. More importantly, they overlook the whole Biblical theology of worship, festival, and

---

3. G. I. Williamson argues against the use of musical instruments by asserting that their use in Scripture was always *merely* ceremonial or else *merely* symbolic. The problem here is a modern, rationalistic view of both ceremony and symbol, and the view that such things are "inferior" to internal, heart worship. See Williamson, "Instrumental Music in Worship: Commanded or Not Commanded?", in *The Biblical Doctrine of Worship* (n.p.: The Reformed Presbyterian Church of North America, 1974).

time. Actually, Biblical teaching as a whole is quite favorable to Christmas as an annual ecclesiastical festival. Too often one finds that, the real reason for doing away with Christmas is that "Rome does it." In such a case the authority of Scripture is replaced by the authority of Rome, an authority that functions by way of reaction against whatever Rome says and does.[4]

Aspects of Worship

In the remainder of this essay, I wish to take up several areas of Biblical teaching on worship that are generally ignored in Protestantism today, at least in Baptist and Reformed circles (which are the circles in which I live, and which constitute the large majority of people reading this essay). As I study Scripture, I find that Lutheran and Anglican churches are more Biblical in their worship, despite some problems. From my experience, though, I suspect that the Biblical foundation for what they do has often been forgotten.

By way of introduction, however, let me say that it is clear from Scripture that worship is acceptable to God even in the most humble of settings. An ignorant Arminian Pentecostal, trying to lead a Bible study in a home, and celebrating communion with saltines and grape juice, may very well be more pleasing to God than a learned orthodox Calvinist conducting worship in a Biblically-designed church, and using Biblical elements in communion. We all know this, and it is not at issue in this essay.

Rather, I am making two points. First, given the opportunity, we ought to improve our theology and our worship along the lines taught and indicated by Scripture. There is to be an eschatological development of the kingdom of God, progressive glorification, and theology and worship should become richer with the

---

4. I have argued this at length in an essay entitled, "The Menace of Chinese Food: Observations on Christmas and Christmas Trees." This essay is available for a contribution from Geneva Ministries, Box 131300, Tyler, TX 75713. My own position is that the Puritans were correct in arguing against either state or ecclesiastical *imposition* of annual festivals, but they threw the baby out with the bath in rejecting *voluntary* observances.

years. That is, the Bible not only teaches us what is essential (*esse*) for the worship of the church, but what is good for her well being (*bene esse*) and her full being (*plene esse*). Second point: Conservative Protestantism has generally rejected the opportunity to grow and develop Biblically, in spite of loud affirmations of Biblical rigorism. I maintain Biblical rigorism as my position, but Biblical rigorism is not the same as cultic minimalism (which is influenced by Western stoic philosophy, and unfortunately is all too often the posture of Reformed and Anabaptist worship).

The Act of Crossing Oneself

Throughout all the centuries of the Christian church, the cross has been a prominent symbol of the faith. It is probably the most prominent "mere symbol" in the church, once we have excluded the sacramental signs of Holy Baptism and Holy Communion. The cross has been used in three distinct but interrelated ways: as an architectural design, as a symbol, and as an action. Churches were built in a cruciform shape. A cross was put on the front wall and on the steeple. People crossed themselves to invoke the protection of the covenant God.

The Reformers did not object to the act of crossing oneself, provided it was not done superstitiously. They recognized that it might simply be an external bodily action that accompanies an inward prayer for protection. To be under the sign of the cross is to be under the blood of Christ, under the protection of His wings. A man in distress might pray, "Lord Jesus Christ, protect me from harm, for I am Your child, under Your protection," and he might cross himself as an external physical act while he thus prays.[5]

This may make little sense to a modern man, however. Under the influence of Greek philosophy, primarily Stoic asceticism and

---

5. Thus Martin Bucer, "This sign [of the cross] was not only used in the churches in very ancient times: it is still an admirably simple reminder of the cross of Christ." Bucer writes with respect to making the sign of the cross as part of the rite of holy baptism. In Bucer, *op. cit.*, p. 90.

Neo-platonic mysticism, men despise the body. The only thing that really counts is the inward, mental, psychological motion. An external physical motion, such as crossing oneself while praying for protection, is not only superfluous, but actually evil.

In the Biblical perspective, physical actions are neither evil nor superfluous. When a man repents, he falls to the ground, prostrate before God. When he is horrified at God's judgments, he sits in the dirt and puts dust in his hair, or tears out his hair and rips his garments (cf. e.g., Ezra 9:3). When he is happy at God's blessings, he dances in the streets. And when he wants to invoke God's protection, he . . . well, why don't you fill in the blank?

We may ask, then: When conservative Protestants scream and yell about the act of crossing oneself, are they being true to Scripture, or simply reacting against Rome? True, many Roman Catholics cross themselves superstitiously. The external act is seen magically rather than dynamically, as a way of capturing God's favor rather than as a whole-personed expression of the heart. So what? The wars of religion were centuries ago. What does that have to do with how Protestants are to act today?

I want to make it clear here that I am not *advocating* that conservative Protestants go back to the custom of crossing themselves in prayer. We have not reinstituted this custom in our church. What I am saying is that the custom is not unScriptural, and that the conservative church at large should give it some thought. If we create a Christian culture, one that no longer despises the body and bodily actions, such dancelike gestures and customs may well return.

The Cross Design in Scripture

Let us go on to the basic cross shape, as the Bible sets it out. First of all, as always, we go to Genesis 1 - 4, and in 2:10-14 we find that the fountain in Eden produced a river that split into four heads, and went out to water the four corners of the earth. We may diagram this as follows:

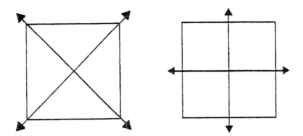

Neither of these diagrams is designed to show what an aerial view of the pre-deluvian world might have looked like. Rather, the diagrams are a symbolic form, showing the basic shape. Later in Scripture, the same picture recurs, with water flowing from a rock, or from the Temple, or the headwaters of the Jordan flowing from the great rock at Caesarea Philippi. The theological continuity among all these pictures lies in their symbolic form.

Notice in the two diagrams how the fundamental cross or X form produces a square. The square fills out the space that is fundamentally defined by the cross. The cross has a center, and it has four extensions, which are either the corners of the square, or the centers of the sides of the square. The Bible repeatedly uses this fundamental shape to portray the kingdom of God.

At the center is the initial sanctuary. Adam and Eve would follow the four rivers out, extending dominion along their lines, and branching out to fill and cultivate the whole world. One of the most common ways of portraying the cross as the center of the world, with influences spreading everywhere, is the labyrinth design. Here the four rivers of influence are shown "curving" around the world in ever expanding squares, until the whole (square) world is transformed.

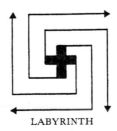

LABYRINTH

The Cross in Architecture

In addition to the Edenic manifestation of this cosmic cross/ square design, we also find it in the architecture of the Tabernacle. The holy of holies was, of course, a square (actually, a cube). The holy place was a rectangle twice as long as it was wide. The entire court area was also a rectangle twice as long as wide. Within the Tabernacle, the furniture was arranged in a fundamentally cross shape, with the Ark and Incense Altar at the head, the Showbread and Lampstand forming the crosspiece, and the Altar of Burnt Sacrifice at the feet.

Arranged around this sanctuary was a gigantic cross, which might have been visible to Moses from Mount Horeb. According to Numbers 2, the camp on the east side numbered 186,400 men, while the camp on the west numbered 108,100. The camp on the north numbered 157,600, while that on the south numbered 151,450.

NORTH CAMP
OF DAN

(EAGLE FACE)

157,600

WEST CAMP
OF EPHRAIM

(BULL FACE)

108,100

LEVITES,
PRIESTS,
TABERNACLE

EAST CAMP
OF JUDAH

(LION FACE)

186,400

SOUTH CAMP
OF REUBEN

(MAN FACE)

151,450

Even if we were to modify this configuration, to fill in the empty spaces and form more of a rectangle, it would still retain a cross shape, with the shortest side west and the longest side east.

The cross shape is that of a man with his arms extended. It is the shape of the body of Christ, incarnate, and of the church of Christ, His body mystical. The church is "one new man" according to Ephesians 2:15. Cruciformity is humaniformity. Naturally, then, the shape of the church in the wilderness was that of one large man, a cross shape. To be *in* Christ is to be *in* a cross shaped architectural model.

In the diagram I have pointed out that the four faces of the Cherubim, according to Ezekiel 1:10 and Revelation 4:7 may also fit here. Judah is compared to a lion in Gen. 49:9, and Ephraim to a bull in Dt. 33:17. Even if the correspondences prove inexact, the general configuration is the same: four directions pointing away from a central location.

The humaniformity of the kingdom of God is also seen from another fact. The kingdom is to be organized with elders over 10s, 50s, 100s, 1000s, and 10,000s, according to Exodus 18. Notice that there are not elders over 500s and 5000s, as we might expect. The reason for this is not apparent, until we realize that this is also the system of organization for the army. When Israel marched out of Egypt, she marched five in a rank. The term translated "battle array" in Exodus 13:18 actually means "five in a rank" (cf. also Josh. 1:14; 4:12; Jud. 7:11; Num. 32:17).[6]

Five squads of ten men, marching in ranks, form a platoon of fifty men. The dimensions of such a platoon are 5 men by 10 men, or a ratio of 1:2. This is one of the common dimensions used in the Tabernacle and its furniture. Two platoons of 50 men form a company of 100 men. Arranged side by side, the dimension is 10 by 10, or 1:1, a square, another common dimension of the house of God. Ten companies gives us a battalion, which we could arrange five in a rank, two companies deep. This gives us the dimension 20 by

---

6. In Hebrew, *hmsh*. Lexicons sometimes make this out to be a separate root from the *hmsh* meaning "five," but there is no reason to think this. The lexicographers simply have not taken into account military organization.

50, or 2:5. I am not aware of the occurrence of this shape in the Tabernacle, but if we form a brigade of ten battalions, again arranging them five in a rank, two battalions deep, we get another square 100 by 100.

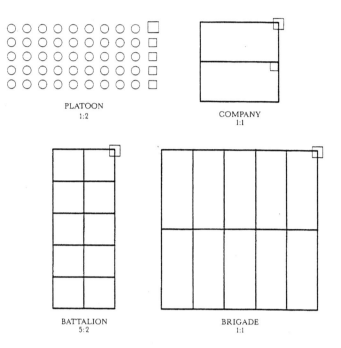

Of course, the Bible repeatedly tells us that God's house is built of people, that we are living stones in His temple, etc. It is interesting, however, to see how this was signified to the people of old. The arrangement of the army in groups of five explains the prominence of the number five in the dimensions of the Tabernacle. Five seems to be the number for preeminence and power.[7] Here again, to sum up, we see the humaniformity of the house of God, and thus the appropriateness of the use of the cross shape in church architecture.

---

7. See the discussion of this in my book, *The Law of the Covenant: An Exposition of Exodus 21-23* (Tyler, TX: Institute for Christian Economics, 1984), pp. 261ff.

We can easily coalesce the cosmic cross with the humaniform cross. At the center, in the Tabernacle, was a spring of water, the laver of cleansing. In Ezekiel 47, that fountain pours life to all the world. As Israel was to be a priest to the nations, the water can be seen to flow through the tribes, the limbs of the cross, to the four corners of the earth—just as the rivers flowed from the Garden of Eden.

Defilement spreads similarly. Thus, the world is cursed all the way from the center to its four ends. Accordingly, atoning blood had to be placed on the four horns of the altar. Accordingly also, our Lord's visible wounds were positioned at the extremities of his body: hands, feet, and head. Thus, the ends of the earth, signified by the ends of the cross, are covered by His blood.

Why should we fear this type of symbolism, since the Bible abounds in it? If Protestants truly believe in Biblical worship and theology, they need to take such things seriously. It should be clear that the cross is not simply a symbol of the death of Christ. It is a symbol of dominion, that His death and victory extend to the ends of the world. It is a symbol of His body, the new man, the church, and of His rule over it. Thus, it is entirely appropriate to use the cross as a symbol of the church.[8]

The second commandment forbids bowing down and serving anything made by human hands in an attempt to conjure and manipulate God. It does not forbid the making of artistic or symbolic objects, nor does it forbid their placement in the environment of worship. There is no Biblical principle against placing a cross at the front of the place of worship, especially since the cross is a God-ordained, not a man made, sign.

How practical is the cross shape for architecture? If we start with the concept of people gathered around the Word and Sacra-

---

8. Anti-cross churches frequently have weathervanes on their steeples. The cock that surmounts these is an ambiguous symbol, recalling both Peter's denial (the sin of man) and the rising of the sun (the coming of the Kingdom). The weathervane proper points in four directions, and while it turns whatever way the wind blows (pointing to the vacillation of the church?), it could also remind us of the wind of the Spirit. All in all, I think that the cross, as a symbol of the death of Christ and of the cosmic extent of His dominion, is a preferable symbol. I doubt if many people have ever reflected on the meaning of the weathervane!

ment, we come up initially with a "church in the round" design. Since we don't want people staring at each other in worship, generally the church in the round is not a complete circle. The cross shape easily lends itself to this, particularly if we modify it by expanding the center into a square or circle. We thus retain the gathering of people around the Word and Sacraments, which is both practical and theologically satisfying.

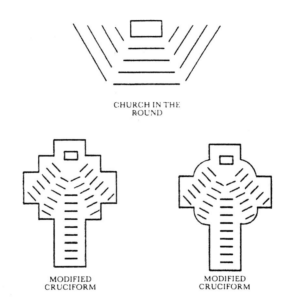

CHURCH IN THE
ROUND

MODIFIED
CRUCIFORM

MODIFIED
CRUCIFORM

Posture and Gesture

I mentioned the act of crossing oneself above. I am not necessarily recommending this, but I am saying that there is no reason to reject it out of hand. Christianity does not separate the soul from the body, but teaches the resurrection of the body, and affirms that we worship God in the whole person, which includes bodily movement. As Romano Guardini put it, "The man who is moved by emotion will kneel, bow, clasp his hands or impose them, stretch forth his arms, strike his breast, make an offering of something, and so on. These elementary gestures are capable of richer development and expansion, or else of amalgamation. . . . Finally, a whole series of such movements may be coordinated. This gives rise to religious action. . . ."[9]

Historically, the church has always stood during certain parts of worship, knelt during others, and sat during others. Men stood for the reading of the word and for the reciting of the covenant in the law, the creed, and hymns of covenant recitation. Men knelt for prayer. Men sat to hear the Word expounded, and to eat of the Lord's Table. For some strange reason, modern evangelical Protestants sit for prayer and for the reading of Scriptures, something even their never-kneeling Protestant forebears would have been shocked at.

Gestures have traditionally been reserved for the officiant leading the service. As Moses prayed with hands uplifted, and as Paul enjoins (1 Tim. 2:8), hands were raised in the two-pillar position during prayer. Biblically, the two pillars signify two witnesses, God's Word and Oath (Hebrews 6:13-18).[10] Thus, two pulpits in the church, with two readings from the Word during worship; two sacraments; two elements in the Holy Communion; etc. Presbyterians sometimes retain the lifting up of hands in prayer; most other conservative Protestants do not.

In the benediction, when the office bearer places (not invokes) God's blessing upon his people (Numbers 6:22-27), the hands are also held in the two pillar position. Traditionally, the phrase "in the Name of the Father, and of the Son, and of the Holy Spirit" has been added to the Aaronic benediction, and the sign of the cross made while it is said. Presbyterians often object to this part, but as we noted above, there is really no reason to do so, for it is but an outward gesture showing that the people are members of the cruciform body of Christ, under His government and protection.

The most obvious bodily movement missing from "Bible believing Protestant" culture and worship is the sacred dance. The

---

9. Romano Guardini, *The Spirit of the Liturgy* (London, 1935), p. 168.

10. See my essay, "Rebellion, Tyranny, and Dominion in the Book of Genesis," in Gary North, ed., *Tactics of Christian Resistance.* Christianity & Civilization No. 3 (Tyler, TX: Geneva Ministries, 1984), p. 50.

psalms repeatedly enjoin dancing, yet psalm-singing churches do not dance, and neither do hymn-singing churches. If there was ever proof that a Greek rationalistic intellectualism has robbed the church of her Biblical foundations, this is it. The African churches, which have not been ruined by rationalism, use dancing. Perhaps we shall learn from them.[11] Some churches still retain a shadow of the dance in the procession that begins worship. That is not much, but it is better than nothing.

The purpose of this essay is not to survey every single area where Protestantism has tended to overlook Biblical teaching. The illustrations above have been selected simply to enhance the basic point, which is that Biblical worship is a far cry from modern conservative evangelical worship. There are a variety of pastoral considerations that must be taken into account if we are to reform our worship, and some of these dictate that we should proceed carefully, and not try to do everything at once. I am not arguing that we should institute sacred dancing tomorrow, but that we need to think seriously about eventually doing so.

I close with one final illustration. The Reformed and Presbyterian churches rejoice in their heritage of singing the psalms. Few still retain this heritage. Yet the heritage itself is suspect. Why sing the psalms in versified form? To versify the psalms is to change them, and to lose much of the content. Why not simply chant them? Chanting is very easy to learn and to do; it is simply an enhanced form of reading. When we chant the psalms, we are using the exact words of God.

Why not? *Because that's what Romans and Anglicans do!* Thus, in spite of all the brave talk, the fact is that we Reformed people are less Biblical in our worship, at some points, than are the Anglicans and the post-Vatican II Roman Catholics. And this is not even to mention the fact that most Presbyterian churches do not have the Lord's Supper every week!

---

11. An interesting essay on this subject is Boka di Mpasi Londi, "Freedom of Bodily Expression in the African Liturgy," in Maldonado and Power, ed., *Symbol and Art in Worship.* Concilium 132 (New York: Seabury, 1980).

11

GOD'S HOSPITALITY
AND HOLISTIC EVANGELISM

The thesis of this essay is that one of the most important Christian virtues possessed by the effective evangelist is hospitality. The practice of household hospitality by Christian saints and elders is an image or copy of God's hospitality, seen as He invites us into His house to eat at His table. Because the modern church does not understand the importance of the Lord's table, and because Christ's supper is not visibly displayed week by week, the virtue of hospitality is not clearly understood in our day. As a result, numerous less-than-effective evangelistic techniques have developed that do not take advantage of the Biblical model. In order to reform our evangelism, we need to reform our churches, so that God's hospitality is made visible to all.

The virtue of hospitality is repeatedly enjoined in the New Testament. Elders in particular are to be given over to hospitality (1 Tim. 3:2; Tit. 1:8), for they especially are to display the grace of God in the world. Every Christian is to practise hospitality, however (Rom. 12:13; 1 Pet. 4:9). The presence of these exhortations to practise hospitality presupposes the need for such exhortations: it is easy to lapse into a convenient lifestyle and ignore hospitality; thus, the exhortation is needed. Especial praise is accorded those who show hospitality to strangers. In some cases, hospitality to strangers means hospitality to travelling Christians (Matt. 25:35, 40 + Matt. 12:50). Other verses speak more generally of entertaining strangers (Heb. 13:2), and in yet other places, the entertainment of unbelievers is clearly in view (Job 31:32; 1 Tim. 5:10).

The last verse mentioned, 1 Timothy 5:10, distinguishes be-

221

tween hospitality shown to the saints and that shown to outsiders, for the phrase "washed the saints' feet" is in part a reference to the practice of hospitality (cf. Gen. 18:4; 19:2; 24:32; 43:24; 1 Sam. 25:41; 2 Sam. 11:8; Luke 7:44; John 13:5). Here as elsewhere we are enjoined to do good to all men, but especially to those of the household of the faith (Gal. 6:10).

The repeated injunctions in the Old Testament to care for the alien and sojourner in the land are reflections of the concept of hospitality (see, for example, Ex. 22:21; Lev. 19:34; 25:35; Num. 35:15; Deut. 10:19; 27:19; 31:12; Jer. 7:6). The stranger was under the protection of the LORD, in His house (land), having crossed the threshold of His house (the Jordan), and thus being entitled to hospitality.

The only persons excluded from Christian hospitality were excommunicated persons (1 Cor. 5:9-13) and perhaps false teachers (2 John 10). As regards the latter passage, John Stott in his fine commentary on the epistles of John points out, first, that it is only teachers, not all adherents to false teaching, who are to be excluded. Stott also points out that the specific heresy was the denial of the true doctrine of incarnation, not some lesser matter. Third, Stott calls attention to the fact that the epistle is written to a house-church, and thus it is likely that the prohibition is actually to the church, not to individual households. The church must not extend an official welcome to a false teacher (*i.e.*, allow him to teach in their midst); possibly an individual Christian household might show hospitality to the false teacher in an effort to correct his errors.[1]

Holistic Man

The Biblical virtue of hospitality, specifically, ministry to the whole person in a structured environment, points us to the Biblical concept of man. Here we arrive at one of the major errors that has cropped up historically in the church, for the Bible teaches neither a bipartite nor a tripartite view of man. Rather, the Scripture teaches that man is a unity, not composed of several parts, but acting in several dimensions or spheres of life. Man is a spirit

---

1. John R. W. Stott, *The Epistles of John*. The Tyndale New Testament Commentaries 19 (Grand Rapids: Eerdmans, 1974), *comm. ad loc.*

in bodily state, not a spirit housed in a body. It is Greek philosophy that teaches that man is a soul or spirit housed in a body. The reason for this is not hard to understand.

Pagan man senses, indeed knows, that he will continue to survive after death. It is clear from his experience, however, that the physical body will die. Thus, pagan man assumes that there is some immortal soul living inside his body, which soul or spirit is his true self, and this soul will go on living in some other place after the physical body dies. These conclusions are very logical, but are founded on the false premise that death is a natural phenomenon. The Bible teaches that God never intended man to die, so that death is a most unnatural phenomenon. True, the personal self-awareness of each human being is sustained by God apart from his body after death, but this is an unnatural situation that will be remedied finally with the resurrection of all bodies at the last day.

What makes men different from animals is not that man has a spirit but that man is the image of God. Both animals and men are quickened and kept alive by the Holy Spirit, and this is the meaning of such often misinterpreted passages as Genesis 2:7, 7:22, Ecclesiastes 12:7. The Bible has a holistic view of man.

This is not to say that all aspects of human life are equally important for all purposes. It is the religious dimension of human life, man's relationship to God, positive or negative, that is primary above all else. For this reason, cultural and personal transformation must begin with, and be ever grounded in, a proper relationship with God. The religious dimension of life is most important, not because the soul is the most important "part" of man, but because the whole man's relationship with God is the most important of all aspects of his life.

Under the influence of Greek thought, Christianity began to hold that man is divided into various parts or faculties, and that the most important of these parts is the intellect.[2] This notion is

---

2. For a brief and helpful introduction to the problem of Greek influence on Christianity, see Rousas J. Rushdoony, *The Flight from Humanity* (Fairfax, VA: Thoburn Press, 1973).

called the doctrine of the primacy of the intellect. Because the brain was regarded as the most important part of man, the most important work of the church was to communicate intellectual information to that brain. Thus, instead of the primacy of the Word, the church fell into the primacy of preaching.

What the Bible teaches, however, is the primacy of the Word in the work and worship of the church. This means, of course, the Word read, proclaimed, and taught, but it also means the Word sung (in Psalms, Bible songs, and Psalm-like hymns), the Word prayed, the Word obeyed and implemented from house to house, and the Word made visible and experienced (in the sacraments). A church that practices the primacy of the Word will have a healthy balance among all the elements of worship and life, and will not be a preacher-centered church. The primacy of preaching, however, leads to the primacy of the preacher, the so-called "three office view," and all the problems attendant with that.[3]

The Primacy of the Preacher

There are two large problems that afflict the overly intellectualized church: the primacy of preaching and the problem of revivalism (next section). The primacy of preaching means the primacy of the preacher. It is understandable that the Reformation resulted in a great emphasis on preaching and teaching the Word. For centuries, little or no such instruction had been carried on. Incredible ignorance prevailed all over Europe. Moreover, when the Reform began, the established church strongly opposed the teaching of the Bible. Thus, the Reformation was forged in a crucible in which one of the principle elements was preaching. All the same, the Reformers did not hold to the primacy of preaching in the sense that their later followers did. John Calvin, for instance, wanted the Lord's Supper to be administered in connection with every preaching service, for the Word should always be made visible when it is preached. The Reformers emphasized the singing of the Word, and the congregational praying of the Word in the use

---

3. See the End Note at end of this essay.

of set prayers drawn from Biblical language.

The magistrates in Geneva and elsewhere did not want the sacraments to be administered regularly, however, and Calvin, having no choice, had to go along. As a result, Christ was less visible and the preacher more visible. As time went along, the Reformed churches, especially in the English-speaking world, lost sight of the value of frequent communion, and often relegated the Lord's Supper to an annual observance. The use of prayerbooks came to be frowned upon, out of reaction against the abusive enforcement of their use by the English state, and thus Biblical praying was lost. In time, the book of Psalms came to be viewed as a strange, Old Testament book, not really suited for New Covenant worship. Isaac Watts produced "New Testament paraphrases" of the Psalms, inserting the name of Christ (and "Great Britain") at those points he deemed appropriate. Eventually the Psalms fell into total disuse, and all that was left were non-inspired hymns. The early Reformation hymns were very Psalm-like in character, preserving the primacy of the Word; later hymns became more and more light and frothy, less and less like the Psalms.

Thus, we face a situation today in most evangelical and Reformed churches in which the reading and preaching of Scripture is the only way in which the Word is made manifest in the lives of the saints. This is a real loss for the people of God. The result is the primacy of the preacher. The preacher not only does the only really important thing in the service (preach), he also composes (if he even does that) the prayers that are prayed, and he prays them by himself. It boils down very often to worship by proxy, exactly what the Reformation fought against. Only in the Lutheran and Episcopal churches is there more than a minimum of congregational participation, because of the use of prayer books.

Since all that is left is preaching, the act of preaching takes on dimensions foreign to the Bible. Preaching has become a great rhetorical event. Sermons ought to open with a stunning introduction, proceed through three alliterating points, and conclude with a gripping application. People should be stirred, moved, etc. The full-orbed worship of Scripture, with congregational prayer, singing, and the Supper has been lost, and this leaves the people psychologically starved, so the preaching must make up for it. The history of the church becomes the history of preachers. People leave one church and seek another on the basis of who is preaching. If one is in a church with bad preaching, there is nothing else to look forward to in going to church: no worship, no real singing of the Word, no sacrament. Everything hangs on a man, and that man is not the Lord Jesus Christ.

There is a story of a certain young preacher who was not very effective at his task. One Sunday he ascended into the pulpit to find a note that read, "Sir, we would see Jesus." After several weeks of this, the young man broke down and began to preach Christ in earnest. Doubtless the young man needed some such exhortation, but the request to see Jesus was erroneously directed to the pulpit. The reading and preaching of the Word is that we might *hear* Jesus. The Bible emphasizes the hearing of the Master's voice, not the seeing of His face. Jesus Himself was so ordinary looking that He could, at times, disappear into the crowds. After arguing with Him for three years, the Pharisees could still not remember what He looked like — He looked like everybody else — so they had to hire Judas to lead them to Him. On the road to Emmaus, His disciples did not recognize His face, but their hearts burned when He taught them the Word. It was when He broke bread (the Lord's Supper) that they had the experience of recognition, that they "saw" Him (Luke 24:13-32). If we would see Jesus, we need to restore the visible Word as the complement to the audible Word.

What about preaching? In the New Testament and in the early church, preaching (heralding) was something done to outsiders, persuading them to repent and believe the gospel. Preaching is recorded for us in the book of Acts, for instance. Within the church, however, what went on was teaching. The teaching elder did not stand to teach, though all stood for the reading of the Word. Rather, the teacher sat enthroned while he explained the text in simple language, without rhetoric, and made some applications. It was a family meeting. (See, for instance, Luke 4:16, 20.) When the Gospel became established in the Roman world, the influence of Greek rhetoric began to be felt, and ministers began standing to "preach" to God's people, delivering polished oratory for edification of the saints. Augustine, for instance, initially went to hear Ambrose preach not because he wanted to learn about the Bible, but because he wanted to improve his rhetoric and Ambrose was greatly remarked as an orator.

Because so much of the Reformation occurred within state churches, the Reformers and preachers treated the churchmembers as if they were unsaved people in need of the new birth. This was doubtless necessary at that time, but it is not the normal Biblical way to view the church. The Baptist churches to this day continue to treat their churchmembers as if they were unsaved, and so they *preach* to them. If the churches are healthy, however, with good doctrine and sound discipline, the elders should not treat the people as goats-in-disguise but as true sheep, and teach them. Those who are not truly converted will eventually rebel against the teaching of the Word. There is no need for rhetoric and flamboyance, for "preaching." What is needed is simple, direct teaching. The notion that there must always be "a word to the unconverted" during a *worship* service is unBiblical rubbish.

All this is to say that *of course* the Word must be read and expounded in worship, whether the minister stands or sits enthroned. Such exposition should, however, be direct and simple, not rhetorical. Spurgeon must not be our model in this respect. Let the preacher keep the people's noses in the Book, not their eyes on his posturing. Many of us enjoy listening to good rhetoric and brilliant "preaching," but as often as not this kind of thing only gets in the way of simple Bible exposition and application. The Word, not the preacher, must be paramount.

The Tragedy of Revivalism

An intellect-centered ministry of worship leaves holistic man unsatisfied. His emotional and physical aspects are not dealt with on a normal, regular basis. Thus, the second problem that afflicts such churches is that the "irrational" side of man manifests itself in unhealthy ways. The situation in early America was very often this: the weekly service consisted of a few verses of a Psalm or two, droned in the slowest singing imaginable, together with a very long prayer (one hour), either prepared by the preacher or made up on the spot, followed by a very long sermon (two hours or more). Then, once in a great while, there was a "communion season." The Lord's Supper, a great mystical event, would be administered, and there would be many special sermons leading up to it over the first couple of days of the conference. The people tended to get all worked up in anticipation of this extraordinary event. It is no accident that the earliest revivals broke out at communion seasons.

Soon the revivals were a regular part of church life, regular in the sense of being expected from time to time. At the revival, people's physical and emotional outbursts were given full play, from "barking" to the jerks (and after the revival, illicit sex).[4] Eventually there came a split between the anti-intellectual churches and the anti-emotional ones. The emotionalistic churches drifted into liberalism, since they had no real doctrinal interest. The intellectual churches also drifted into liberalism, because their emphasis on the intellect left them open to the supposedly irrefutable fruits of modern Biblical research. Small groups of conservatives have remained in both groups: mystical pentecostalists, and intellectualistic Calvinists and dispensationalists. Men were making an unnatural and unBiblical choice between the mind and the heart.

The rationalistic or intellectualistic conservatives have been plagued by irrational movements in their midst for a great many years now. Psychologically starved members, unfed by lecture-sermons, seek out more fulfilling ministries, and sink into the

---

4. As Gary North has noted, after the revival "passions waned, leaving cynicism and unwed or newly wed mothers in the wake. In the town of Bristol, Rhode Island, from 1680 through 1720, there was not a single recorded instance of a baby arriving less than eight months after marriage. From 1720-40, the percentage rose to 10%. From 1740-60, in the Great Awakening era, it hit 49%, trailing off to 44%, 1760-80. This story was repeated throughout the colonies according to one as yet unpublished manuscript I have seen." Gary North, "Revival: True and False," in *Biblical Economics Today* 8:6 (Oct./Nov., 1985). North does refer to one published essay by John Demos, "Families in Colonial Bristol, Rhode Island: An Exercise in Historical Demography," *William and Mary Quarterly*, 3rd Series, 25 (January, 1968): 56.

quagmire of American know-nothing-ism. They are attracted by a screaming "fundamentalist" preacher, for at least he stimulates them. They may try tongues, or some other "Spirit-led" movement. They may mix their intellectual religion with screaming at the weekly chaos festivals of the American Football Religion. They may seek meaning in group-grope, touchie-feelie sessions in which all participants are to pare and bare their souls to each other.

Sometimes the irrational is standardized and becomes part of a sadly truncated religious establishment. The primacy of the intellect is replaced with the primacy of the will or of the emotions, and it is the preacher's job to stir up one or the other. Such is the case (pardon my frankness, brethren) with most of the Southern Baptist churches. The "altar call" has become a weekly ritual (pseudo-sacrament). Each sermon is preached as if the congregation were a bunch of goats-in-disguise. Unhappy Christians, searching for more, ritually re-dedicate their lives to Christ, only to find in time that they have lapsed back into the same stale lifestyle. How can Bible teaching take place under such circumstances? The people get a bare minimum of teaching, and a little emotion as well, but are still unsatisfied because the Word is still locked up to a great extent. Pastors pray for reawakening, and redouble their efforts to convert their congregations, but to no avail. What is needed is exposition of the Word, and an emotionally satisfying worship service that matches the psychology of holistic man.

What is needed in all these churches is a restoration of two Reformation principles that have been effectively eclipsed. First, the Word must be restored to primacy, in place of the primacy of the preacher. By this we mean the Word read publicly to a standing congregation, the Word explained simply and quietly to God's people, the Word applied in an encouraging manner to God's people, the Word sung in Psalms (preponderant Psalmody), Bible songs, and genuinely Psalm-like hymns, the Word prayed in prayers drawn from the language and concerns of the Bible, the Word (Christ) made visible and really present every single week, the Word eaten and rejoiced in.

Second, the congregation must be encouraged and *trained* self-consciously to participate in worship. This means (yes, let it be said) *prayerbooks*, so that the people can read aloud in unison the great Bible-based prayers of the church, and can follow the teaching elder when he prays. The congregation needs to be told that Christ is really (in the Spirit) present at His Table, and they need to eat the food Jesus gives them. By eat, we mean *eat*: a good chewable hunk of bread and a good-sized glass of real shalom-inducing wine. This, not the "altar call," is the kind of active participation the Bible sets forth for the people of God.

Fulfilled, well-taught, fed, happy Christians will naturally be better evangelists. No longer will people be invited to "our church" because it has a fine gymnasium or because the preacher dresses up like an Indian chief for the amusement of the congregation. People will be invited to the fellowship of the Word, and the congregation will be excited about the Word. The unsaved visitor cannot, of course, participate in the Lord's Supper, but he will see there displayed to his view the glorious privilege of the saints.

The restoration of the primacy of the Word in the churches is not optional, nor can it wait. There are many desperately important matters that the churches must be about, but none more important than the restoration of the Word and the exaltation of Christ in worship. Worship is the heart and central training ground of the church, for in special worship we come directly to the special presence of Christ, and this is the foundation of all personal and social transformation.

Familistic Culture

The church must not only implement the whole Word of God to the whole man, but it must do so in the proper God-given context. That context is a familistic culture. The family or household reflects the image of God. God is a Trinity, three Persons in One. They share a community of essence and of life, which we call covenant life because this shared life entails a personal-structural bond. The three Persons relate one to another personally by means of love and communication, and structurally by means of conformity to their own character (law), and by means of an order in which the Father begets the Son, and the Father and the Son send the Spirit.[5] They are joined in being, but also joined in a covenant bond, which has only been broken once, when the Son on the cross cried out, "My God, my God, why hast Thou forsaken me?"

Mankind, the image of God, reproduces this pattern at the created level in the family. Right in the Garden of Eden, God established the family and its boundaries (Gen. 2:24). The family is a covenant bond, which includes personal (love and communication) and structural (law and hierarchy) aspects. Ephesians 3:14-15 states that all human families derive their name, that is their character, definition, and interpretation, from God the Father. Human culture is an outworking of religion, and the outworking of the Trinitarian faith is a familistic culture.

Many of the basic powers of society are given by God to the family: children and their rearing, property, inheritance, and care of the poor.[6] The plan of salvation, covenantally administered, is administered familistically, so that the sign of the covenant is administered not individualistically but by households.

The state and the church are different from the family, and have powers and duties that the family does not have. The state has the power of the sword and the church has the power of the sacraments (binding and loosing). *Both state and church, however, are seen in Scripture as organized by households.* It seems that in the Patriarchal era, when all of society was organized by households, the

---

5. Louis Berkhof writes: "The subsistence and operation of the three persons in the Divine Being is marked by a certain definite order. There is a certain order in the ontological Trinity. In personal subsistence the Father is first, the Son second, and the Holy Spirit third. It need hardly be said that this order does not pertain to any priority of time or of essential dignity, but only to the logical order of derivation. . . . Generation and procession take place within the Divine Being, and imply a certain subordination as to the manner of personal subsistence, but no subordination as to the possession of the divine essence is concerned." *Systematic Theology* (Grand Rapids: Eerdmans, 1941), pp. 88f.

6. On the powers of the family, see Rousas J. Rushdoony, "The Family as Trustee," in *The Journal of Christian Reconstruction*, IV:2(1977):8-13; and Rushdoony, *Institutes of Biblical Law* (Nutley, NJ: Craig Press, 1973), pp. 159-218.

father was ruler both of "state" and of "church," with his firstborn
son as deputy and heir (cf. eg., Gen. 13:4; 14:14, 18; 24:15 + 50,
53, 55, 59, 60; 43:33; Deut. 21:17; Heb. 1:2, 5, 6, 13 + Gen.
48:17f.; Heb. 5:1-10). In the providence of God, Moses received
his training under such a patriarch, Jethro (Ex. 2:16, 21). When,
however, Moses attempted to implement the traditional patriarchal mode of government (Ex. 18:13), the sheer number of disputes among over two million people made it impossible. Thus,
Jethro's advice was to establish circles of courts above the household level to handle the *ministry of order*, seen in Ex. 18:21-22. It
must be noted that this power structure is extremely *decentralized*: a
familistic, household-based culture.

As regards the church, the family retained its importance in
sacramental worship, in that the sign of the covenant was placed
upon society at the household level, and in that the celebration of
Passover was organized by families (Ex. 12:4; 2 Chron. 35:12).
Nonetheless, the Lord saw fit to remove the ecclesiastical duties
from the firstborn and erect a special clan, the Levites, to perform
these duties (Num. 3:12-15, 40-51; 8:16-19). The Levites, however,
were only a temporary ecclesiastical arrangement, being a perpetual bloodline, thus typifying the eternality of Christ's Lordship
over the ministry of worship, and being tied to the Aaronic sacrifi-
cial order (Num. 8:19), which has been fulfilled and superseded
(Heb. 7:4-28).

The family was the central institution of society in the Old
Covenant and Old Creation. Adam was head and priest. Society
was organized in a patriarchal fashion. Genealogy was very important. Indeed, the Levitical priesthood, which substituted for
the firstborn, was still maintained according to a genealogical
principle. Because of sin, however, this first family is wrecked. Instead of protecting his wife, Adam set her forward to encounter
the serpent. Instead of agreeing with God that she was fundamentally deceived, Adam tried to escape responsibility by putting the
blame on her. Hatred between husband and wife soon matured to
become the murder of brother by brother. The first family, thus,
was shattered by sin.

Jesus stated that the greatest enemy of His new Kingdom

would not be the Babelic power state, but the old fallen family (Matt. 10:16-21, 34-37; Matt. 12:46-50; John 2:3-4). The new Kingdom would stand as God's new family, and thus directly challenge the claims of the first, fallen family (cf. John 1:12). Thus, the Old Covenant provision that family responsibilities take precedence over holy war is no longer operative in the New Covenant: Allegiance to Christ must come first (compare Luke 14:15-27 with Deut. 20:5-7).

The new family of the Church does not, however, simply replace the biological family. Rather, the new family puts the old to death only to grant it new, resurrection life. It is for this reason that it is so important to practise household baptism. Household baptism confesses that the old family unit is dead, and must be buried, for it is in need of rebirth.

Moreover, not only is this necessary when the family comes into the Kingdom the first time, it is a weekly necessity as well. Just as the bread is ripped in half, and the blood separated from the flesh in the sacrament, so also the family must be torn apart, coming under judgment, and then reconstituted in the sphere of resurrected, transfigured life. Thus, in the ritual of the Lord's Supper, each member of the family must commune independently of the others. In worship, it is Christ as Husband who feeds each member of His bride. It is a false, Mormon-like practice for the husband to take the bread and give it to his wife and children. It is only afterwards, on the basis of the sacrament and what it represents, that the natural family is reconstituted. It is only when the natural family is subordinated to the church — the new family — that the natural family can be restored.

Thus, while the church is governmentally organized by families, it is not liturgically organized by families. During worship, each stands as an individual before Christ, the Divine Husband. The Lord's Day is the Day of the Lord, and on the final Day of Judgment each will stand as an individual. A very good illustration of how this works out in practice is seen in Acts 5. Notice that Sapphira was not judged and found guilty in union with her husband. Rather, she was interviewed separately, on the clear assumption that she was separately responsible for her own actions.

The fact that she chose to stand with her husband rather than with the church is an illustration of what it means to choose the old family over the new. During worship, in times of judgment, the husband never speaks for his wife. When joining the church, both the man and the woman must answer the questions. Both must answer the questions put to them when they bring a child for baptism. The wife must take the sacrament directly from Christ's representatives, not through the mediation of her husband.

Since the church restores the world, however, after worship is completed the natural family is restored. After the transformation that takes place in worship, the principle that the husband is head of the wife is secure. Indeed, it is precisely the breaking down and rebuilding action of the liturgy that secures the order of the natural family, and thus restores Biblical familistic culture.

The baptistic worldview of American evangelicalism does not perceive that the family structure as such is dead and must be renewed in the Kingdom. While evangelicals are very concerned about the family, its structure is not related to the specific work of the church. The church is seen as dealing with individuals, but not seen as taking hold of the family as such and transforming it. Baptistic evangelicalism thus tends to separate the natural family from the foundation and reinforcement of the new family, the church.[7] Books on Christian family life abound, yet few if any refer to God's new family as the foundation for the restoration of the natural family. The natural family is simply enjoined to keep a bunch of rules — good in themselves — apart from the transforming life of the Kingdom. As a result, pressures and expectations are place on the natural family that it cannot bear, and rampant divorce is the present-day result in American evangelicalism.

The restoration of the natural family in the Kingdom is seen in the organization of the New Covenant church (Acts 2:26; Rom. 16:5, 10, 11; 1 Cor. 1:11, 16; Col. 4:15; 1 Tim. 5:13; 2 Tim. 1:16; 4:19; Philem. 2). The logical pattern for organizing the New

---

7. On American evangelicalism, see James B. Jordan, ed., *The Failure of the American Baptist Culture*. Christianity and Civilization No. 1 (Tyler, TX: Geneva Ministries, 1982).

Covenant church is that found in Exodus 18, with the elders over tens (houses), and fifties (local churches) and hundreds (the churches in a city), etc. This seems, indeed, to have been the pattern in the early church.

Early on, however, the church departed from this familistic structure. The higher elders (over hundreds, thousands, myriads; that is, bishops, archbishops, and patriarchs) were to function as *advisors* and *shepherds* to the younger, lower ranks of elders. In the event of a judicial case appealed to them, the elders would sit together as a court, for adjudication is a joint power. There would be little legislation in the church, for the Bible was the legislation, and there would be little administration, for the Spirit was the Administrator. Soon, however, in naiveté perhaps, the church adopted the imperial form of the Roman empire. Bishops became monarchs, not shepherds. This is the imperial stage of the church, and it continued down to the Reformation. These monarchs tended to replace the Bible and Christ as the Law and King of the church.

The Reformation broke with the imperial form and substituted the bureaucratic form of the church. Instead of familistic elders over tens, the elders sat as bureaus, boards, and committees, ruling over the churches. Or else the pastor acted as dictator. Instead of being courts of appeal, presbyteries and synods became ruling bodies in a legislative and bureaucratic sense, again tending to replace Scripture with church laws.

This bureaucratic form of the church is thankfully dying now. Churches are instinctively returning to cell groups, meeting in homes of elders, and in small groups.

The bureaucratic form of the church turns rulers from footwashers into distant dictators.[8] The result is that people do not really know any of the elders, and suspicion abounds as to what the elders are doing. This is aggravated when the board of elders becomes close-mouthed and secretive. The problem, however, is in the structure. Rule in the church is to be by means of footwashing (hospitality) as much as by giving orders (Mark 10:42-45;

---

8. See Mark 10:42-45; John 13:1-17.

John 13). Christ rules by being present with us, by being our Host and having us over to His house for dinner, even by being our Servant! The elders, who are to imitate Christ, must do the same.

Why do churches assume that all the elders must be acceptable to and rule over the entire congregation? This is not the pattern seen in the Bible (cf. Acts 6:1-6). If a congregation has several sub-groups, each sub-group should elect its own elder to be elder over that particular house-church. These elders over tens (or twelves)[9] will meet together to compare notes and to settle judicial cases, but it is not necessary that the elder over the poorer people be regarded as socially perfect in the eyes of the upper class people. Paradoxical as it may seem, such a decentralized structure will not lead to greater divisions but to fewer problems, for people's needs will be met effectively, and suspicion will disappear.

The house-church is not the only level at which the churches are to be organized. After all, the church "at Ephesus" was also considered a church, not simply a court of the church. At each level, however, the church is a household and its primary gathering is at a meal.[10]

The Gospel Invitation

Is there a Gospel invitation? To many evangelical Christians, the answer to that question is an unqualified "yes." Some Calvinists, reacting against the misleading character of the "altar call," seem less interested in inviting men to anything than they are in sending men away to think about the message they have heard. The answer to this conflict is to understand that the Gospel invitation is an invitation to come into Jesus' house and have supper

---

9. The Biblical pattern appears to be that the civil structure of Christian society is to be organized by tens and the ecclesiastical or covenantal structure by twelves. There were twelve tribes and twelve apostles. If we use Jesus and the twelve as our model, we shall have elders over 12s, 60s, 120s, 1,200s, and 12,000s.

10. Many valuable insights into the concept of the church as a house are to be found in two works by Meredith G. Kline, *The Structure of Biblical Authority* (Grand Rapids: Baker, 1975); and *Images of the Spirit* (Grand Rapids: Eerdmans, 1980). The present writer does not agree with Dr. Kline's overly dispensational approach to the relationship between the Old and New Covenants, and it should not be assumed that Dr. Kline would agree with everything in this essay.

with Him. The psychological instinct in the "altar call" is correct: Men should *do* something and *come* somewhere in response to the call of the Gospel. Physical response, holistic response by the whole person, is the proper response to the Gospel. It is a perversion to hide the Lord's Supper from view and to ask men to make some hidden, inward motion of the "soul" in coming to Christ. The Biblical gospel addresses the whole man, and the whole person is expected to respond.

To come into Jesus' house to eat His Supper, a person has to cross the threshold of the house. That threshold crossing is the sacrament of Baptism. We do not invite men to be baptized; we invite them to come in and eat, but they must cross the threshold and be baptized before they can sit down. In the parable of the wedding supper (Matt. 22:1-13), one man shows up without the proper garment. Obviously, he did not come in through the door, or he would have been washed and given one (cf. also John 10:1-9).

It is interesting to note how the Greek philosophical influence has gutted Scripture of its clear meaning for so much of Christendom. In Revelation 3:20, for example, Christ asks to be admitted to the church so that He can participate in His own Supper! This, however, is instinctively read by the modern mind as "asking Jesus into your heart," which the passage really has next to nothing to do with. Revelation 3:20 is speaking of the covenant meal.

Similarly, the parable of the wedding feast (Matt. 22:1-13) and the entire discussion of the Gospel in Luke 14:1-24, as well as such passages as Isaiah 55, are read as if only some inward "spiritual" matter were under consideration. Not at all. The invitation is to a real meal, one at which Christ is present as Host. Real food, physical food, is to be eaten.

From the Garden of Eden to the Tree of Life in the book of Revelation, shared food is a sign of the covenant between God and His people. The Scriptures have so much to say on this that one scarcely knows where to begin. Melchizedek shared bread and wine with Abram (Gen. 14:18). God shared a meal with Abraham (Gen. 18). When Jacob and Laban made their covenant, they shared a meal (Gen. 31:44-46). The Passover meal was the sign of God's covenant to Israel in Egypt, and down through the

ages thereafter. At Sinai, when God established the covenant with
Israel, Moses and the elders ate with God (Ex. 24). At the Feast of
Tabernacles, the people were to eat in the presence of God and re-
joice (Deut. 14:22-27). In the wilderness, the people ate manna
and drank water from the rock, both of which were sacraments of
Christ (John 6; 1 Cor. 10:1-5). The milk and honey in the land
(house) of promise were tokens of God's presence and blessing.
And we can go on and on, not to speak of the other feasts in
Israel, and the Peace Sacrifice that the family shared with the
priest and with the Lord.

Are these all "spiritual" meals? Away with such internalized
Greek nonsense! *Of course* what matters most is the presence of
Christ, and fellowship with Him, but He has ordained that fellowship to take place *at a meal*. He invites us over for supper every
week, and we decide to eat with Him four times a year. Do you
think He might possibly be offended? He invites His enemies, in
the Gospel, to join Him for dinner, but we encourage men to contemplate an absent Christ in their souls. Is our evangelistic display askew?

The Lord's Supper is not some mystery kept hidden from the
view of the world. Nor is it some mystical rite to be kept "special"
by infrequent observance. It is as simple as dinner with Jesus, and
more profound than any theologian can ever fully understand.

The Lord's Supper does not have an exclusively backward
orientation. It is a Medieval perversion to focus only on the death
of Christ in the Lord's Supper. The emphasis in Scripture is
equally on the active presence of Christ at His Supper, and on the
Supper's prophecy that He will return. Holy Communion is not a
morbid event, but a feast. Let the churches celebrate it as a feast,
before the eyes of the world, so that the unconverted will realize
the full extent of what they are being invited to partake of.

The Time of the Feast

Christ, as God, is present everywhere. Christ, as King and
elder Brother and Guide to His people is present with them all the
time. The question is whether there is any special presence of

Christ associated with special worship, or is all worship the same?

The church has always affirmed, because of clear Biblical indication, that there is a distinction to be drawn between Christ's general presence and His special presence, between general six-day worship and special sabbatical worship. The presence of God is marked by special blessing and curse (Ex. 3:7-14; 6:1-8; 20:5, 7, 12; Ps. 135:13f.; Is. 26:4-8; Hos. 12:4-9; 13:4ff.; Mal. 3:6; John 8:31-59). In the New Covenant, this special blessing and curse is attached to the Lord's Supper (1 Cor. 10:16; 11:17-34). Christ, then, is specially present at His Table.

Also, the Day of the Lord is the great time of blessing and curse. The sabbath day is the Day of the Lord, or the Lord's Day. The association is all important. We are told in 1 Cor. 11:31 that judgment is associated with Lord's Day worship and the Supper. This is the time of the coming of the Lord, when He comes specially to be present with His people.

Everything in sabbatical worship stems from the concept of special presence. The special regulative principle of worship is an expression of the special regulation of special worship. The special day is an expression of the special time of special nearness of the Lord. Special blessing and curse is attached to the observation of sacramental worship. The special institution of worship (the church), with its special officers (elders), flows from special presence.

Historically, Calvinism has not always been clear on this. Some, such as John Calvin himself, affirm the special regulative principle of worship, but do not distinguish between the sabbath or Lord's Day and the other days. If we take a consistently sabbatarian approach, then the special regulative principle only applies to special sabbath worship. Thus, informal voluntary feasts, such as Hanukkah (John 10) or the festival of the incarnation (Christmas) are not bound to the rules governing special sabbatical worship.

The special time is clearly the sabbath. Some have argued that just as space has been decentralized in the New Covenant (no more central sanctuary, but now Christ is present wherever two or three gather), so also time has been decentralized, so that we choose the time of special worship. Against this notion are two considerations. First, it does not follow that the decentralization

of space means the flattening of time. Time has no "center," and
the sabbath is not one center but a repeated series of special times.
Moreover, second, the references in the New Testament to the
Lord's Day imply that the special time for worship continues.

The testimony of the book of Revelation is particularly important here. John says he was in the Spirit on the Lord's Day. The
reference to being "in the Spirit" (1:10) is a clear reference to Special Presence, particularly since John was caught up into heaven
and participated in the heavenly worship service (Rev. 4, 5). The
sound of the trumpet (1:10) was the call to special assembly (Num.
10:3, 4).

Further, we ought simply to recognize that we do not meet
with God for special worship when we choose, but when He ap-
points. That appointment is the sabbath or Lord's Day.

Man is a cyclical being, and the seven-day and seven-year
work-rest cycles are part of his makeup. Violations of that cycle
lead to sickness and death. God will have the entire cosmos operating together on that cycle, angels included (Rev. 4, 5). Thus, we
do not choose our own personal sabbath, unless we are engaged in
some unavoidable work of "mercy or necessity."

When does the sabbath begin? The Biblical day seems most
clearly to begin at sundown, according to the testimony of creation (Gen. 1:5, etc.) and of redemption (Ex. 12:6, 14). Passover
was held beginning at sundown, and the Day of Atonement, specifically called a sabbath, ran from evening to evening (Lev.
23:32). Since the Day of Atonement was the preeminent sabbath
of sabbaths in the Old Covenant, coming in the seventh month,
and characterized by fasting as well as rest, the rule of evening to
evening is surely established for the sabbath.

The New Testament clearly teaches that the Old Covenant
sabbaths are abolished (Col. 2:16-17). Interestingly, the New Testament institutes the Lord's Day, or Day of the Lord, in the place
of the Old Covenant sabbath, so that it is proper to speak of the
Lord's Day as the Christian sabbath.[11] The Lord's Day, however,

---

11. See my monograph, *Sabbath Breaking and the Death Penalty: A Theological Investigation* (Tyler, TX: Geneva Ministries, 1986).

is not spoken of as a day of rest but as a day of worship. This raises the possibility that the day of rest, for some people, might be another day than the day of worship — as indeed is the case for ministers and for those engaged in works of mercy and necessity. For the most part, worship and rest should coincide, as they do in Christ.

The Lord's Day clearly begins with sunrise and continues after sunset. The sunrise is a sign or token of the New Covenant (Mal. 4:2; 2 Sam. 23:4; Is. 60:1-3). On the first Lord's Day, Jesus met with the disciples after sunset and shared bread and wine with them then (Luke 24:29-43; John 20:19). The preaching of the Day of Pentecost came in the morning (Acts 2:15), while the Lord's Supper was eaten on the evening of the Lord's Day (1 Cor. 11:20-22, 33-34).

On balance, then, it seems that we should ideally begin our restored-creation-sabbath rest on Saturday night (unless we must rest some other day), have a preaching service Sunday morning, and the Lord's Supper Sunday night. All things considered, the Lord's Supper is an evening meal, as was the Passover, so the most appropriate time for special Eucharistic worship is Sunday evening. The fact that people brought their meals to the Agape Feast (Love Feast) before eating the Lord's Supper shows that preparation of food is not forbidden on the Lord's Day. Thus, we may wisely and joyfully reinstitute the Biblical Agape Feast (covered dish supper) for Sunday nights, at least occasionally.

The Lord's Supper is not optional on the Lord's Day. The Bible never contemplates divorcing these things. God commands our presence at His table. Ordinarily, it is not wise to set up extra communion services on other days of the week. It is true that the New Covenant is a kind of perpetual sabbath and Lord's Day, but this does not eliminate the special weekly Lord's Day. In times of revival, such as are seen in Acts 2:42, 46 and in Calvin's Geneva, daily preaching services may occur, and perhaps the Lord's Supper would be appropriate on a daily basis.

In the writings of theologians, there is a preoccupation with the question of whether or not the efficacy of the sacrament is the same as or different from that of the preached Word and general daily faith. This question arises only because the Biblical unity of sabbath, proclamation, sacrament, and gathered priesthood has been ripped asunder. The Bible cannot answer questions concerning the supposed sacramental status of the sabbath, or what there is "extra" about the communion service. As Calvin pointed out, the sacrament is in the nature of a miraculous visible seal to the preached word.[12] Just as Word (authority), Presence, and miracle (power, control) go together in the Scripture, so Word, Presence, and sacrament go together in the New Covenant.

If we distinguish the sabbath day from the six cultural days, and sabbatical activity (special worship, rest, and recreational delight in the works of God and man) from cultural activity (creative work and labor in restraining the curse), we can also distinguish the special presence of Christ, as heaven is opened on the sabbath, from His general presence with His people on the cultural days. Thus, we can distinguish an informal Bible study or a Wednesday night meeting from a sabbath worship festival. Moreover, we can distinguish the official gathering of the priesthood under the leadership of special priests (elders) from general informal gatherings of the priesthood on the six cultural days for Bible study. It is the power of the special priest to bind and loose, to admit to sealing ordinances or to excommunicate, to place God's blessing on the people (not merely to invoke it, Num. 6:23-27) and to curse God's enemies.

Thus, the special efficacy of the sacraments is part and parcel of the special efficacy of sabbath worship, the blessing of special priests, the special "official" proclamation of the Word, and preeminently the special presence of Jesus. The difference between this and daily Christian experience is not normative, as if something different in the way of principle were involved; nor is it existential, as if we exercise some other kind of faith; but it is situational, carried out on the sabbath day in the special presence of God, the angels, the spirits of just men made perfect, and the gathered priesthood (Heb. 12:22-25).

---

12. Roland S. Wallace, *Calvin's Doctrine of the Word and Sacrament* (Tyler, TX: Geneva Ministries, 1982), pp. 137-141.

To rip the eating of the sacrament out of this setting has two effects. First, it perverts the revelation of Christ in worship, just as to have ripped out a piece of the Tabernacle furniture would have perverted the revelation of Christ under the Old Covenant. Thus, God's people are confused, and do not experience the fulness of revelation, of the Word. Nor is their need for the covenant meal, and for sealing ordinances, satisfied. As a result, God's people will seek substitute experiences elsewhere.

Second, ripping the sacrament out of this regular sabbath worship setting makes it into something special and mysterious. The question is then raised, what is the special mysterious efficacy of the sacrament? This tends toward superstition among the people, whereas weekly observance and rejoicing in the covenant meal would prevent that.

The Lord's Supper is the covenant meal, and the Lord's Day is the day of judgment. As we break the covenant through sin during the week, we come to the Lord on the sabbath, confessing our sin, accepting His judgment, and renewing the covenant. The broken covenant is reratified ceremonially on the sabbath. Thus, there is a covenant recital, rehearsing the deeds and the law of the covenant. We rehearse the deeds of the covenant when we say the Creed, and we rehearse the law when we hear the proclamation of the Word. The covenant is renewed, and sealed once again by the covenant meal. This is not to say that we lose our salvation during the week, only to regain it on the sabbath as a result of covenant renewal. Rather, we must distinguish among three different things. First, there is the total removal of sin from us in Christ, as He died for our sins on the cross, and as this is applied to us definitively when we are born again. Second, there is the daily cleansing from experienced sin that comes, based always on the work of Christ, as a result of our confession and repentance (1 John 1:9). Third, there is the sacramental signing and sealing of cleansing. It is not only baptism that serves as a sign and a seal. The weekly sacramental cleansing from sin adds, as it were, a seal to the daily repentance we have engaged in during the week. The weekly covenant renewal is a weekly (sacramental) clearing of the deck.

This is why the Corinthian church was in such gross sin: They came to the covenant renewal supper, but refused to forgive one another, holding grudges right into the next week. The meaning of the weekly sacramental cleaning of the slate was lost on them. The faithful Christian rejoices in the fact that God has not only forgiven him all sin in Christ, but God forgives his daily sins as he confesses them, and seals that forgiveness in the weekly covenant renewal.

Covenant Bonding

Man was created to participate in the covenant life of God, though obviously not in the being of God. Adam was created the son of God (Luke 3:38), and a son is a member of the family covenant. Sin broke that covenant, and since life itself is a covenant phenomenon, given by the Holy Spirit, the breaking of the family covenant community spelled death for the ones cast outside (Gen. 2:17). The restoration of covenant community and life was only possible if God Himself should become the substitute for man's punishment, and experience covenant exile and death on man's behalf. This the Lord Jesus Christ did for His people (Mark 15:34). As a result of His death and resurrection, God's people are restored to covenant fellowship and life (John 17:21-23). The covenant is reestablished through blood unto resurrection life.

All covenant bonding in human life is an extension and replica of the covenant life of God. This means that the covenant of marriage, of the family, and of the household involves a community of life. Since ordinary life comes to us through food, a community of life is a life of shared food. The boundary of the household covenant is established by the supper table. Those who eat at the same table on a regular basis are in covenant union, sharing covenant life, which life comes through food. (Notice the emphasis on food in the Bible, starting in Genesis 2. The household of Israel shared common food, having been told in Leviticus 11 and Deuteronomy 14 what to eat and what not to eat.)

Because of sin, however, all covenant bonding is destroyed. The man attacks his wife, and she attacks him (Gen. 3). The children fight and kill each other (Gen. 4). Thus, all covenant bonding must be reestablished in the sphere of resurrection life and through blood. The marriage bond is reestablished through the blood and pain of the wedding night. The parent-child bond is reestablished through the bloodied birth of the infant. The bond of adoption is permanently established through the bloody boring of the servant's ear at the master's doorpost (Ex. 21:6). The God-man bond is reestablished through the blood of the sacrifice and of circumcision.

These are all threshold experiences, in which a person passes through a door into a house. Because of sin, the door must be bloodied, so that the passage through the threshold is a passage through death to resurrection life. Thus, the door of the human body is bloodied in marriage and in childbirth, and the door of the house is bloodied when the slave is adopted into the family (from then on being known as a "homeborn" slave).[13] Once established through blood, the covenant is renewed through the evening meal — those of the same household eating the same food together. This is simply an extension into common life of what we find in the church as well: the threshold experience of entering the land was the passage through the Jordan river, and the daily food was the milk and honey of the land. The threshold experience of entering the special priestly covenant with God was circumcision, and the covenant renewal was the Passover. In the New Covenant, the threshold experience of entering the house is the cleansing of baptism, and the covenant renewal is the Lord's Supper.

Thus, *covenant bonding is a resurrection phenomenon*, and covenant life is in the sphere of the resurrection. To the extent that the unbeliever experiences covenant bonding in his marriage, family, business, etc., to that extent he is borrowing capital from the resurrection, crumbs that fall from the Lord's Table. This is common grace, the goodness of God that leads to repentance. If he will not improve on these graces, he will lose all covenant life, and be isolated apart from all community by himself in hell forever.

Covenant life, resurrection life, then, entails *a social bond*, a bond between God and man and between man and man. Thus,

---

13. On this whole matter, see my book *The Law of the Covenant*, (Tyler, TX: Institute for Christian Economics, 1984), chapter 5.

the idea of community is inseparable from that of resurrection life. The sacrament of life, in which Christ's resurrection life is imparted to us, cannot but be a community-creating experience.

To eat Christ's body and drink His blood, then, entails participation both in His *death* and in His *resurrection*. These cannot be separated. In that the body and blood are separated, we participate in His death, *covenant renewal*. At the same time, the bread represents the unbroken life of the church, and the wine represents the life that is in the blood (Lev. 17:11, John 6:53). The Spirit is the life. As life is in the blood, and as the blood sustains the body, so the Holy Spirit sustained Christ, and now sustains us. To drink His blood is not only to participate in His death, but also *to drink the life of the Spirit, resurrection life*. This resurrection life is *covenantally bonding*, and creates the community symbolized by the one loaf (1 Cor. 10:17).

In the Bible, the entrance of a man across the threshold of God's kingdom and into covenant life also meant *bringing his whole household with him*. The boundaries of that household can be seen from Genesis 2:24 and those passages indicating that slaves were included in the household. When a son or daughter leaves the household and cleaves to a spouse, a new household is established. Before such a time, the son or daughter is included in the father's household, for as long as he or she eats at the father's table.

All those who eat at the household table are included in the covenant with God, at least during the historical administration of the covenant. (If a son or a slave does not mix faith with the covenant promises, he will be cut off from the eschatological fulfillment of the covenant.) Both children and slaves were circumcised (baptized), and both participated in the sacramental meals (Passover, Peace Sacrifice, Feast of Tabernacles, Lord's Supper).

The Scripture plainly states that the infants and children under the Old Covenant ate at the Lord's Table. This is found in 1 Corinthians 10:1-5 and John 6:31-65. In these passages, both Paul and Jesus teach us that the manna and the water provided for Israel during the wilderness were true Spiritual food, the same food as the Lord's Supper. It is not the precise substance of food that matters, but the Spirit Who comes to be with the sacramental food and Who gives life. The Spirit came to be with the manna and water in the wilderness, with the Passover meal, with other Old Covenant meals, and He comes to be with the Lord's Supper today.

What this means is clear enough. The children ate the manna and drank the water. Indeed, there was nothing else to eat or drink. The passage in 1 Corinthians 10:1-5 associates this with baptism: all those baptized in the Old Covenant were entitled to eat the Lord's Supper (Note that it does not say that all, including children, were circumcised in the Red Sea crossing, but that they were baptized. This is a proof text for infant baptism.) This does not mean that all were saved, for "with most of them God was not well pleased; for they were laid low in the wilderness." Those who were initially included in the historical administration of the covenant by baptism did not all persevere in faith so as to attain to the eschatological fulfillment of the covenant. At any rate, we can see that the Lord has invited the children to His table; do we dare to turn them away, as the disciples did, and received Christ's rebuke (Matt. 19:13-15)?

Slaves, including those not personally converted, also ate the Passover in the Old Covenant. All purchased slaves were circumcised when they became part of the master's household, according to the express command of God. (Ex. 12:44; Gen. 17:12f). The act of circumcision made the slave into a covenant member, in the same class as the "native of the land" or Israelite (Ex. 12:48; Lev. 15:29), able to partake of the Passover, which no foreigner could partake of (Ex. 12:43-45).

A newly purchased slave would not even know the Hebrew language, let alone be inwardly converted. It would take time to teach him Hebrew, and then to explain the covenant of God to him. Notice, however, that the slave was circumcised in ignorance, and admitted to the Lord's Table in ignorance.

This seems strange to modern Americans because of the influence of individualism. The Bible however, is covenantal, not individualistic. The household is included in the decision of the covenant head, and it is only as the members of the household mature that they are expected to continue in the covenant on their own. Under the influence of humanistic individualism, however,

Baptist theology has grown up. The Baptist doctrine is that baptism symbolizes a person's individual faith and regeneration, so that only such persons can come to the Table of the Lord. This, however, is not what baptism means in the Bible. In Scripture, baptism is God's claim of ownership and God's promise of salvation. In the sense that it is a claim, baptism creates an obligation to obey God's Word. In the sense that it is a promise, baptism is the Gospel, and creates an obligation to exercise faith in God. Thus, the Reformation faith exhorts its children (and slaves, if there are any) to improve on their baptisms, to mix faith with the promises. The promise is for you and to your children, we are told (Acts 2:39), just as it was for Abraham. The promise must be mixed with faith to be effective, for there is no automatic salvation. Baptism, however, is not man-centered, a sign of faith, but God-centered, a sign of the promise. Thus, baptism is administered first, and then faith is to follow. The Bible does not teach us to baptize indiscriminately, but to baptize by households. Those who share table fellowship with the covenant head of the household (wife, children, and slaves) are included in the household covenant, and baptized. They also belong at the Lord's Table.

When Jesus invites us over to His house for a dinner, He does not tell us to get a babysitter and leave the kids at home. They are invited, too. They cross the threshold with their parents, and sit with them at the meals.

Current-day practice, however, often assumes that baptized children must go through some experience, to the satisfaction of some spiritual examiner, before they can be admitted to the Lord's Table. There is not a shred of evidence in Scripture for this additional demand. If we are going to treat our children as unregenerate until they have gone through some mystical experience, we had better not teach them to pray, or even permit them to pray. Away with such hymns as "Jesus loves *me*, this I know, for *the Bible tells me so*. Little ones to Him *belong*; they are weak, but He is strong." That song is a lie, if children are not even allowed to eat Jesus' food.

The Biblical perspective is clear. We teach our children that Jesus is their God and Savior. We teach them to pray, and we teach them the laws and precepts of the kingdom. Baptism is God's seal of covenant membership, and entitles the child to all the benefits of the covenant. If the child later on breaks the seal and rejects the covenant, he is to be excommunicated; and this presupposes that he is already a communicant member.

Indeed, the Bible indicates that the foetus participates in Jesus' Supper. We all know that unborn children get their food from their mothers, in the "natural" sense. Indeed, one of the traditional ways to calm down a violently active foetus is for the mother to sip a small glass of wine; it puts the baby right to sleep. But, does this fact really apply to "Spiritual" food, in the sense of the Lord's Supper?

Yes, there is Scriptural evidence that it does, and it is found in Judges 13:7, 14. When the angel of the Lord appeared to the wife of Manoah and told her that her son (Samson) would be a Nazirite from his earliest days, He told her not to eat or drink anything a Nazirite should not eat or drink. Now, the reason the Nazirite was forbidden to drink wine and eat raisins was not because of any physical influence these would have (Numbers 6), because there is no special physical influence associated with raisins and grapes. The reason was quasi-sacramental: During the course of his work, the Nazirite was not to participate in the good fruits and blessings of the Lord. This was as a type of the Lord Jesus Christ, Who took upon Himself the curse of the covenant during His life, so that we might experience the blessings of the covenant during our lives.[14]

The fact that the mother of the Nazirite was to abstain from the fruit of the vine means that the Spiritual-symbolic character of food pertains to the child as much as to the mother. Indeed, this would be obvious if we were faithful to the Scripture and used wine in communion, for then the effect on the foetus would be noticeable. At any rate, those who believe that children do not belong at Jesus' table should excommunicate all pregnant women during the terms of their pregnancies. Only in this way can we be

---

14. On the Nazirite, see my book, *Judges: God's War Against Humanism* (Tyler, TX: Geneva Ministries, 1985), chapter 12.

sure that no children are partaking. If this seems extreme, it is only because the theological position that prohibits children from eating the Lord's Supper is extreme.

What is the relevance of this for evangelism? It should be obvious. In an age when the family is breaking down as never before, and when there is, moreover, great alarm over this breakdown, the church must make clear that Christianity has the answer. Evangelism is not exclusively individualistic, but covenantal. We are not out simply to convert individual people; we are also out to convert families. Part of the display of the Lord's Supper week by week needs to be its familial character. Away with the nauseating individualism which has done so much to wreck the family during the last two centuries! The invitation to the wedding feast is extended to the whole family.

Analogical Hospitality

Now that we have considered how God would have us display His hospitality in worship, let us return to a consideration of how we as Christians should evangelize by hospitality. Just as we are to think God's thoughts after Him, so we are to live God's life after Him. This "imaging" of God is called analogical living. Just as God sets a pattern of hospitality, inviting people over to His house for dinner, so we should imitate that pattern. The perfect context for evangelism is the Christian home.

We may contrast this practice with the more common method of going door to door. When we knock on the stranger's door, we are at his mercy. He may or may not let us in. He is immediately suspicious of us: What are these people doing? Are they Mormons or Jehovah's Witnesses, or some new cult (like *serious* Presbyterians)? Moreover, if he lets us in, we are on his turf. It is his house, his castle. And this is as it should be. God in His common grace grants to the unbeliever the joys and privileges of having a family and a household. It is indeed his house, and we are invaders. We are speaking to him in his context. Moreover, he cannot see anything of how Christians live, so we cannot give him a whole-life message. The situation is not only awkward, but it is relatively ineffectual. The gains to the church from this method are minimal. That is not to say that God never blesses visitation evangelism, but that it is not a very strong way to witness.

Now, if I have a neighbor family over to my house, I have the opportunity to display Christian hospitality to them from the moment they cross my threshold. I am in control of the situation, and it is a Christian environment. They observe Christianity in action. They eat my food. They observe the devotions conducted at my table. Without invading their privacy, I can explain Christianity to them. And even if I do not give them the Gospel with a direct verbal appeal, it is set before them unmistakably in all that they experience while in a Christian home. The advantages of this method of evangelism are obvious.

Of course, this means that I must have my Christian household in order. Probably the main deterrent to hospitality evangelism, and hospitality in general, is the fact that the Christian family sees itself as too disorderly and not a good witness. An untidy house with a sloppy housekeeper will effectively keep the covenant head of the home from inviting people over. Bickering parents, undisciplined children, poor leadership by the father, are all too often found in Christian homes as well as in pagan ones. The Christian household, however, must analogically reflect the order found in the kingdom of Christ. Christians must honestly face up to the disorder in their own lives and homes, for judgment begins at the house of God. Then hospitality will be a real possibility. Most children will act up when company is visiting the home, because the children are made to feel insecure by the attention the parents are giving to outsiders. The issue is not whether children act up or not, but whether the outsider will see Christian parents handling the problem in a Christian manner (e.g., giving extra love to the kids). The churches must double their efforts to raise up orderly Christian homes, as a prelude to hospitality in general and hospitality evangelism in particular.

Since elders should be the leaders in the church in her imitation of God, no one should be an elder who is not given to hospitality. The diaconate, the apprenticeship for the elders, is characterized by "waiting on tables," or training in hospitality. Because there are great expenses connected with frequent hospitality, all elders (and deacons also) should be given money to help with this. (See 1 Tim. 5:17, which presupposes that all elders are given some honor [money].)

If it is questioned whether we should invite unbelievers to our table, the answer is that our table is not the Lord's Table. It is related to the Lord's Table analogically, but it is not the same thing. The household table is a feature of common grace and of common life, an outflow from the Lord's Table. It is a blessing that partakes of covenant bonding and is a benefit of the resurrection, but until the end of history it is an institution of common grace. Abraham extended Patriarchal hospitality to any stranger travelling by. The stranger in the ancient near east was always entitled to three days of hospitality, regardless of his religion. While in Abraham's house, the stranger was under the protection of Abraham's household God, who in his case was the Lord.

Similarly, our hospitality can be and is to be extended to anyone except persons excommunicated from the church. When in our houses, the visitors are under the protection of our God, the Lord Jesus Christ. This enables us to tell them about Him, and to invite them to put their own households under His covenantal canopy. In this way, the unbeliever sees the whole Christian lifestyle, a style of life which he cannot help but wish were his own, since his own marriage and family life is in bad shape.

It is much more difficult and takes much more skill to witness for Christ in a strange house, with its own alien household gods. Such a difficult task is not for every Christian, but requires gifts and skills of a special sort, akin to the work of casting out demons, since going into a strange house is often going into a demonized environment. The space enclosed by a house is a real defined space, a place. For this reason, the question of what gods or God is ruling in the house-place is not an idle question. There are such things as demonized or haunted houses. How much better is hospitality evangelism, when the stranger is in a Christian house!

One of the sad side-effects of the notion that every Christian should be involved in visitation evangelism has been the production of truncated, simplified presentations of the Gospel. This kind of thing goes hand in hand with the Greek notion of the soul and the primacy of the intellect, since the Gospel is reduced to a personal individual decision to accept Jesus into one's "soul," and not the adoption of a new lifestyle. As a result, the actual message gotten out this way is only a small part of the whole Gospel. Hospitality evangelism, on the other hand, addresses the whole man in the context of his whole family, and in the environment of the Christian household. Hospitality evangelism is more natural and conversational, and can range over the whole spectrum of the Christian life. The Gospel is as wide as all of life, and hospitality evangelism enables us to make that point clear in a way that visitation evangelism usually cannot.

Summary and Applications

The modern church has confused preaching and teaching, so that it preaches to the saints instead of teaching them and building them up. The proper place for preaching is the marketplace, the highways and byways, which today means primarily the media. If the local newspaper will not give you a weekly column, then take out advertisement space and put in a brief, hard-hitting message for the times. Remember that you are not advertising your own church, but you are heralding the good news in the marketplace. The same thing applies to the use of radio and television.

At the same time, the media is not the place to conduct a worship service. When worship services are broadcast, the teacher tends to become a preacher, trying to save the lost instead of building up God's people. Also, worship services should not be broadcast because the people of God are supposed to gather for worship, not sit at home. The Lord's Supper is an indispensable part of worship, and can only be partaken of at the church.

The modern church has failed to make visible the Word of God, confusing the saints as to the meaning of the Lord's Supper, and confusing the holistic nature of the evangelistic invitation. The Gospel addresses the whole man, invites him and his family to the Lord's feast. This is sadly obscured today. The mysteries of the kingdom of God are open public "mysteries." The Word is displayed through preaching the Gospel to the unbeliever. This is the active form of evangelism. All of the Christian life, however, and especially worship, are passive forms of evangelism. The unbeliever who visits the service of worship should hear the Word taught and sung and prayed, and should see the covenant meal displayed before his eyes, even though he does not participate in it. In this way, the worship service, though not oriented toward evangelism, performs an evangelistic function in displaying the worship of God.

The emphasis on visitation evangelism has produced a lot of simplified Gospel tracts and methods, but little transformation of society. While door-knocking is usually necessary in starting a church from scratch, the Bible indicates that hospitality evangelism is a much preferable method under ordinary circumstances. While it is true that Christ is a Visitor, the Biblical concept of visitation is usually connected with judgment. While it is still day, we should show Christ as the gracious Host, Who invites people to His home for a feast.

End Note

Although the Bible gives no evidence to support the so-called three-office view, it does not thereby exclude the possibility of experts and specialists among the elders. It is clear that all elders have the same powers and authority. The modern notion that only a teaching elder can "preach" is rubbish. The idea that ruling elders admit to the Lord's Table but only teaching elders can administer the Table is nonsense, and nowhere to be found in Scripture. The tendency of this error is once again to surround the Lord's Table with superstition, so that the teaching elder "consecrates the elements" or "sets the elements apart from ordinary use." What is supposed to happen at this point in the service? There is no ritual of consecrating the elements in the Bible or in Protestant theology. It is the people, not the elements, that are to be consecrated to God, and set apart.

Expertise is another matter. In 1 Timothy 5:17 three levels of reward for expert service are mentioned: the normal situation in which the elder receives some pay to offset the time and money he puts into kingdom work, the elder who does exceptionally good work and should receive double pay, and the elder whose expertise lies in the area of Biblical teaching and who should also receive double pay.

In a largely illiterate (pre-Gutenberg) society, the man who could read and write had a real skill. Such was the scribe in the Old Testament, such as Shaphan in 2 Kings 22:8, 10. He read the Law of God for Hilkiah and Josiah, who apparently could not read it for themselves. The scribes, by New Testament times, were expert students of the written Word. This expertise continued into the New Testament church. Special expertise does not, however, qualify any elder for special powers. Indeed, the qualifications for elders are almost entirely moral, not intellectual (1 Tim. 3; Tit. 1). The notion that the primary skills of the eldership are intellectual, the three-office view, is a byproduct of the Greek primacy-of-the-intellect philosophy.

In the post-Gutenberg era of universal literacy, it is to be expected that whatever boundaries between teaching and ruling elders have grown up should begin to break down. This is a good thing, and a real bonus for the churches. It should be encouraged and enhanced.

Public teaching, however, need not be the only area of expertise recognized by the churches; counselling is another. Throughout its history, the church has always labored in the "cure of souls," and the ministry of counselling is not only a real skill that should be remunerated, but it is also an excellent means of evangelism, particularly in an age of social collapse.

If we employ the model set out in Exodus 18, we might have higher ranks of elders. It must be kept in mind, however, that the elders have two functions: shepherding by means of teaching and advice, and rendering judgments in judicial cases. The former is a personal function, the latter a joint power that requires the elders to sit together as a court. The concept of ascending courts does not place in the hands of higher elders any special powers, such as the power to administer sacraments, or to administer the "rite of confirmation." Nor are the higher elders either administrators or legislators for the churches under them, since the Spirit is to administer the loosely-organized churches, and the Bible is her legislation. Higher elders give advice and counsel to junior elders, and handle appeals from lower courts. That is all.

The Bible actually teaches, by the way, only one office in the church: the office of ruler (priest-king-prophet). The church ruler guards the sacraments (priestly), rules (kingly), and teaches (prophetic). The only other office in Scripture is the office of ruler in the state (see Zech. 6:13). Each elder should have a diaconal assistant, and the deacons should assist the elders generally in their work. This would be more obvious to us if we lived in an age in which job training was by apprenticeship instead of by university education. Some of the great deacons in the Bible who later became elders are Joshua, Elisha, the twelve apostles, and the seven deacons of Acts 6.

The notion that elders rule and deacons serve is unBiblical and pagan, and completely contradicts the message of Mark 10:42-45. The idea that elders minister to spiritual needs and deacons minister to material needs is a nice, tidy piece of Greek philosophy, but has no foundation in the Biblical holistic view of man. Since the deacon is the apprentice, he will wind up doing the "dirty" work, and this means the more material and less directly Word-related tasks (2 Kings 3:11; Mark 6:41-43; Acts 6:2ff.) These are not two offices, however, but the relation between master and apprenticeship.

While we are on this subject, it might be well to note that the minimum age for rule in Scripture is 30 years of age (Gen. 41:46; 2 Sam. 5:4; Luke 3:23). They *marvelled at Christ's wisdom* when He was twelve, but He did not ask them to submit to His authority until He was thirty. He was wise; the modern evangelical and Reformed churches are incredibly stupid in this regard. They ordain men to become super-elders (three-office "ministers") who have no experience at all, have never been deacons, have had only three years of *book*learning, and are about 25 years old. A more incredibly moronic system of training can scarcely be imagined. It is no wonder that the church is in the shape it is in. Paul told Timothy not to let people despise his youth, when Timothy was at least 35, and Rehoboam was called a youth when he was 41 years old (1 Kings 12:8; 14:21). The word 'elder,' after all, does mean *older*.

Of course, after a century of ignorance and compromise there are very few older elders in the churches. It may be and usually is necessary for younger men to take the lead; this is not the Biblical norm, however, and the young men should be aware of the dangers in their undertaking.

12

TRIUMPHALISTIC INVESTITURE

Since the time of the Vestarian Controversy in Elizabethan England, and even earlier, the wearing of vestments has been viewed as a "Romish error" by many evangelicals, particularly those in the Puritan, Presbyterian, and Baptist traditions, as well as those influenced by them. The purpose of this essay is to take another look at the issue. We need to distinguish between two different matters at the outset. The first is the question of the use of distinctive clerical garb, and the second is the question of the use of liturgical vestments (special clothing used in worship by the officiating elder).

Clerical Garb

Virtually all churches in America expect their ministers to wear special clothing, to have a special look. Just to illustrate this, let me briefly describe three common forms of distinctive clerical garb. First, there is the fundamental baptist's clerical garb, which I call the "flashy" look. It often involves, for instance, white or maroon shoes, a white or maroon belt, a loud necktie, and some form of relatively loud suit. This flashy (almost "superfly") look is found not only among fundamental baptists, but also among pentecostals of all sorts. Clearly not all fundamentalist and pentecostal preachers dress this way, but many do.

Second, there is the young evangelical preacher look. This involves a more conservative business suit, but not black. It also involves a particular styling of the hair, this being perhaps the most distinctive aspect of the YEP look. One of my colleagues, Elder

Lewis Bulkeley, has referred to this as the "helmet haircut." Each time I go to a pastors conference of the Gothard Institute, I am struck by the cloned appearance of the crowd, because virtually all the men have "Yeppie" helmet haircuts. The hair is blow-dried into a seemingly perfect mold.

Third, there is the conservative presbyterian minister's garb. This means a black or very dark blue suit, a white shirt, and a conservative necktie; rather like the kind of clothing worn by lawyers.

Now, this is what people expect their pastors to dress like, if not every day, at least in the pulpit — and it most certainly is distinctive clerical garb.

There are three aspects to these clerical costumes: high quality, conservatism, and distinctiveness. First, people want their pastors to dress well, whatever dressing well means to them. For people in lower social and economic brackets, dressing well means dressing loudly; for more upper class types, it means dressing in severe, tasteful dark suits. In other words, people want to see their clergy adorned in fine clothing.

The second aspect is no less important, though more subtle. Clerical garb generally lags behind the latest styles. There seem to be several reasons for this. One is that the leading clergy are always older men, whose tastes were set in youth, and who are thus naturally disposed to the forms and fashions of an earlier time. After a number of generations, this conservative tendency can result in a "clerical costume" that actually had been the public fashion generations earlier.

A second reason for conservative garb is that most churches keep their pastors poor. This is no myth; it is reality, and has been for centuries. A result of it is that clergymen cannot afford a lot of clothing, and so tend to avoid fashion and fad, going for clothes that are less likely to go out of date. A black suit, white shirt, moderate necktie — these never go out of style, because they are never really *in* style; but white shoes, green suits, very wide or very narrow lapels, very wide or very narrow neckties, very wide or very narrow belts, etc. — these do not last more than a few years before they change. Lack of funds keeps clerical garb conservative.

But third, probably the most important reason for conservatism is that people rightly expect their elders and pastors to display a bearing and lifestyle that is relatively more sober than that of the rest of society, because the church and her ministers are seen as a stabilizing element in society. Thus, except where the need for a flashy look has overwhelmed this conservative tendency, people expect their pastors to dress in a more "quiet" fashion than society roundabout.

This last observation leads us to the third aspect of clerical garb mentioned above: distinctiveness. People want their pastors to look different. People need to repose some kind of secondary confidence in their pastors (primary trust in God and His Word, of course). An outward sign of office is helpful in this, and people desire it, even when they do not realize it. An example will help: People want physicians and nurses to dress in white. They have more confidence in what the physician or nurse says if he or she is dressed in medical garb. People *want* to believe their physicians, because they *want* to believe that they can be cured of whatever afflicts them. And since confidence is a large part of any cure, it is a sound and healthy thing for physicians to maintain a slight degree of mystique about their work. The uniform helps quite a bit in this.

Now, the same thing is true in the church. People want to believe that their elders and pastors can help them; they want to repose a secondary kind of trust and confidence in them; and thus they want their pastors to dress in a distinctive way. Pastors represent the church as Mother to the people, and the people want to trust their Mother, just as they put primary trust in their heavenly Father. This has been true throughout all of church history, and it does not go away just because we fail to take notice of it. We need to become "epistemologically self-conscious" in this area of clerical symbolism and garb.

Since this is so, shouldn't we pastors just take the bull by the horns, and dress like clergymen? The customary apparel of the clergy in English-speaking lands, and indeed worldwide, for the past century or so, has been the black shirt with a white tab in the front, or a white ring collar around the neck. (The tab collar is more common in both Catholic and Protestant circles, though one sees the ring collar sometimes in both circles also.) Recently, due to the influence of the Liturgical Movement, the medieval black has been supplemented by shirts of various colors.

The ring collar makes a particularly appropriate uniform because the "dog collar" is the mark of a slave. The clergy are to serve God's people as servant priests to the royal priesthood. Those who are to rule, must do so by becoming servants, said our Lord (Mark 10:43-44).

Vestments

Properly speaking, a vestment is a special garment, generally some form of cape, worn during the celebration of Holy Communion by the officiating elder (priest, presbyter, minister, elder, pastor, bishop, you-name-it). What we usually think of as vestments — the black robe (cassock), with a white shirt over it (surplice), and with a colored strip of cloth around the neck and down the sides (stole) — are not properly speaking vestments but are called "choir" attire. For our purposes, however, let's just stick with ordinary, non-specialist language, and call them all vestments. For our purposes, a vestment is a special costume worn by the elders during worship, but not every day.

Why wear special clothing? Because the elder, during the worship service, carries out a symbolic role. When he prays for the people, he symbolizes Christ as the Head of the church, praying to the Father. Thus, his garments of glory and beauty remind the congregation that the prayer offered up during worship is not only the prayer of a sinful man, but it is also the prayer of Christ before the Father. Our own prayers would not be heard if they were not offered in union with those of the Son (see Revelation 7:3, 4).

Second, when the elder reads Scripture and proclaims the Word to the congregation, he symbolizes Christ the Husband of the church, instructing the Bride. Here again, vestments of glory and beauty serve to remind us that we are not listening to the mere opinions of men, but to the very Word of God.

Thus, vestments remind us, and reinforce to us at a deep psychological level, that the man conducting the service is not just our good buddy Joe-Bob Smith, but during this hour he is the Angel of the church (Rev. 1:20f.), the Apostle (emissary) of Christ, the Bishop (overseer) of the congregation, the Elder (wise one) guiding the flock, etc. Conservative French Calvinist theologian Richard Paquier has this to say about it: "Whoever leads in the act of worship does not perform as a private party but as a minister of the church; he is the representative of the community and the spokesman of the Lord. Hence, an especially prescribed vestment, a sort of ecclesiastical 'uniform,' is useful for reminding both the faithful and himself that in this act he is not Mr. So-and-so, but a minister of the church in the midst of a multitude of others."[1]

Biblical Regulation of Vestments

The primary opponents of vestments, historically, have been the presbyterians, baptists, and Puritans. In America, their influence has spread to most of evangelicalism. The popular but erroneous view of the regulative principle of worship to which most evangelicals subscribe, is this: Whatever is not explicitly commanded in the New Testament is absolutely prohibited, in the area of worship. Not only is this version of the regulative principle utterly unBiblical, it is also unworkable, and has no foundation in the Reformation. The actual Principle is this: We are to do in worship only those things that can be substantiated from the whole Bible by precept, principle, or example. As arch-presbyterian Samuel Miller wrote in his book *Presbyterianism* (1835), "the Scriptures being the only infallible rule of faith and practice, no rite or ceremony ought to have a place in the public worship of God, which is not warranted in Scripture, either by direct precept or example, or by good and sufficient inference" (p. 65).

Note that Miller does not insist that every matter "warranted" in Scripture *must* be applied in all times and seasons, as if God had spelled out every detail for all time. Not at all. Rather, whatever we do should have Scriptural backing. Such is the regulative prin-

---

1. Richard Paquier, *Dynamics of Worship: Foundations and Uses of Liturgy* (Philadelphia: Fortress, [1954] English trans. 1967], p. 138.

ciple. Thus, the Bible may *indicate* that clerical garb and/or vestments are a good thing, without *commanding* that the church must always use them, or *describing* what they must look like.

The main problem we have understanding dress in Biblical times is that the industrial revolution, coupled with democratic notions of society, have completely separated us from all human traditions in this area. Nowadays, men dress in "business suits" regardless of their profession; earlier, this was not so. In traditional societies, clothing gave a visible indication of the status of a person, in two regards. First, it gave an indication either of his occupation, or of the kind of occupation he held. Particularly on special occasions, the guild of blacksmiths dressed one way, the guild of bakers another, and the guild of barber-physicians another, and so forth. Clothing marked calling. Democracy has impoverished us to the extent that this no longer is so.

Second, clothing marked clan. Among the Scots, as every presbyterian knows, the plaid tartan is different for each clan. This custom is not unique to Scotland. Now, looking back into the Bible, even if the Bible said nothing about it, we may be virtually certain that the various tribes had different patterns of clothing. This means that the Levites dressed differently from everyone else, and since the Levites became the clergy in Israel, their distinctive tribal garb became the clerical garb of Israel.

We can go further than this general inference, however. God marked out the various ranks of clergy with special clothing, during the Old Covenant. Because every Israelite was a priest to the nations, every Israelite was to wear special clerical garb, consisting of a blue tassel at the corners of his outer garment (Num. 15:37-41). Moreover, the house of Aaron were the priests to Israel, and they were all dressed in special clothing (Ex. 28:4, 40, 41; 1 Sam. 22:18). Finally, the high priest, as priest to all Israel including the Aaronic house, had extra-special vestments to wear (Ex. 28:6-39). Now of course, this was in the Old Testament, but there is no reason to presume any change in principle here. We do not simply reject something just because we do not find it explicitly repeated in the New Testament.

Is there a continuity in this area? Certainly. A priest was not someone who mediated between God and the sinner: That was the role of the prophet (Gen. 20:7). Rather, the priest was a representative of the people to God, and of God to the people. We have seen that the elder in the church today has the same liturgical role, offering prayers on behalf of the people (leading them in prayer), and representing Christ to them in the preaching of the Word. Since the symbolic role is still with us, the outward sign of the symbolic role is still appropriate.

We may go further and notice that in the Bible special clothing was used to designate special office in the political area also. Thus, in setting Joseph over his brothers, Jacob made him a special cloak, and later Pharaoh did the same (Gen. 37:3, 23; 41:42). Similarly, the royal house in Israel wore special clothing (2 Sam. 13:18). Thus, the Bible shows us that it is appropriate and desirable for the leaders in a society (including the church) to dress in a way that displays their office and its glory.

Man was created naked, but as God's image he would eventually have been invested with a robe like God's own glorious "cloud" robe. God's throne is enrobed in the rainbow. Glorious colors mark His garment, and should that of His image. Also, we are told that the stars differ in glory, as do men (1 Cor. 15:41). Christians are called stars in Philippians 2:15, and pastors are called stars in Revelation 1-3. Thus, varieties of garments are appropriate for men in various stations and callings in life. The rejection of distinctive and glorious apparel in our society is a result of the exclusive preoccupation of the church with justification and sanctification, to the exclusion of glorification and dominion.[2]

What we have shown is that both clerical garb and liturgical vestments are fully acceptable in terms of the protestant regulative principle of worship.

---

2. For some of the wider theological ramifications of the doctrine of investiture, see my essay "Rebellion, Tyranny, and Dominion in the Book of Genesis," in Gary North, ed., *Tactics of Christian Resistance*. Christianity & Civilization No. 3 (Tyler, TX: Geneva Ministries, 1983); and Ray R. Sutton, "Clothing and Calling," in James B. Jordan, ed., *The Reconstruction of the Church*. Christianity & Civilization No. 4 (Tyler, TX: Geneva Ministries, 1985).

History and Controversy

We now turn to a brief survey of the history of clerical garb and vestments in the church, and in particular we want to consider the Reformation controversies in this area.

In the early post-apostolic church, it seems that the clergy did not wear distinctive clothing. (This at least is the belief of most scholars, though it can be debated.) Why this was so, we cannot say for certain, but after Constantine Christianized the Roman Empire, the clergy did begin to wear clothing that befitted their office and role. It seems most likely, thus, that clerical garb did not develop in the early church because of persecution, and the desire to keep the clergy as invisible from the state as possible. The clergy were given special recognition during the worship service, however, in that they were marked out by the spatial location they assumed during the meeting. Following the pattern of worship in heaven ("Thy will be done on earth as it is in heaven"), especially as seen in Revelation 5:8-14, the congregation was divided into four groups. Those who held the general office of all believers formed one choir, those who held the office of deacon another choir, and those who held the office of elder or presbyter formed the third choir. Presiding over the meeting was that elder who was set aside to be the officiant in that particular service. Each of these four groups had a specific role to play in the performance of public worship before the throne of God.

Thus, it is no surprise that when circumstances permitted it, the officers of the church began to wear special clerical garb and vestments. At this point a comment by W. Jardine Grisbrooke is worth quoting: "In case one is tempted to regard this development as due to the influence of pagan usage, it is worth nothing that one of the charges levelled by the Emperor Julian the Apostate against the Christians was that they dressed up in special clothes to worship God!"[3] Originally these special clothes were simply conservative Roman apparel of high quality, but as time went along and fashions changed, the clergy continued to wear the old Roman

---

3. "Vestments," in Jones, Wainwright, and Yarnold, ed., *The Study of Liturgy* (New York: Oxford, 1978), p. 489.

clothing, and these came to be the distinctive mark of the clergy.

Let us now leap forward to the time of the Reformation. The Swiss Reformers, including Calvin, were not in favor of retaining traditional vestments. This was not because they believed that the regulative principle forbad them, but because they felt that vestments had been so abused that it was better to do away with them, at least for a while. Calvin opposed fighting over this issue, so that when the newly elected bishop John Hooper spent time in prison (!) rather than wear traditional vestments, Calvin wrote to Bullinger, "While I admire his firmness in refusing the anointing, I had rather he had not carried his opposition so far with respect to the cap and the linen vestment, even though I do not approve of these."[4] Martin Bucer, Peter Martyr, and Heinrich Bullinger took the same basic position.[5]

But what was at issue here? Calvin and the other Swiss Reformers wore the "Genevan gown," which was an academic robe, when they conducted worship. Moreover, I have not been able to find out whether or not Calvin refused all distinctive clerical garb for daily use. Thus, the controversy over vestments does not seem to have been over the principle of special clothing, but rather over certain particular items that the Reformers wanted done away with. Indeed, down to the present time the clergy in Reformed churches in every country of the world wear distinctive garb, and also a gown in the pulpit. It is only in America that the custom has arisen of the clergy pretending to dress just like everybody else (and as I showed above, this is not really practiced by anybody.

On the cover of my copy of James Bannerman's *The Church of Christ*, published by Banner of Truth Trust, there is a painting by John Lorimer called "The Ordination of Elders." The clergyman in the painting is wearing a black gown, and he also has a peculiar

---

4. John Calvin, *Letters*, translated by David Constable (Philadelphia: Presbyterian Board of Publication, 1858; reprinted by Baker Book House, 1983), Vol. 2, p. 307.

5. See Bucer, *Censura*, trans. by E. C. Whitaker in *Martin Bucer and the Book of Common Prayer*. Alcuin Club Collections No. 55 (London: SPCK, 1974), p. 18f. In general, see Peter Milward, *Religious Controversies of the Elizabethan Age: A Survey of Printed Sources* (Lincoln: University of Nebraska Press, 1977), p. 26f.

collar with two white tabs sticking out from it. Nobody else is dressed that way. Thus, in Scotland, the heartland of super-presbyterianism, clerical garb and vestments were used.

So, I'd like to know just what Bishop Hooper was fighting about. Was he opposed to *all* clerical garb, or just to some items? Was he opposed to *all* liturgical vestments, or just to some of them? Apparently he opposed those that were associated with the separate office of bishop, and those associated in the popular mind with the performance of the "sacrifice of the Mass."[6]

It is instructive to continue looking at the history of vestments in England. James Hastings Nichols points to the problem the Reformer's encountered, commenting on how the first *Book of Common Prayer* was received: "While Cranmer repudiated any idea of priestly consecration or of a propitiatory sacrifice, he was scandalized to find that his Romanizing opponents could read these meanings back into his service by means of the ceremonial and ritual of the Mass, altars, vestments, lights, gestures. In the very year of its publication he began a revision of the Prayer Book to make its theology more explicit."[7] The problem was that any ceremonial action or symbol can be understood in a variety of ways, because in and of themselves ceremonies and symbols are silent.[8]

To take an example, let us consider the lifting up of the elements in worship. In the Bible, the gifts given to God were lifted up to heaven, and then received back from Him. This was called "heave offering" when the gift was lifted upward and back down, or "wave offering" when the gift was waved forward toward the throne and then received back. There was nothing magical about this; it was simply an external action that accompanied and displayed the act of giving a gift to God. The priest lifted the gift

---

6. See the discussion in A. H. Drysdale, *History of the Presbyterians in England: Their Rise, Decline, and Revival* (London: Publication Committee of the Presbyterian Church of England, 1889), pp. 52ff.

7. James Hastings Nichols, *Corporate Worship in the Reformed Tradition* (Philadelphia: Westminster, 1968), p. 63.

8. On how "liturgical piety" changes the way rites are perceived, see my essay "Christian Piety: Deformed and Reformed," in *The Geneva Papers*, Vol. 2, No. 1 (Tyler, TX: Geneva Ministries, 1985).

up to God, and then received it back for the use of the church of the Old Testament.

Now, clearly there is nothing wrong, then, with lifting up the collection plates, and the bread and wine to be used later in the Lord's Supper, toward heaven during the offertory prayer. The gifts are given to God, and then He gives them back to the elders to administer. When we look at it this way, lifting up the offering and the elements is thoroughly evangelical, Biblical, and Reformed.

But, it is possible to go through the same actions with the bread and wine, but with a different purpose. They can be lifted up so that people can worship and adore them, as if the bread and wine have been transubstantiated into the re-sacrificed body of Christ. Thus, the Westminster Confession of Faith states in 29:4, that "worshipping the elements, the lifting them up, or carrying them about for adoration . . . are all contrary to the nature of this sacrament, and to the institution of Christ." Notice that the WCF only forbids lifting them up for the purpose of adoration; it does not forbid lifting them up in the Biblical manner of a heave offering.

On this subject, Bucer wrote, "We read that the Lord took bread in his hands and blessed it, that is to say, he gave thanks: and this was the custom of the religion of ancient times. For in order to arouse in the people a greater disposition to offer thanks to God, the men who presided over the sacred rite used to lift up the gifts of God for which thanks were due for all the Lord's blessings (as the gifts themselves suggested): and they set them forward in the sight of the people." Because of the practice of adoring the elements, however, Bucer wanted the practice set aside, at least temporarily.[9]

Now, the Reformers found out that the people had been programmed through decades (even centuries) of bad teaching to view the ceremonial in this wrong way. When the people saw the bishop or the presbyter robed in glorious vestments, they did not

---

9. Bucer, *Censura*, pp. 56ff. Bucer's explanation of the rite is, unfortunately, overly psychological. Bucer does not see any value in bodily action as part of worship, but reduces the relevance of the action to a means of stimulating the people.

think of him as representing the Bride adorned for the Husband, nor did they think of him as representing Christ to them; rather, they thought of him as someone who mediated between them and God. The vestments were (wrongly) associated in peoples' minds with a false and destructive view of the clergy, the idea that people may not approach God directly, but must go through the priest. Because of this, many of the Reformers wanted to do away with vestments altogether, at least for a time.

Concerning the Reformed and Puritan reaction against full vestments, we should also bear in mind what Nichols reminds us: "[These matters] must be interpreted against the background of massacre and torture, of galley slaves, kidnapped children, the wheel and gallows, the smell of burning flesh and hair. The ceremonial of their persecutors became especially distasteful to the Reformed. Those lines of robed monks chanting, the tapers, images of the Virgin, the crucifixes used to escort the martyrs to the stake, were recognized and . . . classified with devil worship."[10]

Another matter soon intruded itself. The Puritans, being in part a catholicizing movement (desiring a Reformed international church), resisted the notion that the King was the chief legislator for the church. At least in the early days, the Puritans were not opposed to prayer-book worship as such, but they were opposed to statist imposition of any kind of worship. The Vestarian Controversy that broke out in 1565 during the reign of Elizabeth must be understood in this light. It was Elizabeth's desire to rule the church and enforce absolute ceremonial uniformity that caused the controversy. Many of the bishops opposed her, and tried to protect the right of local churches to vary the ceremonial and vestments as they pleased, but Elizabeth had her way in time.

"The more earnest Puritans perceived that there was more involved in this struggle than 'merely disputing about a cap or a surplice'. . . . A tract of 1566 raised the question of whether in the scriptural plan for the church the magistrate was not subordinate to the church."[11] The larger issue was the relation of church to

---

10. Nichols, p. 88.
11. Powel Mills Dawley, *John Whitgift and the English Reformation* (New York: Scribner's, 1954), p. 77.

state, and the discussion of vestments was soon absorbed by that larger conflict.

From what I have been able to uncover about the Vestarian controversies, it does not seem that the early Puritans rejected vestments on the grounds of the regulative principle of worship. Rather, these Puritan Reformers were pastorally concerned lest their people be led astray by the continuance of customs long associated with error, and they wanted at least a fast from these customs for a time. More importantly, the Puritans asserted that the local churches, or at least bishoprics, had the right to decide these matters for themselves, without statist interference. Since the state insisted on certain kinds of vestments, the Puritans insisted that they had the right, maybe even the duty at this point, not to wear them. They wore the Genevan gown instead. [12]

(Later radicals, baptists, and congregationalists found ways to make everything under the sun a matter of the regulative principle; but if that is the case, then vestments would be *mandatory*, since the Bible teaches that the church of the Old Testament used them!)

To summarize: Because of serious abuses connected with traditional vestments, the Swiss and many English and Scottish Reformers wanted either to replace these with other kinds of vestments (the Genevan gown) or do away with them altogether. I put this under the category of fasting from an abuse. If a man finds he is watching too much television, he may decide to sell his TV and fast from it for a while. Later on, he may get another TV and learn to use it moderately. Similarly with alcohol. Fasting from an abuse is a proper way to learn to control part of God's world. The principle of fasting is the opposite of the doctrine of demons, "touch not, taste not" (Col. 2:21; 1 Tim. 4:1-5). The goal of fasting from a thing is to learn proper use of it, not to avoid the thing altogether. There is nothing inherently wrong with alcohol, television, or traditional catholic forms of worship and vestments. Indeed, the Old Catholic forms are a whole lot more Biblical and edifying than what generally goes on in conservative evangelical churches today.

The Reformation was four centuries ago. There is no need to-

---

12. Janet Mayo, *A History of Ecclesiastical Dress* (New York: Holmes and Meier Pub., 1984), p. 72.

day to set distance between ourselves and Roman Catholic customs. After 400 years, people in our churches are not still caught up in Medieval superstitions. If you pastors wear a collar, and a surplice and stole in worship, nobody is going to think that you and you alone can mediate between him and Christ. It simply is not a problem today. Thus, pastoral concern about Medieval influences is a non-issue in the discussion of vestments today.

Priestcraft?

I think we have a problem in letting Roman Catholic theology tell us what a priest is and was. In traditional Roman Catholic theology, a priest "mediates" between God and man in the sense of having *power to negotiate* between the two, in some sense. This is more than mere representation. Representation, we may say, is purely *official*. A representative speaks for the people to God, and for God to the people, but a representative does not have any power to alter the covenantal arrangement. He has no power in himself; he is only a speaker.

Roman theology is vague at the point, but clearly gives to the priest more than merely a speaker's role. The Roman Catholic priest has in some sense the power to bind things on earth, in the assurance that God will hearken to him and bind the same things in heaven. Taking Matthew 16:19 more literally, and as a command, the protestant "priest" knows that he may only bind on earth what he knows (from the Bible) has already been bound in heaven.

Now, the question is this: What was the priest of the Old Testament like? I think protestants very often assume that that the Old Testament priest was like a Roman Catholic priest, and that some great change in administration has come with the New Testament, so that now we have the "priesthood of all believers." This, I believe, is an error. Rather, the Old Testament priest was never a "mediator," but only a representative. He spoke to God for the people, and to the people for God, but he never had any power to negotiate. Moreover, there was a priesthood of all believers in the Old Covenant just as there is in the New — after all, anyone could pray to God.

Thus, I assert that the New Testament elder has the same basic position as the priest of the Old Covenant, as a representative of God and of the people. Let me explain further how I think that works out. First, as God's special representative, the elder has a formal role of speaking God's Word to the congregation. Symbolically, this is the ministry of the Groom to the Bride, and thus no woman may ever take up this role (1 Cor. 14:34; 1 Tim. 2:12). I believe that the elders may delegate the role of liturgical officiant to any man in the church, but not to a woman. Possibly then we should entertain the notion that any man may wear liturgical vestments while he performs the role of officiant. If we say this, then the tab collar would be a sign of the office of elder or overseer, and worn only by them, while liturgical vestments might be worn by any man who conducts worship.

Second, as a representative of the people to God, the elder is not in a position of being *sole* representative. Under both the Old and the New Covenants, any believer may approach God on his knees and be heard at any time. This does not eliminate the fact that there are also special times appointed by God for the ceremony of public worship, and that there are certain persons appointed by God to oversee (and normally to lead in) the *public* ceremony of command-performance worship. These were the priests of the Old Covenant, and the elder-bishops of the New.

There is a difference: Under the Old Covenant, public formal worship was highly restricted. Only the high priest might come into the Holiest Place, and then only once a year, not without blood, etc. Now, however, every Christian may come into the Holiest Place (heaven itself) in public worship. The Old Covenant priest represented an absent congregation, kept away by the cherubim with flaming sword. The New Covenant priest (elder) represents a present congregation, readily admitted to God's throne room.

Well, then, why have representatives at all? As one correspondent wrote me, interacting with the original publication of this essay, "It would seem that the New Testament pattern would be not one man representing (symbolically) between God and the people, but all believers approaching directly to the throne of Grace with the officiant acting as the 'orchestra director,' leading the people in their worship, so that worship is done decently and in order." Let me make two comments on this.

First, if the minister at any point prays a prayer in which all the people do not join, he is in some sense "representing" them to God. Only if all the prayers are choral would this principle of representation be avoided. In fact, of course, the principle that the minister represents the people in prayer, and they join in at the end by saying "Amen," is totally "protestant" (as is the principle of representation in general). If we grant this, though, then we have granted some kind of representation, and that's all I need argue for.

Second, however, I think the New Testament indicates the propriety of an officiant who collects prayers and offers them to God as the peoples' representative during worship. The primary New Testament document designed to teach us about worship is the Book of Revelation, which takes place on the Lord's Day, and which shows us how worship is conducted in heaven. Revelation starts out by identifying the "angels" or messengers of the churches as the presiding pastors of seven local churches. The letters to the seven churches are addressed to the seven angel/bishops, as representatives of the churches. Then, in heaven, we repeatedly see these seven angels (or their heavenly counterparts and archetypes) performing liturgical acts — specifically, blowing trumpets (reading the Word to the earth/congregation) and pouring out chalices (administering the Sacraments, in this case negatively, to the earth). All of this indicates a continuing New Testament principle of liturgical representation. (And see Revelation 8:3, which seems to refer to Christ, but which by calling Him an "Angel" links this part of His ministry to the ministry of the seven angels of the churches.)

Most evangelicals readily grant that there are special as well as general officers in the church: servant priests who minister to the royal priesthood. Against ecclesiastical anarchists, we argue for officers and government in the church. I believe that this same principle holds true in worship, and that there is good Old and New Testament evidence for it. Some people feel that if we have officers in the church, it destroys the "kingship of all believers." Historic protestantism argues back that this is not so, but that the bipolarity of special and general kingship is a reflection of the Trinity (one and manyness) of God. Similarly, the special servant priesthood of the officers does not destroy the general royal priesthood of all believers. Nor does the role of the officiant as the representative between God and man in public worship contradict the general priesthood of all believers.

Reacting against Rome for its own sake is idolatry, since it replaces the regulative principle of Scripture with a regulative principle of not doing whatever Rome does. We need to be able to read the Bible and do our theology and worship without constantly looking to what Rome thinks or does.

Arguments for the Reintroduction of Vestments

There are a number of reasons why I think that conservative evangelicals should seriously consider wearing clerical garb (the collar) and using some form of vestments in the celebration of worship. To simplify the discussion, I list them here:

1. The Bible indicates that symbolizing special office in clothing is a good thing, as we have seen above. All things being equal, we should move in that direction. Since Rome is no longer a problem, all things are equal.

2. Biblical teaching as a whole links clothing and calling. Just as physicians, policemen, judges, and auto mechanics wear clothing that befits their calling, so should the clergy.

3. A church officer is neither a professor nor a civil judge. Thus, wearing an academic gown (the Genevan gown) into the pulpit is inappropriate. The clergyman needs his own vestment, distinct from that of the academy and civil magistrate. (The use of academic regalia in the pulpit has gone along with turning the worship of the church into a lecture hour. We need to get away from this.)

4. Distinctive clerical garb makes the church symbolically visible in our society. This is important for evangelism (people come up to you when you wear the collar and want to talk about

their problems) and for social restraint (people behave more properly around those they recognize as clergy).

5. As the state shows its contempt for the church and her officers, as in Nebraska, the church should make its signs of power and office more visible. Nebraska's storm troopers felt free to invade a little Baptist church, because all the clergy there were dressed like businessmen. If everybody had been wearing collars, I think the thugs would have been much more intimidated. Intimidation is a good thing. People should be intimidated by the church, because on Judgment Day, they are definitely going to be intimidated by Her Lord!

I want to expand on this point just a little. Historical circumstances led the Reformers to make visible distinctions between their liturgies and the Roman Mass. We do not live in those same circumstances. In our circumstances, the Christian church is treated with contempt by the tyrannical state. When a Christian minister in a business suit is confronted by a statist judge in robes, the church is at a disadvantage. We need to make it visible and clear that the church is a true government on the earth, equal with the state. There is nothing like black shirts and collars to make that point!

6. The slave collar is important to the minister in that it reminds him constantly of his status as a special slave of Christ. A slave does not speak his own mind, but that of his master. A slave does not do his own will, but that of his master. While this is true of all Christians, it is true in a special way of the peculiar duties of the servant priesthood.

7. Similarly, wearing glorious vestments in worship, and generally adorning the place of worship in a beautiful and impressive fashion, is an important witness. During worship, the church building becomes the palace of the King of kings. He is graciously willing to meet us even in the humblest dwelling, but it is more fitting that He meet with us in a beautiful place. An impressive church building displays the triumph of Christ, as well it should.

8. The symbolism of vestments is also helpful in our day. True Christian theology is always triumphalistic. Christ is risen, and is enthroned King. He is arrayed in glory and beauty, and He

also arrays His bride in glory and beauty. All of us could wear glorious apparel, but it would be pretty expensive. (This, though, is why people wear their "Sunday best" to worship.) In worship, the officiant represents the people, the Bride. Let him be gloriously arrayed, then. This is part of the public witness of the church before the watching world.

Presbyterians, with their heritage of postmillennial triumphalism, should be in the forefront of restoring splendor to the church, which is His Throne and Bride. Let the nations tremble!

9. Practically speaking, we should be careful not to introduce too much, but bring the people along. In the area of vestments, a simple white alb or surplice (the white robe of the Bible) and a colored stole (the strip of cloth that represents the "easy yoke" of Christ's service, the colors variable with the liturgical season) should be sufficient. But we should not be afraid to think about more glorious apparel at some later time. The Bride is most certainly and triumphantly to be adorned, and this is most aptly indicated by the vestments worn by the officiant while he leads in worship.

Conclusion

The church needs more governmental and institutional visibility in America, as she confronts the state and attempts to safeguard Christian liberties. The reintroduction of clerical garb and liturgical vestments would be very helpful along these lines, in my opinion. The use of such special clothing is supported by Scripture, and does not contradict historic protestant teaching on the subject, when we take historic protestantism in context.

13

A LITURGY OF MALEDICTION

Malediction is the opposite of benediction, and means "curse." In the Book of Revelation, "seven stars" are seen in the right hand of the enthroned Jesus Christ (1:16,17), and these are identified as the "angels of the seven churches" (1:20). Since the letters are addressed to these angels (2:1,8,12,etc.), the angels clearly are rulers in the church on earth. Probably each was the presiding elder (later called "bishop") for all the congregations in his city, according to the pattern set out in Exodus 18:21.

This unmistakably sets up the theology of the Book of Revelation. Sadly, the point is almost universally missed, and it is assumed that the word "angel" as used in the remainder of the book has reference only to heavenly, spiritual beings. We have to remember, however, that the Christian church, particularly during sacramental public worship, exists "in the heavenlies" (Eph. 2:6; Heb. 12:22-24). Thus, John's being caught up to heaven on the Lord's Day (Rev. 1:10; 4:1) is at least analogous to the position of the church during worship each Lord's Day.

The Book of Revelation as a whole is organized as a worship service, and is a model for us. Jesus taught us to pray, "Thy will be done on earth as it is in heaven." Thus, the heavenly model is to be reproduced on earth. In light of this, the seven angels who sound trumpets in Revelation 8 are to be connected with the proclamations of the angels (officers) of the seven churches. Either what is pictured is the actual work of church officers, or else it is the heavenly model that earthly church officers are to emulate. Either way, it is of immediate practical import for the church.

It is the church that binds and looses on earth, and the Book of Revelation shows how she is to do so: by proclamation and prayer. She is only to bind on earth what she knows has been bound in heaven, but concerning that there is no mystery, for she has been given the Word of God, the Bible, to show her how to act (Matt. 16:17-19).

As various agencies of state and federal government bring attacks against the church, church officers need to hold formal services of malediction to call down the curse of God upon those persecuting His bride. To rehearse an example: The elders at my church were forced to excommunicate a woman who had been a teacher in the church-run Christian school. At that time, she resigned her employment with the school. Later, she formed a conspiracy with a couple of other excommunicated persons and appealed to the Texas Employment Commission for unemployment compensation in connection with her employment at our school.

This was a deliberate attempt to get our church engaged in controversy with the state. The state does not have any jurisdiction over the church at all, for the church is established by Christ, not by the state. This is particularly the case concerning hiring and firing practices of the church, since employment by the church is determined by God's office-bearers, and entails Spiritual considerations that the state has no right to judge.

Initially, it appeared as if the state were summoning the church to a hearing. The proper initial response of a church in such a situation is to go before the state and explain that the state has no jurisdiction, and that the church cannot be summoned. We have to fight on the issue of jurisdiction. It appeared to us, thus, as if a long and bitter conflict might be brewing.

Of course, in extreme circumstances, we might go along with the state's pretended assertion of jurisdiction, because we know that in fact the state cannot in the nature of the case ever really take jurisdiction over the church. The state did its worst to Jesus Christ, but in spite of the apparent triumph of the Jewish and Roman states, in fact they could do nothing except what had been given them (John 19:11). Moreover, it was God the Father Who put Jesus Christ to death, for us. And, of course, the apparent victory of the state was very temporary (less than three days). Thus, the state cannot really threaten the church at all. All the same, for the good of society, the church should resist the jurisdictional encroachments of the state.

Before the hearing, a special service was held to ask God to confound the wicked efforts of the conspirators. After the reading of several passages of Scripture (2 Chronicles 26:1-23; Acts 4:1-31; Psalm 59), interspersed with the singing of several appropriate psalms (Ps. 2, 72, 79, 80, 83, 94), the following form was used:

Presiding Elder: "Dearly Beloved, our Lord Jesus Christ has assured us that His church is built upon Himself, the Rock, and that the gates of hell shall never prevail against it. To His church He has committed the keys of the kingdom of heaven, saying 'whatever you shall bind on earth shall have been bound in heaven, and whatever you shall loose on earth shall have been loosed in heaven.'

"In the Book of Revelation, the office-bearers of the church are called the angels of the churches, and in the eighth chapter of that Book, these office-bearers are shown blowing the trumpets of the Word of God. As the office-bearers proclaim the Word of God, signified by these trumpets, and as the people of God pray for salvation, signified by incense that ascends to heaven, God is faithful and pours out fiery wrath upon His and their enemies on the earth.

"Tonight we bring before you the names of_____, who have attacked the church of Jesus Christ. We ask you to join with us in praying that God will pour out His wrath upon them, and upon all in alliance with them in this sinful act. When I have prayed God to deal with them, I shall ask the other elders to join me in solemn Amen, and then I shall ask the congregation to join with us in solemn Amen. Let us pray.

(praying) "Almighty and Most Terrible God, Judge of all men living and dead, we bring before you _____ (here name the persons being cursed), who have brought an attack upon the integrity of Your holy government on the earth. We as Your anointed office-bearers now ask that You place Your especial curse upon these people, and upon all in alliance with them. We ask You to pour out the fire of Your wrath upon them, and destroy them, that Your church may be left in peace, and our time free to pursue the advancement of Your Kingdom. We ask that You visibly and swiftly vindicate the government of Your only Son, Jesus Christ our Lord, Who lives and reigns with You and the Holy Spirit, ever one God, world without end. Amen.

(addressing the other elders) "Elders _____ (here say the names of the elders), do you join with me in invoking the wrath of God upon these people? If so, answer Amen."

Elders: "Amen."

Presiding Elder: "Congregation of the Lord Jesus Christ, do you join with us in asking God to visit His wrath upon these people? If so, answer Amen."

Congregation: "Amen."

The next day, when the hearing was held, representatives of the church attended, explaining that the church was not under the jurisdiction of the Texas Employment Commission, and that our appearance should be regarded as a "special appearance," and a courtesy. The Texas Employment Commission agreed, and stated that the church is not under its jurisdiction. The enemies of the church were put to confusion.

We dare not expect that every situation will work out as easily, but we should confidently ask our God to fight for us in these and like battles.

14

A LITURGY OF HEALING

The Bible has a great deal to say about sickness and healing. To understand it rightly, we have to bear in mind that man was created as the particular symbol of God (Gen. 1:26,27), and the universe is the general symbol of God (since all creation reveals — symbolizes — its Creator). Thus, the foundational level of all human intellectual apprehension is the symbolic. The true meaning of any thing or event can be found only when it is seen as revealing (signifying or symbolizing) God and His relations to man and the cosmos.[1] This Biblical creationist perspective inverts the normal (sinful) way of thinking, which assumes that things and events have meaning *in themselves*, and that any symbolic dimension (which may or may not be present) is *added to* the fundamental non-symbolic and self-contained meaning of things and events.

Applying this to the subject of sickness and healing, we find that under the influence of rationalism, the orthodox churches in recent centuries have often maintained the following notions. First, that since the healings in the Bible invariably have a symbolic and typological meaning, such healings were appropriate only for the periods in which special revelation was being given.

---

1. This is the doctrine of natural revelation, particularly as developed in consistent creationist form throughout the writings of Cornelius Van Til. For a good discussion of this matter from another slant, showing its importance to the Church Fathers, see Alexander Schmemann, *For the Life of the World* (New York: St. Vladimir's Seminary Press, 1973), appendix 2, "Sacrament and Symbol." My own thoughts on this can be obtained by writing to Geneva Ministries, Box 131300, Tyler, TX 75713, and asking for the paper, "Symbolism: A Manifesto."

With the completion of the work of redemption and the close of the canon of Scripture, no such sign-healings are needed. This approach *assumes* that the symbolic dimension is special, and adventitious to the "brute fact" of healing itself. In fact, the symbolic dimension is the primary one.

Secondly, following on this, rationalistic orthodoxy has downplayed the Biblical evidence that indicates that the coming of the New Covenant is the coming of an age of healing, and that a healing ministry is part of the normal work of the church. The tendency in rationalistic orthodoxy is to eliminate as much as possible the mystical or non-rational element in faith and worship. This tendency is nowhere better seen than in the "Zwinglian" view of the presence of Christ in the Holy Eucharist, advocated by virtually all evangelical and Reformed groups for several centuries now.[2] In view of this, it is no wonder that the healing ministry has all but disappeared from such churches.

Predictably there has been a reaction against the rationalism of orthodoxy, and we see it in the cultivated non-rational experientialism of the charismatic movement. Unfortunately, the charismatic movement tends to err as much on the one side as orthodoxy does on the other. Not infrequently, hard theological reflection is seen as damaging to the irrational work of the "Spirit," and all too often, irrational experiences are sought for their own sake, and in terms of what we must call (with severe frankness) a pleasure principle. The massive quest for pleasurable ecstatic experiences is part and parcel of a uniquely American kind of Christianity, which is of a piece with the American "fun and games ethic" as a whole.

All the same, charismatic theologians note rightly that the New Covenant is a time of healing, and that the Bible indicates a certain expectation that God will heal the diseases and afflictions of His people. Such promises were found in the provisional administration of grace to Israel under the Old Covenant (as in Ex. 15:26; Dt. 7:15; Prov. 4:22). It is particularly with the ministry of Christ and His disciples, however, that we find abundant healings

---

2. For a corrective to this view, see Ronald Wallace, *Calvin's Doctrine of the Word and Sacrament* (Tyler, TX: Geneva Ministries, 1982).

manifested, as tokens of the nature of the New Covenant era.

The problem that most charismatic theologians have with applying this data is that they are Americans, afflicted with the overly-individualistic approach to life that characterizes "American Baptist Culture."[3] In fact, all sickness signifies and manifests the curse on man for original sin, and all healing signifies salvation in Christ. As Job's friends had to learn, however, this does not mean that any particular affliction that comes upon an individual indicates some particular sin on his part. And it follows, then, that we cannot say to each and every afflicted Christian, "Jesus wants *you* well." There may be many reasons why Jesus does not want a particular person well at a particular time.

By itself, this fact eliminates virtually all encouragement to pray for healing. We may well just seek to relax fatalistically in whatever Providence seems to decree for us. It is at this point that the charismatic theologians have a salutary corrective to offer, for in fact we do have a general (not a particular) warrant for believing that the normal Christian experience is one of health, not of sickness. This is especially true in terms of the coming of the New Covenant. God has judicially declared the world cleansed of evil; that is, God has re-symbolized the world from darkness to light. This re-symbolization or redefinition is the foundation for the re-creation of the world. God has re-symbolized man as healed, and since the symbolic dimension is primary, this means that man is to be healed physically as a consequence. Thus, the healings performed by Jesus were not "merely" symbols of Spiritual healing, but were tokens of the fact that physical healing is normally a consequence of Spiritual healing.

Rampant illness in our society as a whole simply indicates that we are under the Egyptian curse, because of secular humanism and the refusal of the Christian churches to deal seriously with it.[4]

---

3. This phenomenon is discussed at length in James B. Jordan, ed., *The Failure of the American Baptist Culture*. Christianity and Civilization No. 1 (Tyler, TX: Geneva Ministries, 1982).

4. For instance, in spite of all the yelling about abortion, and all the rhetoric about abortion's being murder, how many evangelical leaders have come out and *demanded the death penalty for conspiracy to commit abortion?* Has *anybody?* No wonder God does not take evangelicalism seriously!

The Sociology of the Church

Reformation and revival will do the most to bring about deliverance from disease. All the same, since the church is the society of the saved, a ministry of physical healing is an important part of the work of the church, both ministerially and evangelistically.

Problems with the Modern Healing Movement

The preeminent problem with the modern healing movement in America is the fact that it is not connected with the God-ordained sacramental ministry of the church. This is part and parcel of the American ecclesiological heresy, as seen in the abundance of "parachurch" organizations that siphon off time, money, and personnel from the church.[5] Briefly, we may say that this basic problem has manifested itself in three plagues.

1. The healing movement has been plagued with autonomous man-centered ministries. The Biblical method is for the elders of the church as a group to pray over an individual, with confession of sin. The modern movement focuses attention on the claims of a few "Spiritual giants" who ostensibly carry a gift of healing around with themselves. 1 Corinthians 12:9 does refer to a gift of healing that is bestowed on certain members of the church for the benefit of all. There is no Biblical warrant, however, for such persons to leave the church and engage in personality-cult oriented, parachurch "healing crusades" of their own.[6] The circus-like atmosphere that pervades such meetings and television ministries serves to alienate sober Christians, and turn them away from any consideration of the Biblical healing ministry.

2. Part and parcel of the previous plague is the plague of charlatanry. A few years back, it was possible to write and obtain a

---

5. I am not opposed to all parachurch ministries. They are the Protestant equivalent to the monastic orders of the Catholic churches, and are an inevitable sociological bipolar counterpart to the fragmented ecclesiological situation in American protestantism. The problem lies in the normalization of these abnormal parachurch ministries, and their exaltation over the supposed deadness of "churchianity." On parachurch, see pp. 77-81 of this book.

6. In England, persons with such gifts have normally functioned within the church. See Charles W. Gusmer, *The Ministry of Healing in the Church of England.* Alcuin Club Collections No. 56 (London: SPCK, 1974).

"healer's kit" that would teach one how to become rich as a charlatan healer.[7] It is well known, and has been repeatedly documented, that certain famous "healers" have carefully worked out methods of controlling what kinds of afflicted persons are permitted to "come forward" to be healed. Woe to the person who tries to get in line without an approval slip that indicates he has been checked out beforehand! Well-known healing ministry hospitals refuse to take under care any but the simplest kinds of sicknesses, to keep their rate of success high. The phenomenon of "slaying in the Spirit" is, sometimes at least, accomplished with the assistance of cattle prods. Naturally, this type of fakery serves to put off sober-minded Christians.

3. The third plague is demonism. Demonism accompanies the charismatic movement for the simple reason that pleasure-seeking irrationalism provides an open door to the demonic. When one hears a nationally respected charismatic leader state that "Jesus" appeared to her and told her to quit reading her Bible and just yield to "him" moment by moment, one realizes that one is dealing with the Arch-deceiver, who can appear as an "angel of light" (2 Cor. 11:14).[8] Satan can grant temporary physical healing, and those who seek health for reasons of personal pleasure may thus find their latter state worse than their former. The rationalistic orthodox never fail to note this, and it only serves to arouse further suspicion regarding *any* kind of ministry of healing.

Let me say that certain recent trends in some charismatic circles indicate a return to a church-centered form of ministry, and a desire to downplay the fabulous and ecstatic in favor of the theological and practical. This is all very encouraging.

A Biblical Philosophy of Healing

The Bible prescribes the use of oil in healing.[9] There is no need to "consecrate" such oil, and what kind of oil is used does not

---

7. This was brought to light by Carroll Stegall in a privately published pamphlet, "The Modern Tongues and Healing Movement," which is long out of print.

8. This incident reportedly occurred in New Zealand. The charismatic leader was national head (female!) of a Pelagian (heretical) youth mission group.

9. Mark 6:13; James 5:13-16. Note the symbolic connection between the Eucharist and healing in Luke 10:34. The meaning of this is discussed later in this essay.

matter. (Olive Oil and Baby Oil are two we can recommend.) The use of oil is not medicinal, contrary to the assertions of some in the camp of rationalistic orthodoxy. The Bible distinguishes between the proper ministry of physicians (such as Luke) and the proper ministry of elders. The anointing with oil is a ceremony, performed "in the name of the Lord," by the elders. It does not conflict with or take the place of the labor of physicians. Rather, the healing ministry of the church forms the (symbolic) foundation and (whole-life Christian) context for medicinal help.

This answers a fourth problem with the modern healing movement, which is its tendency to despise God-appointed ordinary means of healing (and in extreme cases, the rejection of medicine altogether). It is true that the Bible condemns King Asa for consulting physicians, but only because He did not first consult the Lord (2 Chron. 16:12). Paul had no problem making use of the services of Luke.

It is important to understand that *only* the gospel gives men health. The labor of physicians is important, but only as a means of holding back the curse. *Physicians cannot give men true health.* Nor can eating "health foods," fasting, exercise, colonics, or any other feature of the Old Creation. The first creation is decaying. It is only the New Creation that can bring true health, through *transfiguration*. It is only in Christ, and in eating His Spiritual food, that healing can take place.

The ministry of the Holy Spirit is to move men into the New Creation. In that New Creation, in its fullest form, men have new, deathless, transfigured bodies, as did Jesus Christ after His resurrection. During the gospel era, the New Creation does not wipe out the original creation, but rather sustains and renews it. Thus, the "normal" effect of the healing work of the New Creation is the restoration of the sick body to health. At the same time, such restoration to health is not of preeminent importance. The primary thing is to live in the New Creation, by faith. Thus, the healing ministry of the church is not finally to give people physical health, but is primarily to enable them to *transform* their experience for the glory of God. Anointing with oil is a sign to the sick or dying person that enables him to turn his suffering into true martyrdom, true witness to the transforming health of the gospel as New Creation.

The coming of the New Covenant does indeed mean that, in a general sense, "Jesus wants us well." The *norm* in the Kingdom is physical health. God wants the cultural mandate to be fulfilled. He wants us to be working to bring the world to its fullest fruition. We can legitimately argue with Him that He should give us good health so that we can be about His business. Thus Paul, in order not to be a burden to the churches and in order to carry out his ministry, asked that his "thorn in the flesh" be removed (2 Cor. 12:8). What was true of Paul's particular ministry is also true of any labor performed by Christians in God's world: We should desire strength and health so that we can do the best possible job.

Accordingly, sickness and other physical problems are an *exception* in the Kingdom. The person who is sick, or who has some particular physical problem, has been called to a special, exceptional ministry. All Christians are martyrs (witnesses) in the general sense, but the suffering Christian is a martyr (witness) in a special, exceptional sense.

The person who is sick, or blind, or has some other physical problem, is *supposed* to ask God for healing. He should not rest content with his "thorn in the flesh." He should approach God for healing, because he should desire to be in the best possible condition to labor in the Kingdom. If God chooses, however, not to grant his request for healing, then he is to understand that the problem has been given him for a special purpose, and rest in that assurance.

God is most specific. If we need healing, we are to approach the elders (plural) of our local church, with confession of sin, and ask to be anointed with oil. If God turns down our request the first time, should we come back and try again? Paul states that he came to the Lord three times (2 Cor. 12:8; and cf. Luke 18:1-7 on perseverance in prayer). Paul did not make a fourth request. I think this indicates a rule for us.

I should also point out that, theologically, unction is not a sacrament in the special sense, since it is not a seal of the New Covenant as such. On the other hand, the ministry of special healing flows from the general healing that comes from Christ, made physically manifest in the sacraments. Thus, Christians should not come to healing services and ask for unction repeatedly, "just in case," or for general health. It is only in specific circumstances that unction is to be requested.

In summary, God generally wants His people able, strong, and healthy. He has instituted the rite of unction to take care of illnesses and other maladies. We are not to despise this provision, but make full use of it. If God does not grant healing the first time, we should return with renewed petition two more times. If, after three requests, God still does not grant health, then we are to understand that He has a special purpose for us, and rejoice in that exceptional calling, and view the rite of unction as a means of transforming our problem from a manifestation of the curse into a special manifestation of the Kingdom, for our good and for the good of others. It is not my purpose here to discuss all the benefits that come from suffering, according to Scripture. Suffice it to say that our Lord Jesus Christ is said through suffering to have learned to sympathize with our weaknesses and to have learned obedience (Heb. 4:15; 5:8). Thus, all Christian suffering should be in union with Christ, a means to learning submission to God, and a means of learning better to feel for others.

Services of Healing

There is no reason to think that healing services have to be conducted as part of the weekly liturgy, but there is no reason to think that such should not be done either. In some churches, persons are invited to come forward during the long prayer (called the Pastoral Prayer, or the Prayer of the Church), and at that point they make confession of their sin or of their need, and are prayed over by the elders, while the rest of the congregation engages in silent prayer. God has blessed this where it has been done. This could also be done at the beginning of the liturgy, in connection with the initial confession of sin. Such a thing could also be done during a Wednesday evening vespers service.

It is also possible, of course, for the elders to visit a sick person at home or in the hospital, and administer the rite of healing. The elements set forth by James are confession of sin, request for healing, prayer for healing, and anointing with oil. James also indicates that several elders should be present, and this again works against the modern one-man-show approach.

No particular rite is set out in Scripture. It is always well, however, to explain to people what is going on, and that is the main purpose of the ritual accompaniments to unction. Before administering the rite, the sick person (here called the penitent) should be interviewed by the elders and given opportunity to confess any particular sins that may be on his mind. The following example of such a rite is a modification of the Order for the Ministration to the Sick, found in the *Book of Common Prayer* (New Edition).

An Order for the Ministration to the Sick

Officiant: Dearly beloved, the apostle James tells us that if anyone is sick, "let him call for the elders of the church, and let them pray over him, having anointed him with oil in the name of the Lord, and the prayer of faith will restore the one who is sick, and the Lord will raise him up, and if he has committed sins, it will be forgiven him. Therefore, confess your sins to one another, and pray for one another, so that you may be healed." [James 5:14-16]

Also we read of our Lord Jesus Christ, in the Gospel of Mark, that He sent out His disciples, "and they were casting out many demons, and were anointing with oil many sick people and healing them." [Mark 6:13]

In Scripture, anointing with oil is a sign of the gracious work of the Holy Spirit, the Lord and Giver of Life. Anointing with oil, and the laying on of hands, is not a sacrament, since though it is a sign, is it not the seal of the New Covenant. At the same time, however, this outward rite finds expression in the New Covenant as an act of confession, a confession that only the power of the Holy Spirit can heal men of sickness, and a confession that God's ordained government of elders is, ordinarily, the place at which an appeal for special healing should be made.

The apostle James indicates that the person seeking special healing should confess sin, be anointed with oil, and
then be prayed over by the elders of the church. [If done
publicly, here should follow a general explanation of the circumstances of the present ministration, for instance, "Mr.
N. has approached the session and asked to be anointed with
a view to his coming heart surgery"; or, "Mrs. N. has approached the session and asked to be anointed and prayed
over concerning a certain affliction from which she has
suffered for a long time"; or, "Mr. and Mrs. N. have brought
their child, N., to the session because. . . ."]

[Then, addressing the sick person, or the parents of the
child]: We therefore ask you the following:

Do you (on behalf of this child)[10] confess that you have
sinned against God, not only in outward transgressions, but
also in secret thoughts and desires, which you cannot fully
understand, but which are all known to Him? If so, answer:
I confess my sin.

Penitent: I confess my sin.

Officiant: Do you (on behalf of this child) confess that you
are deserving of all misery and wrath in this world, and even
of the eternal fire of hell, for your sins? If so, answer: I confess it.

Penitent: I confess it.

Officiant: Do you (on behalf of this child) flee for refuge to
God's infinite mercy, seeking and imploring His grace and
healing, for the sake of our Lord Jesus Christ? If so, answer:
I do.

Penitent: I do.

---

10. This formula is used when parents are speaking on behalf of children too
young to speak for themselves. Since children are members of the New Covenant
by baptism, they are counted as and treated as having faith, and thus as desiring
to serve Christ in wholeness of health. The parent articulates what the child is
assumed to desire, but cannot as yet articulate. Of course, it is not really necessary to ask such children any questions at all. Children who are not baptized, of
course, cannot be the recipients of the ministry of healing, since they are outside
of Christ.

Officiant: [The officiant shall dip his finger in the oil, and place it upon the head or forehead of the penitent, saying:] (Name,) I anoint you with oil in the Name of the Father, and of the Son, and of the Holy Spirit. As you are outwardly anointed with this holy oil, so may our heavenly Father grant you the inward anointing of the Holy Spirit. Of His great mercy, may He forgive you your sins, release you from suffering, and restore you to wholeness and strength. May he deliver you from all evil, preserve you in all goodness, and bring you to everlasting life; through Jesus Christ our Lord. Amen.

[Then shall the elders place their hands upon the penitent, and the officiant shall pray one or more of the following prayers, as appropriate:] (The prayers are taken from pages 458-460 of the *Book of Common Prayer*.)

Should the Sign of the Cross be Used?

How should the oil be placed on the forehead? If we are going to smear it on, will God be angry if we smear it in the sign of the cross? I don't see any necessity here one way or another. Since, however, it is generally assumed in presbyterian circles that signing with the cross is wrong, I should like to insert here a quotation from Martin Bucer, the man who taught John Calvin, and one of the four foremost Reformers. Bucer is actually writing concerning the sign of the cross in baptism, but what he says is relevant elsewhere: "This sign was not only used in the churches in very ancient times: it is still an admirably simple reminder of the cross of Christ. For these reasons I do not consider that its use is either unsuitable or valueless, so long as it is accepted and used with a strict understanding of its meaning, untainted by any admixture of superstition or servitude of an element or casual adherence to common custom."[11] The point here is that the protestant Reformers did not interpret the "regulative principle of Scripture" in such a minimalist way as to exclude all simple gestures.

---

11. Bucer, *Censura*; found in E. C. Whitaker, *Martin Bucer and The Book of Common Prayer*. Alcuin Club Collections No. 55 (London: SPCK, 1974), p. 90.

Appendix A

BIBLICAL TERMINOLOGY FOR THE CHURCH

The most general term in Scripture for those who belong to God is "the people of God." The term "people" does not contemplate a mere mass of particular individuals, but in terms of the equal ultimacy of the one and the many, the word may have either a collective or a distributive use. In Hebrew, it may take a singular or a plural verb (e.g., Is. 9:13 + 9:2).

The people of God are constituted such by Him (2 Cor. 6:16). The first actual reference to a people as God's own peculiar people is in Exodus 3:7, but this reference assumes that the people were already in existence. Depending on context, "the people of God" is not necessarily a synonym for "Israel," as in Psalm 47:9: "The princes of the peoples (pl.) have assembled themselves — the people of the God of Abraham. . . ." Thus, Israel may be cut out of the people of God (Hos. 1:9; Rom. 11:1-32) and other ethnic groups included (Rom. 9:25f.).

The differentiating mark of God's people is that they belong to Him, live in His presence, and obey His laws. The sin of man brought expulsion from Eden, from the "good life" of the covenant, and brought the curse of death. Salvation restores man to Eden, to the Presence of God and the outflow therefrom, restores him to the "good life," and delivers him from death. Thus the differentiating mark of the people of God is life, ethical and vital. It is that range of things denoted by the Biblical concept of blessing. The people of God live in His blessing, while the enemies of God live under His curse.

Accordingly we may note that the concept of "the people of God" does not in and of itself have any peculiar focus on the worshipping function of man. Rather it contemplates life under God in the whole range of human activities, what are often in modern evangelical thought termed "kingdom" activities. Obedience to God covers the gamut of life, the six days of labor and "cultural mandate activity," as well as the one day of sabbatical rest and worship. From this perspective, "people of God" is the broadest sociological aspect of the church.

When the people of God gather, they form a gathering or assembly. The Hebrew term is *qahal*. In Judges 20:2 the two terms are juxtaposed: ". . . the assembly of the people of God." Some notion of coming together, whether representative or comprehensive, is designated by this term. There may be gatherings for many purposes: to receive the Word of God (Dt. 18:6), to journey together (Ex. 16:3), for worship (2 Chr. 1:3), for war (Jud. 20:2), and so forth. The gathering may be by representatives (Dt. 5:22f.), but this is still considered the gathering of the people.

Seemingly problematic are Genesis 28:3; 35:11; and 48:4. The force of these passages, however, seems to be that many tribes (peoples, nations) would come out of Jacob, but all would form one assembly. We may see the great gathering of Israel at Mount Horeb before the face of God, at the Exodus, as a fulfillment of these prophecies. Three verses in Deuteronomy (9:10; 10:4; 18:16) look back to the Horeb assembly as a peculiarly great occasion, because of its covenant-making significance. Hebrews 12:18-21 isolates this particular assembly as summary of the Old Testament condition of the people of God.

An examination of all uses of *qahal* will disclose that the term invariably has in view an actual gathering of people, usually for some stated purpose.

The other Hebrew term we must consider is *'edah*. If *qahal* contemplates an actual gathering, *'edah* refers to what is gathered, considered as an organized people. Correlating these two nouns with their verbal forms, the following relationships are possibilities:

nouns:

		'edah		*qahal*	
verbs:	*ya'ad*	1.	Num. 16:11	4.	no usage
	qahal	2.	Num. 16:42	3.	Num. 10:7

1. One may assembly by appointment (*ya'ad*) the organized people (*'edah*).
2. One may gather together (*qahal*) the organized people (*'edah*).
3. One may gather together (*qahal*) a gathering (*qahal*).
4. One may not assemble by appointment (*ya'ad*) a gathering (*qahal*), since a gathering is by definition already assembled.

'Edah contemplates the people of God as an organized body, gathered or ungathered, but subject to gathering. As a result, this word is used far more prominently than *qahal* in the book of Numbers, since that book is concerned with the actual organization of the people of God. In view of this, while no *qahal* (gathering) is spoken of as having rulers, the *'edah* often is (e.g., Ex. 16:22). The people of God may be an *'edah* in either a political or an ecclesiastical (sabbatical) sense. Thus there are princes of the *'edah* (Josh. 9:15) as well as elders of the *'edah* (Lev. 4:15).

In view of this we should like to propose (tentatively) the following model for consideration. The people of God may be organized for sabbatical purposes and for civil purposes. Thus there are two organizations, one people. The sabbatical organization excludes visible sinners and unbelievers. The civil organization incorporates them insofar as it rules over them. In view of the two organizations, two kinds of assemblies (among others) may be called. Civil assemblies exercise judgment and prosecute war. Sabbatical assemblies are gatherings "before the face of the Lord," or in the Presence of God. The sabbatical assembly has two functions: to expose the people to the Word of God, and to expose God to the worship of the people. The sabbatical organization also has two functions: to solicit all men to the Presence of God, and to exclude those who must be chastised for sin. The sabbatical assemblies in the Old Testament are principally noted as the great solemn feasts, and as certain great occasions in the history of the people (e.g., the dedication of the Temple, the assembly of Jehoshaphat, the crowning of Joash, the great gatherings under Hezekiah, and the assembly under Nehemiah). Finally, it would seem from the New Testament (1 Cor. 11:10; Heb. 12:22f.) that the angels, though a different people of God and though in a different organization (*'edah*), join in the sabbatical assembly (*qahal*) of the people of God.

It is important to note that these distinctions between civil and sabbatical organizations and assemblies are not to be found in the terms themselves. The Old Testament does not speak of "church and state" as we do. Rather, one must examine in context what "the organization" or "the assembly" is said to be doing in order to know if a civil or sabbatical activity is intended.

The Old Testament usage of *'edah* and *qahal* is primarily sabbatical. The reason for this is not far to seek. Man's primary and all-determining relationship in life is his God-ward relationship. The severing of that relationship in the Fall was the wellspring of all other disabilities that have come upon the human race. The restoration of that relationship, and its maintenance, is thus of central and all-determining importance for the life of man. Thus, although the people of God function in all areas of life, the civil included, it remains that there is a primacy to the sabbatical that is determinative of all else.

It remains only to note that the New Testament notion of "church" — *ekklesia* — involves all of these Old Testament ideas. The notions of the church as the people of God in the broad sense and as the general *'edah* or community of saints are very close, and in certain passages a clear distinction cannot be drawn.[1] (Indeed,

---

1. In fact, let me stress here that I am not claiming a sharp distinction between *'edah* and *qahal* in the Hebrew. I do believe, however, that the evidence warrants seeing a *general* or *vague* distinction in meaning. Some terms are very precise in meaning (e.g., "propitiation") and some are very vague (e.g., driving "pretty fast"). Languages need both vague and precise terms, and terms in between. It is easy to make a mistake by trying to read too much precision into a relatively vague term. All I am claiming is that *'edah* generally focuses on government and organization, while *qahal* generally focuses on an actually assembled group.

the very fact that one term — *ekklesia* — is used in these several over-lapping senses points to the unity and diversity in the concept of the church.) The *'edah* or community concept does embody, how-ever, certain organizational and disciplinary aspects that are not in focus in the term "people of God."

First, we find that in 2 Corinthians 6:16 "the people of God" is identified with the "temple of God." The same idea is found in 1 Corinthians 3:16, where the people as a whole are called "temple," and in 1 Corinthians 6:19, where each individual Christian is called a "temple." This usage highlights the equal ultimacy of the one and the many. An extended commentary on the concept of the people of God is found in Ephesians 2:11-22. Generally speak-ing, both Ephesians and Colossians contemplate the church as the general people of God, and this is seen clearly in that the applica-tory portions of these books address the Christian's walk in all areas of life. Other passages that use "church" in this most general sense include Acts 5:11 and 8:1, 3.

Acts 20:28 may contemplate the church as merely a group of people, but since rulers are noted, it is probably best to take this in the sense of *'edah*. Exodus 15:16, however, to which this verse refers, uses "people" rather than *'edah*. The same kind of usage is found in Titus 2:14.

Second, having moved to this point, we notice some passages that contemplate the church as a general or universal *'edah* or com-munity of saints. Matthew 16:18f. should be read in these terms, since discipline is in view. Also, Hebrews 12:23 speaks of the church as those enrolled.

Third, we note passages that contemplate the church as a universal or general *qahal* or assembly of the saints for sabbatical purposes. Hebrews 12:23 uses the term "general assembly," and this is parallel with the Mount Horeb *qahal*. Hebrews 2:12 also considers all the people of God as gathered together for worship, and while this cannot be physically the case until the Judgment, it is really the case by virtue of the omnipresence of Christ through the Holy Spirit. Since all special worship takes place "in heaven," all churches are indeed, in the most profound sense, gathered at the same location during Lord's Day worship. Another general *qahal* usage is Acts 7:38, where "church" is used for the Mount Horeb assembly.

Fourth, we note passages that use "church" for a local *'edah* or community of saints. Matthew 18:17 is one, for local discipline is in view. Clear usages are seen in Acts 9:31; 11:22; Romans 16:1, 4, 5, 16; and especially in 1 Corinthians 14:4, 5, 15, 23. Unlike Ephesians and Colossians, the book of 1 Corinthians focuses attention upon the local community of saints and upon their local worship assembly. In 14:23 a clear Old Testament formula is utilized when the "church" is said to assemble together. General rules for the government of the church as *'edah* are found especially in 1 and 2 Timothy and Titus.

Of especial note is 1 Corinthians 6:4, which shadows the civil notion of *'edah* and *qahal* in the Old Testament. After noting that the saints are to rule the world, the Holy Spirit admonishes the saints not to utilize the pagan civil courts to exercise discipline, but to construct their own. The notion of the passage is not, at it is so often misinterpreted to mean, that Christians should never take other Christians before civil magistrates. Since this passage, and the New Testament generally, does not distinguish explicitly the civil from the sabbatical function of discipline, we may be justified in seeing here the germ of Christian civil government as well as a clear case of Christian sabbatical government. In a pagan society, the local Christian *'edah* may try and sentence an offender, but it can only punish him in terms of the power of the sabbatical government (to wit, excommunication). When Christianity is ascendant, it is incumbent upon the *'edah* to try and punish offenders through both its civil and sabbatical magistrates. The New Testament ever envisions that the nations will be discipled and that the saints will emerge as the world's rulers. In that event, the Old Testament notion of the *'edah* will emerge, at least in its general delineations.

Fifth and finally we come to the local *qahal* or gathering of the saints for sabbatical purposes. This can be seen in 2 Thessalonians 2:1, Acts 11:26, and again in many verses in 1 Corinthians, as 1:2; 4:17; 11:18, 22; and 14:16, 18, 19, 33, 34, 35. The last verses contrast the gathering of the saints with their lives at home.

The result of this survey is to reinforce our model of the church of God. The church as the people of God includes all that Christians are and do, and is thus synonymous with what the term "kingdom" is used to denote in much evangelical literature. The same is true, though in a more specialized sense, of the church as an organized universal people. The church as locally organized must primarily be organized sabbatically, but may and eventually will be organized for other duties as well. The rise and development of Christian orphanages, hospitals, colleges, and so forth is evidence of this. In one sense all these things are part of the church, though they may not be under the government of the sabbatical *'edah*. The church as a local assembly in the Presence of God evinces the actual sabbatical function of man. Finally there is the collective sense in which all the people of God are contemplated as in a great assembly before the throne of God.

The failure to keep these distinctions straight has had recurring ill effects on the church. Those who fail to distinguish the church as a people from the church as an organized sabbatical community, have tended to ascribe to the institutional sabbatical *'edah*, and to it alone, all the various aspects of the church. We readily grant that the church as gathered for worship concentrates in itself in a primary fashion all the multiform aspects of the church. We also grant that, from the standpoint of historical maturation, the institutional church is the nursery of the kingdom in its broader manifestations. We deny, however, that all church functions are only carried out properly when performed by the sabbatical *'edah*. It is not obvious from Scripture that all Christian orphanages, hospitals, schools, families, etc., must be under the command of the officers of the sabbatical *'edah*. The precise delineation of responsibilities has proven difficult historically, and we must, therefore, attempt it anew.

Errors in interpreting and applying Scripture can rise from a failure to understand the various senses of the word "church." Reformed theologians have for a long time used the term "kingdom" for the church as "people of God," and this usage has now become common in evangelical circles. This shorthand has its place, perhaps, but it often leads to misinterpretations of Scripture, for

Scripture does not use "church" and "kingdom" in this way. In Scripture, "church" and "kingdom" have the same referent (the same object in mind), but entail different senses (different aspects of this object). "Church" focuses on the community, "kingdom" on the rule of the Lord. Both terms have a broader "people of God" and a narrower "sabbatical" use.

Appendix B

THREE PERSPECTIVES ON THE
CHURCH IN THE OLD COVENANT

In an attempt to do justice to everything the Bible says about the church in the Old Covenant, I suggest we keep in mind three perspectives. I am under no illusion that this is the last word to be said on the subject, but I believe it is a helpful word. At any rate, Perspective One is as follows: After the sin of Adam, the whole world is fallen and cursed. After the Flood,[1] that whole world system includes both the provisional, temporary, "Eden-sanctuary" restorations and also the downstream locations; that is, it includes both Israel and the Nations. Both are in a fallen situation, and compared to the glories of the New Covenant, both can jointly be said to be "in bondage to the elementary principles of the world" (the Old Covenant arrangement, fallen Adam; Col. 2:8, 20; Gal. 4:3).[2] From this perspective, there was no church in the Old Covenant; the church was born on Pentecost.

Perspective Two is this: For symbolic and pedagogical purposes, God set apart a priestly people for Himself. Compared to the nations, Israel was redeemed and they were not. Israel was the church, in the "olive tree," and the nations were not (Rom. 11).

---

1. Assuming that the Flood washed away the primordial Garden and land of Eden, which were off-limits to fallen man.

2. Interpreters have debated what the "elementary principles of the world" are. Do they have to do with paganism, or with Old Covenant Israel? The reason for the debate is that in both the Colossians and Galatians passages, paganism and Old Covenant religion are conflated. In Colossians Paul speaks of circumcision (2:11) and of sabbaths (2:16) as well as of pagan asceticism (2:22f.). In Galatians, those under the law are slaves/children (3:24ff.), but so are those who did not know God and were slaves to idols (4:8ff.). The "elementary principles" are the principles of the Old Adamic Covenant, in its duality. That entire first or elementary system has been transfigured in Christ.

Israelites were saved; gentiles were not. We might draw from this perspective an inference that to be saved, you had to be circumcised and become an Israelite. This, however, would be a wrong inference, because of what Perspective Three tells us. From Perspective Two, though, the New Covenant church continues the Old Covenant sanctuary of Israel. That is, from this perspective, Israel was the church of the Old Covenant. Israelites were saved by *being* in the church; gentiles were saved by *looking* into the church (*i.e.*, trusting in what God was doing through Israel).

Perspective Three: Israel sustained a relationship to the nations analogous to the relationship between the Garden of Eden and the world. Believers in the nations were ministered to by the priests in Israel. Gracious influences spread from Israel to the nations. To be saved, one did not have to become an Israelite and be circumcised, but one did have to put faith in the system God had set up, and permit the Israelites to function as one's priests. From this perspective, there were both faithful and unfaithful persons in both Israel and the nations. Abraham was the "father" of both groups, the faithful circumcised and the faithful uncircumcised. There were spiritual leaders (priests) among the nations (such as Jethro), but these always had to look to Israel (Eden) as the special priests God had established in the center of the earth. From this perspective, the whole church-system of the Old Covenant, in its duality, is transfigured in the New Covenant.

In summary:

Perspective One: The entire world is fallen. No one really knows God in the Old Covenant. There are no people of God, in the sense that no one is permitted into His abiding presence.

Perspective Two: Only Israel knows God during the Old Covenant. All those outside Israel are in the cursed "world." Only Israel is the people of God.

Perspective Three: There are those among the gentiles who know God, and there are those in Israel who do not. Israel is to feed the nations. God has His people in both places.

SCRIPTURE INDEX

OLD TESTAMENT

NEW TESTAMENT

GENERAL INDEX

(The reader may also wish to consult the Annotated Table
of Contents that follows this index, pp. 321-336.)

315

ANNOTATED TABLE OF CONTENTS

Women rule as women, not as men
Nature of priesthood as guard
    Women are the ones guarded, not the ones guarding
    Women are priest-guards for children, not for the Bride
Deaconesses
Conclusion, 49
    Architecture, catechisms, church & state, preaching

The Three-fold Nature of the Church, 51
    1. Government tied to sacraments
    2. Worship flows from presence of Christ
    3. The people of God in all they do
Recognizing the Church, 53
    Different kinds of visibility
    Belgic Confession versus Westminster Confession on true and false
        churches
    Bible does not give "marks" for the church, as abstract formulae
Wave, Particle, and Field, 54
        Basic concept of each of these
    The People of God, 55
        Particle: live holy lives
        Field: versus enemies of God
        Wave: more or less faithful
        Hierarchies: individuals, families, schools, etc.
    The Gathered Church, 56
        Particle: worship meetings
        Field: versus other Christian activities
        Wave: liturgical sequence
    The Church as a Government, 57
        Particle: visible sacraments and officers
        Field: versus other types of government (school, state, etc.)
        Wave: more or less faithful as government
The "Wave" of Church History, 58
    The church as a whole tends to move together, despite apparent diversity
    Sectarianism: Pilgrims versus Puritans
    The church creates social "shells"
Local and Larger, 61
    Bipolarity in Israel: central Temple and local synagogues
    Elders: hierarchy; two court systems (civil and ecclesiastical)
    The one and many question
    New Testament localistic language
Schism and the "Visible" Church, 64
    Kinds of visibility: moral and dominical, gathered, and institutional

Three aspects of clerical garb:
 1. High quality: People want their pastors to dress well
 2. Conservative look
   a. Clerical garb generally lags behind the latest styles
   b. Most churches keep their pastors poor
   c. People want an appearance of stability
 3. Distinctiveness: People want their pastors to look like pastors
   The ring collar = the mark of God's slave

Vestments, 262

During worship the elders symbolizes Christ to the people
He also symbolizes the Bride, adorned, to Christ

Biblical Regulation of Vestments, 263

True and false forms of the Regulative Principle
Modern men ignore the value of clothing
 1. In pre-modern times, clothing marked calling
 2. In Bible times, clothing marked clan
All Israelites were priests, and all wore special clothing
The Biblical conception of a priest is still relevant today
In the Bible, special clothing marks rulers
In the Bible, clothing marks degrees of glory
Conclusion: vestments are thoroughly Biblical and protestant

History and Controversy, 266

Vestments appeared after Constantine, when the church became more visible
Earlier, spacial arrangement marked special officers during worship
The Reformers did not oppose all vestments, but preferred the Genevan Gown
The English Vestarian Controversy
 1. Opposition to things that were associated with Roman abuses
 2. Opposition to statist imposition of vestments
A parallel example: lifting up the communion elements in worship
It can be done superstitiously
Or it can be a Biblical "heave offering" gesture
Martin Bucer did not oppose it
The Puritans wore the Genevan Gown
Since we are 400 years removed from these controversies, they should not totally govern us

Priestcraft?, 272

Traditional Roman Catholic theology errs in its understanding of what a priest is and does
The Biblical priest was never a mediator, but a representative
The New Covenant elder is also a representative, in some senses
 1. As God's special representative, the elder formally speaks the Word to the Bride
 2. As the Bride's special representative, the elder formally speaks prayers to God